SOLDIERS OF DIPLOMACY

JOCELYN COULON

Soldiers of Diplomacy: The United Nations, Peacekeeping, and the New World Order

Translated by Phyllis Aronoff and Howard Scott

UNIVERSITY OF TORONTO PRESS
Toronto Buffalo London

Originally published as *Les casques bleus* © 1994, Éditions Fides

English translation © Phyllis Aronoff and Howard Scott 1998

Printed in Canada

ISBN 0-8020-0899-2

Printed on acid-free paper

Canadian Cataloguing in Publication Data

Coulon, Jocelyn
    Soldiers of diplomacy : the United Nations, peacekeeping, and the
    new world order

    Translation of: Les Casques bleus.
    Includes bibliographical references and index.
    ISBN 0-8020-0899-2

    1. United Nations – Armed Forces.   2. International police.
    3. Security, International.   4. International relations.
    5. United Nations – Armed Forces – Canada.   6. Canada – Military
    policy. I. Aronoff, Phyllis, 1945– . II. Scott, Howard. III. Title.

    JX1918.P7C65813 1998   341.5'23   C98-930791-3

University of Toronto Press acknowledges the financial assistance to its
publishing program of the Canada Council for the Arts and the Ontario Arts
Council.

The English translation from the French original was supported by a grant
from the Canada Council.

Contents

vi Contents

Acknowledgments

I would like to thank all those who have contributed to the writing of this book. I think first of Renée Carrier, assistant to the military adviser to the secretary-general of the United Nations in New York, who was unstinting with her time in searching for dozens of documents and tracking down unpublished statistics on the peacekeeping operations. I owe her a great deal. My thanks go also to Fady Atallah for bibliographical research.

To write this book, I travelled, in 1993, to twelve countries and visited seven peacekeeping missions: Somalia, Western Sahara, Cambodia, the former Yugoslavia, the Golan Heights, southern Lebanon, and Jerusalem. I had already been to the missions in Cyprus, in 1990, and Kuwait, in 1991. My research also took me to Ottawa and to UN headquarters in New York several times. On my travels I conducted interviews with dozens of soldiers, diplomats, and experts of twenty different nationalities, all involved in peacekeeping activities. From UN Secretary-General Boutros Boutros-Ghali to the ordinary Fijian Blue Helmet stationed in southern Lebanon, all received me graciously and devoted long hours to telling me about the joys and frustrations of their work. My heartfelt thanks to them all.

I would also like to express my gratitude to everyone who, in the course of more than a year, organized meetings, provided documents, or helped me to make contact with the most inaccessible individuals: Jane Gaffney and Isabelle Broyer of the UN press office; Colonel Douglas Fraser and François Taschereau of the Canadian delegation to the UN; Philippe Coste, the French ambassador to Cambodia; Philippe Martin of the French Foreign Office; Grégoire Chilovsky of the French mission to the UN; Janet Arnold of the International Peace Academy in New York; and Pierre Lizée of York University in Toronto. In the field, I received invaluable assistance from Captain Jacques Poitras in Somalia, Lieutenant-Colonel Pierre Cantin in Cambodia, Lieutenant-Colonel Rémy Landry in Bosnia, Major Normand Desjardins in southern Lebanon, Salwa Assily of the Canadian Consulate in Beirut, and Austrian Captain Franz Walch on the Golan Heights in Syria.

I also wish to express my gratitude for the financial assistance I received from the Canada Council for the Arts and from the Cooperative Security Competition Program; of course, these organizations bear no responsibility for the contents of this book.

My sincere thanks to the publisher of the original edition of this book, Antoine Del Busso, who believed in the project from our first meeting. Finally, many thanks to Harold Scott and Phyllis Aronoff for the translation and the staff at University of Toronto Press for making possible the English edition.

Introduction

A few years ago, the general public rarely heard about the Blue Helmets. At most, there was an occasional story in the print or electronic media about the soldiers keeping the peace in Cyprus, between the Arab countries and Israel, or in some far-off land that most people had barely heard of. The role of the UN soldiers was simple: to act as a buffer force to keep the peace between two consenting warring parties and promote a peaceful settlement of the conflict. Paradoxically, the concept of peacekeeping was not described specifically in the United Nations Charter. This did not stop former Canadian statesman Lester B. Pearson from using that Charter to create the Blue Helmets during the Suez crisis in 1956. The success of this idea earned him a Nobel Peace Prize. The Blue Helmets were awarded the same prize in 1988.

Peacekeeping operations have come a long way since the Suez crisis. Until very recently, peacekeeping was a diplomatic activity full of subtleties for the governments involved and a bit of a romantic adventure for the participating soldiers. That time is past. With the end of the ideological rivalry between East and West and the proliferation of local wars, peacekeeping has become a thriving industry. It has also become a dangerous activity for the Blue Helmets, who find themselves in the midst of wars in which the rules of the past have given way to the anarchy engendered by ethnic and nationalist passions.

In 1991, there were only 11,000 Blue Helmets deployed in eleven peacekeeping missions throughout the world: on 1 September 1994, there were 76,600 deployed in seventeen missions. While the number of soldiers had fallen to 25,000 by June 1997, their mandates have become extremely complex: intervening in civil wars, patrolling dangerous regions, organizing elections, disarming militias, rebuilding infrastructures, protecting minorities, evacuating threatened ethnic groups, exchanging prisoners, drawing borders, and more. Taking on these additional tasks has had serious consequences for the Blue Helmets. At no time since the UN operation in the Congo in the sixties – when about 50 Ghanaian and Italian soldiers were killed, some of them hacked to pieces – have the Blue Helmets faced such hostile environments. There have been bloody tragedies: 25 Pakistani soldiers were killed in cold blood in June 1993 in Somalia, and in Rwanda in April 1994, 10 Belgian soldiers were murdered. While some 400 Blue Helmets were killed between 1948 and 1990, often in accidents, 460 were killed between 1991 and 1995, most of them in combat or attacks.

My investigation focuses on the years 1993 and 1994, a turning point in the history of the UN. At that time, the UN believed that it could be an independent agent, free to make decisions and take actions. It also believed that by strengthening the hand of its Blue Helmets it could police the world. Its activities attracted worldwide attention, and its officials and diplomats had never worked so hard. There was an atmosphere of euphoria in the corridors of UN headquarters and among its many supporters, who had for a long time wanted the UN to play a more interventionist role. But the euphoria was short-lived; the member states, particularly the great powers, were quick to remind the UN that it was only an instrument in their hands.

This book describes the inner workings of the UN and the organization of its peacekeeping operations. It shows how the role of the Blue Helmets as originally conceived by Pearson has evolved over the last forty years. In the beginning, the Blue Helmets were simply peacekeepers. Then, for a short time in Somalia, they were the warriors of the new world order. In Bosnia and Rwanda, however, they were neither, paralysed by the diplomacy of the great powers, who refused to grant them any power, and by ethnic conflicts that made a Somalia-style intervention hazardous. But the UN has also scored many successes. Its presence is much valued, and it is striving valiantly to improve the organization and deployment of the Blue Helmets.

The exceptional role Canadians have played in UN peacekeeping operations emerges clearly in these pages. Their prominence here is due not to the personal choice of the author, but rather to the quality of Canada's participation in peacekeeping initiatives since 1948, which has been a source of pride for all Canadians. For decades, Canada was the top contributor of Blue Helmets in the world and the undisputed leader in peacekeeping, which it made the cornerstone of its foreign policy. However, Canada's central role is threatened today. Cuts to the Canadian Armed Forces and massive participation in peacekeeping operations by dozens of countries with better-equipped or more substantial armed forces have meant that Canada is increasingly being relegated to a secondary role. This decline was no doubt foreseeable, but nothing prevents the government from reversing it.

This book is the English translation of the original edition published in French in 1994. It has been updated where appropriate, particularly in the chapters dealing with the conflict in the former Yugoslavia and in the epilogue. More titles have been added to the bibliography.

The complex history of the Blue Helmets is at times exhilarating; at other times it makes for sombre reading. I have tried to do justice to their story in this book.

JOCELYN COULON
July 1997

Part One:
The Rebirth of the United Nations

1

In the Glass Tower

In New York City, on 1st Avenue between 42nd and 44th Streets in the heart of Manhattan, there is a glass tower some forty stories high and, beside it, a smaller edifice crowned with a white dome. The East River flows slowly by behind these buildings, which house the headquarters of the United Nations. In the past forty-five years, this site has become familiar not only to New Yorkers but to television viewers all over the world. It is here, in the forum of the General Assembly or in the tense meetings of the Security Council, that politicians, diplomats, and officials debate the great political, social, and military questions that affect the whole world. Sometimes the proceedings are flamboyant, as when Soviet leader Nikita Khrushchev, in October 1960 in the General Assembly, took off his tan shoe and pounded his desk with it. Equally dramatic was the triumphal welcome delegates gave to Palestine Liberation Organization leader Yasser Arafat when he spoke there in November 1974, a gun clearly visible on his hip.

When I visited the UN in 1993, the top three floors of the steel and glass structure housed the offices of Secretary-General Boutros Boutros-Ghali, his civilian assistants, and his military adviser, Canadian General Maurice Baril. Baril, a native of Quebec, oversaw the military operations of the peacekeeping missions and was in charge of planning the organization of the future UN army. These men were responsible for all UN peacekeeping activities throughout the world, a heavy burden indeed for, since the collapse of the Communist block in 1989 and the end of the Cold War, the UN had been experiencing a period of unprecedented renewal. The level of UN activity in the world had increased dramatically, and requests for services were being received every day. The UN had never been such a hive of activity. In 1993, the Security Council, the executive body of the organization, met 171 times, a record since its inception in 1945, and the fifteen members of the council acted like ministers in a world government.[1]

***

When I met with him in January 1993, Boutros-Ghali was clearly pleased with the UN's newly won credibility. Moving with assurance, he shook my hand firmly and led me to a small sofa in his office on the thirty-eighth floor of UN headquarters. The room was plain and rather sombre, but the view was magnificent. It was late afternoon and the sun had already set; the New York skyline across the East River sparkled as evening fell.

Slender, and carrying himself slightly bent over in a way that made him look shorter than he actually is, Boutros-Ghali was an austere man. His solemn face was partly concealed by large, thick-lensed glasses. At seventy, he was head of the world's largest international organization. He had fought fiercely to win this position, and it was said that he had already succeeded in making enemies, even among those who once claimed to be his friends and supporters. Enigmatic, authoritarian, and imperial, Boutros-Ghali was much less malleable than some had thought. When he readily won the support of the members of the Security Council in November 1991, Boutros-Ghali was felt by certain countries to be 'their man' – the French liked him because he was a francophile and had dreamed of becoming his country's ambassador to Paris, where he had gone to university; the Americans welcomed him because he was one of the architects of the Camp David Accords and the peace treaty between Egypt and Israel; the Arab countries respected him because he was from their region and understood their problems; and the countries of the Third World believed that the Egyptian would be sensitive to their plight.

But all, to varying degrees, quickly became disenchanted. Boutros-Ghali turned out to be a determined man with his own agenda. He also let it be known that he had no intention of spending his life in that glass tower, and that he would only take the position for a single five-year term, thus undercutting the plans of those who would have demanded favours from him in exchange for their support for a second mandate.* His independent spirit and sudden changes of mood sometimes led to diplomatic incidents. For example, irritated by the uproar in the Western media over

---

*Boutros-Ghali did stand for a second term, but his mandate was not renewed, and he was replaced in January 1997 by Kofi Annan.

the war in the former Yugoslavia, he once launched into a tirade about the fact that this 'war of the rich' was mobilizing the time and resources of the UN at the expense of the wars of the poor, such as the one in Somalia.[2] And there was a persistent rumour that on another occasion Boutros-Ghali had lost his temper with African diplomats who had come to complain to him, denouncing them as imbeciles and saying that if Somalia and other African problems were being ignored, it was because they never called him, whereas the Western diplomats flooded him with calls about the former Yugoslavia.

Because of his brusque manner and sharp tongue, Boutros-Ghali was nicknamed 'the Sphinx' and 'the Pharaoh,' which did not seem to displease this polyglot, cosmopolitan Egyptian who had set himself the task of breathing new life into the UN. It is true that he came from a place where democracy and the spirit of consensus were not cardinal virtues. Accustomed to the Egyptian bureaucratic tradition, Boutros-Ghali would listen to advice and opinions, of course, but in the end he acted as he saw fit. He showed no patience either with the diplomats from the member states or with his close associates. After he took office in January 1992, heads rolled, regardless of nationality. He quickly 'used up' dozens of diplomats, officials, and military personnel, some of whom had made the mistake of openly opposing or criticizing his decisions. Boutros-Ghali not only governed the UN, as many wanted him to; he reigned over it. The Egyptian diplomat scoffed at criticism and quite simply refused to let anyone dictate his behaviour. In his view, the head of the UN had to show initiative. Indeed, Boutros-Ghali had taken to heart article 99 of the UN Charter, which authorized the secretary-general to 'bring to the attention of the Security Council any matter which in his opinion may threaten the maintenance of international peace and security.' Interpreted broadly, this article allows the head of the UN to take a lot of initiative. Boutros-Ghali had no qualms about using any loophole in the UN Charter that might give him a little more power.

Throughout my interview with him Boutros-Ghali expressed himself with ease in impeccable French. He gave me little chance to ask questions, guessing their content from the first words. Although his time was valuable, he did not hesitate, in the middle of an interview, to get up to find a document that he considered important to an understanding of the issues.

'Peacekeeping operations,' he explained, 'are only a fraction of United Nations activities. Most of our energy is devoted to problems related to development, minorities, human rights, the environment, etc. But I'm conscious that the spotlights of the media are focused on the wars and conflicts, and the Blue Helmets the United Nations sends all over the world. And it's a good thing the media take such an interest.'[3]

Boutros-Ghali was well aware of the importance of the UN's role in the prevention of armed conflict. He knew, he said, when he agreed to become secretary-general in 1992, that he would have to deal with a world undergoing enormous changes, including the breakdown of the rules of the Cold War that had for so long governed relations among the great powers and silenced the smaller countries' political, economic, and cultural demands.

'I had been a minister in the Egyptian government since 1977,' he said. 'I could have continued to work for my country, but I could see that the nineties were going to be a turning point in the history of the world. The UN was there. The position of secretary-general was vacant. I made the leap.' Boutros-Ghali was determined to let nothing stand in the way of his rendezvous with history.

The emerging new world order – for some people, a new disorder – paradoxically, provided an opportunity for the UN to reshape the organization of the world. The UN had been created just after World War II to prevent the recurrence of such a catastrophe and to enable the member states to settle their differences peacefully. In reality, however, it never played an important role in any of the conflicts of the Cold War. In fact, stated Boutros-Ghali, 'the United Nations was powerless to deal with many of these crises because of the vetoes – 279 of them – cast in the Security Council.'[4] For a long time the great powers had managed the world as they saw fit, leaving the UN only the narrowest room to manoeuvre. Its interventions were marginal and its soldiers, the Blue Helmets, were relegated to the role of auxiliaries while the great powers negotiated agreements to keep wars from flaring up into conflagrations. That era was now over.

'The political leaders of the world are asking us for help in all areas. They think that the United Nations can solve everything. I don't know if we have solutions, but the United Nations has to respond to these new demands.' The more pressing ones, Boutros-Ghali was forced to admit, were those concerning peacekeeping. In fact, on 31 January 1992, a few days after he took office as secretary-general, the leaders of the fifteen member countries of the Security Council met in New York to ask him for an 'analysis and recommendations on ways of strengthening and making more effective within the framework and provisions of the Charter the capacity of the United Nations for preventive diplomacy, for peacemaking and for peacekeeping.'[5] Boutros-Ghali acted quickly. With a small team of officials headed by a Russian diplomat, Vladimir Petrovsky, he produced a document entitled *An Agenda for Peace*, which he presented to the member states in June 1992. This document breathed new life into provisions of the UN Charter that had lain dormant since 1945 because of the political paralysis of the organization.

'It's all in the Charter,' said Boutros-Ghali. 'You just have to reread it and apply the chapters and articles dealing with conflicts. They are numerous and specific, and they give the United Nations, if the member states so wish, extensive powers. What I did with this *Agenda* was remind the member states that the UN had the tools and it was only a matter of using them.'

The *Agenda* document provided the UN with new ideas for more effectively carrying out its task in the management and settlement of conflicts. Without rejecting the traditional role of the Blue Helmets, Boutros-Ghali wanted to go beyond interventions that consisted simply of patrolling a ceasefire line, as the UN had been doing for many decades. He wanted the organization to be able to intervene as quickly as possible at the start of a conflict. *An Agenda for Peace* examined the mechanisms that could be used at each stage of a crisis in order to keep it from growing and to limit the damage. It focused on the diplomatic and peaceful instruments that the UN had at its disposal. But Boutros-Ghali certainly did not dismiss the use of force. The essence of *An Agenda for Peace* was clearly the determination to establish armed forces at the disposal and under the command of the UN, an army that the secretary-general would be free to use quickly in times of crisis. But Boutros-Ghali objected to my use of the term 'army.'

'An army? No, that is not really what I wrote,' he said, showing me an article he had published in the American journal *Foreign Affairs* (winter 1992–3) that corrected that impression. 'At a time when I'm fighting the proliferation of the UN bureaucracy, I'm not going to start creating an army, with officers, headquarters, etc. What I want is for the member states to make available to the UN military forces that can be deployed rapidly. Today, it takes more than three months after the decision is made to send a peacekeeping force for the Blue Helmets to be deployed in the field. That's too long. The time has to be shortened.'

Boutros-Ghali asked Maurice Baril, his military advisor, to draw up a detailed plan for rapid deployment of the UN forces. The basic idea was simple. The UN would have firm commitments from member states to maintain, in their own countries, fully equipped military units that would be available at the request of the secretary-general. Thus when the Security Council created a peacekeeping mission, the secretary-general would ask the countries concerned to put their forces on alert. The first units of the mission could then be deployed in the field within forty-eight hours and the other components, civilian and military, would arrive within days.

But beyond the desire for greater operational efficiency for peacekeeping missions, the creation of a UN army with the secretary-general as the commander in chief would be in keeping with the more interventionist role the UN had adopted in recent years. *An Agenda for Peace* proposed a significant change in the role of the Blue Helmets: that they become more active, even more aggressive, in the field. Traditionally, since the first mission in 1948 – with the notable exception of the Congo, where the Blue Helmets used weapons to impose their will – the peace soldiers had been deployed after certain basic principles had been agreed upon by the parties: the establishment of a ceasefire and the minimal use of force. In most operations, the Blue Helmets were deployed after the cessation of hostilities, along a line separating the belligerents. They were equipped only with light arms, which they were authorized to use only in self-defence. They had no power to impose peace and even less to impose peace against the will of the belligerents. At most, they could defend their position, holding out as long as possible until the situation cooled down.

But the political and military givens had changed with the transformation of the international order over the last few years. Now, the UN gave its Blue Helmets mandates in which force was often required to implement its decisions. Boutros-Ghali wanted the UN to be better organized and to be able to act more quickly in order to accomplish its new tasks more effectively. To him, the Blue Helmets, for so long the guardians of peace, had to become warriors for peace, heavily armed peacemaking units authorized to use force against recalcitrant factions and able to quickly enforce the decisions of the UN anywhere in the world. Placed under the orders of the secretary-general, these forces would be independent of any government. Boutros-Ghali was careful, however, not to suggest unilateral UN intervention in conflicts. The member states were the real bosses of the UN and nothing could be done without their agreement. But as soon as they gave the green light, the UN machine, supplied with soldiers and equipment, would be set in motion without being dependent on the good will of the member states.

In addition to his innovative demand for new military possibilities for the UN, Boutros-Ghali took an important step forward both for the organization and for the international community: he requested the imposition of UN decisions on recalcitrant parties. The UN had previously intervened in conflicts only when the parties had signed a ceasefire agreement and accepted its involvement. In no instance could the UN force the parties to respect the agreements they had signed. Boutros-Ghali wanted to go further.

'I'll give you an example,' he said. 'There is a conflict between A and B. A and B agree to a ceasefire and the deployment of a peacekeeping mission. But A decides not to respect the ceasefire. The UN then decides to take action against A. I will ask for coercive measures against A.'

Boutros-Ghali set the tone, drew up the plans, defined the programs, and provided the guidelines. Although he sometimes irritated UN bureaucrats and provoked sarcastic comments by certain diplomats and governments, his idea of revitalizing the organization quickly took form, thanks to a handful of loyal advisers and talented military officers.

* * *

Boutros-Ghali's civilian advisers had their offices on the thirty-seventh floor of the UN headquarters. There were about two hundred of them taking care of the political and diplomatic aspects of the seventeen peacekeeping missions deployed throughout the world in 1993. One of them, the Indian Shashi Tharoor, a unique character and a tireless worker, was a special assistant to Kofi Annan when he was in charge of all UN peacekeeping operations.* Tharoor handled the explosive former-Yugoslavia file, which regularly took him to the Balkans and turned his life in New York into a continual shuttle between floors of the glass tower. Arriving at nine in the morning, he rarely left his office before eleven at night, seven days a week. As the sole adviser on Yugoslavian affairs, Tharoor had to know and understand every aspect of one of the most complex situations of the post-Cold War era and present it to his superiors. During informal meetings of the Security Council, where decisions are made before being presented publicly in the big Council Chamber, it was Tharoor who whispered into the ears of officials the data they needed to defend their positions and draw up resolutions. Every day brought telegrams to be answered, reports to be dictated, committee meetings to be attended, keeping Tharoor constantly on the move from the basement to the top floor of UN headquarters. He was the perfect adviser, always available and

*Annan replaced Boutros Boutros-Ghali as secretary-general in January 1997.

never lacking for a new idea or proposal to help his superiors solve the Yugoslavia problem.

In his little office, Tharoor created an atmosphere that broke the monotony of the drab, unoriginal UN decor. Once the door was closed, you felt as though you were in his apartment. He had covered the walls with movie and theatre posters and the laminated covers of all his books – for at thirty-seven years old, Shashi Tharoor was a novelist whose work was very well known in India and beginning to attract attention throughout the world. But what was he doing at the UN?

'There's nothing surprising about a novelist working in a paper factory like the UN,' he said jokingly. 'In fact, I've been in the UN system since I was twenty-two. I spent four years rescuing boat people in southeast Asia before going to the Geneva office. I left that job temporarily to finish my first novel (*The Great Indian Novel*), but the UN came looking for me. In 1990, I moved to New York to work in the Office of Peace-keeping Operations. One year later, I was offered the Yugoslavia file.'[6]

An Indian writer responsible for the former Yugoslavia. Is that strange? Malicious tongues would have it so, saying that the UN should take more care in choosing diplomats in charge of political matters. Tharoor came to the Yugoslavia file almost by chance. When he arrived in the Office of Peace-keeping Operations, he worked on a variety of issues. Then war broke out in the former Yugoslavia and his boss, Marrack Goulding, asked him to devote some time to it. The scope of the problem gradually forced Tharoor to abandon the other matters that had been assigned to him. To those who doubted that an Indian could deal effectively with such a conflict, Tharoor responded that in political and diplomatic affairs, the UN liked to recruit employees with the mental flexibility to adapt to any situation.

'Unlike what one finds in ministries of foreign affairs around the world, here at the United Nations we're generalists,' he said. 'The UN above all seeks people who speak several languages, who have a good understanding of the UN system, and who are versatile. If the Yugoslavia crisis ended tomorrow morning, I would have to be able to be responsible for another part of the world. After all, even though the conflicts are different, the instruments we use to contain them or to encourage a settlement are the same.' He could have added that there was nothing to prove that the choice of a Serb, a Croat, or even a German or a Russian would have been more useful to the UN in its quest for a solution in the former Yugoslavia.

Tharoor did have one asset to compensate for his lack of specialized knowledge of the Balkans. He came from a country whose birth had been difficult and whose communal conflicts were similar to those ravaging the former Yugoslavia. In 1947, when the Indian subcontinent was partitioned to create India and Pakistan, bloody clashes between Hindus and Moslems caused more than a million deaths. Today India is still shaken periodically by conflicts between the two communities, and in some states ethnic quarrels are still very much alive. Tharoor was familiar with this kind of conflict – familiar with its dynamics, the passions that sparked and fuelled it, the compromises that had to be sought and those that could not even be suggested. He was perfectly aware that the former Yugoslavia was a minefield that had to be negotiated with the greatest of care. Too aware, perhaps. Hadn't the UN been accused of producing ineffective, inapplicable solutions to the conflicts in the former Yugoslavia?

'Security Council resolutions first of all reflect the opinions of the member states who propose them and adopt them,' explained Tharoor. 'The UN is not responsible for this. Its role is to obey the orders of the member states.'

A vote in the Security Council is the result of long, tortuous political negotiations among the ten non-permanent members, who are elected every two years by the General Assembly, and the five great powers – the United States, Russia, China, France, and the United Kingdom – who have held seats at the table since 1945. These fifteen countries make up what may be called the executive of the organization. Before a vote, these countries attempt to reach a consensus and draft a resolution that takes into account the demands of each one. When this is not possible, a resolution must receive the support of nine countries – and not be vetoed by any of the five great powers – in order to be adopted.

All the major political decisions are made by the Security Council: admission of new members, suspension or exclusion of members, revision of the Charter, and nomination of the secretary-general. And Security Council decisions regarding international peace and security are binding on all member countries of the UN. For example, when the Security Council decrees an embargo against a country, all the member states must respect it. When a peacekeeping mission is established, the member states must pay the expenses.

Shashi Tharoor may have had the ear of the secretary-general and exercised considerable influence in the UN bureaucracy, but he knew that ultimately the member states would make the decisions. Even if he worked sixteen hours a day, Tharoor was only carrying out orders. But he was able to speak about the UN with a touch of humour. Before coming to New York, he had made some biting remarks about its diplomats, especially the Indian ones. In his first book, *The Great Indian Novel*, the narrator describes the Indian diplomats at the UN to his biographer in the following terms: 'They say the new international organizations set up by the wonderfully optimistic (if oxymoronic) United Nations are full of highly successful Indian officials with quick, subtle minds and mellifluous tongues, for ever able to understand every global crisis from the point of view of each and every one of the contending parties. This is why they do so well, Ganapathi, in any situation that calls for an instinctive awareness of the subjectivity of truth, the relativity of judgement and the impossibility of action.'[7] The words are cruel, Tharoor acknowledged. Brushing back his mane of black hair, he explained that what a character in a novel says does not always reflect the opinion of the novelist, and that it is necessary to be able to find the humour in certain things in life. But there was still an element of truth in the description by the narrator in *The Great Indian Novel*. 'The words are there and I can't do anything about it now,' he said with a smile.

During the period when he was saving Vietnamese boat people on the seas of Southeast Asia, Tharoor had felt a certain satisfaction in doing his duty. Now, he was not so sure that his day-to-day work made any real difference. But the telephone was ringing in his office. 'It's the Security Council calling an emergency meeting. I have to go,' he said, dashing toward the door.

* * *

The offices of the military adviser to the secretary-general of the UN were on the thirty-sixth floor of the glass tower, directly below the offices of the civilian advisers. It was here that the resolutions and decisions on the peacekeeping missions voted by the Security Council ended up and here that the work of the Blue Helmets in the field was planned and managed. Here, too, military personnel had the headache of interpreting the decisions of the Security Council – which often bore little relation to reality. But the military was not concerned with politics. The officers were there to execute orders and salute.

When Boutros-Ghali arrived at the UN in January 1992, the offices of the military adviser consisted of a few rooms at the far end of the thirty-sixth floor. He was hardly aware of their existence. Their staff went about their duties nonchalantly, and sometimes there was not even anyone to answer the telephone. However, peacekeeping operations were becoming increasingly important and the number of missions was growing. With the grandiose plans described in *An Agenda for Peace* and his idea of setting up a sort of army for the UN, Boutros-Ghali needed a team of military people who were a little more dynamic. In the summer of 1992, he asked certain countries to suggest candidates for the position of military adviser, which had been occupied since 1977, without much enthusiasm, by a Ghanaian officer, Brigadier-General Timothy Dibuama. Admittedly, during this period peacekeeping was not the main activity of the UN and calm reigned at most of the missions. Moreover, the UN had indicated as early as 1967 that it saw no need to establish a permanent staff to analyse events, plan the Blue Helmets' activities, and run the peacekeeping missions on a day-to-day basis.[8] Now, despite his years of service, Dibuama was no longer the man for the job, and Boutros-Ghali was looking for new blood.

Canada proposed General Maurice Baril, a native of Saint-Albert-de-Warwick in Quebec, who was then commanding the battle school at Gagetown, New Brunswick. The secretary-general could not easily rule out the candidacy of the Canadian, as he had done with those submitted by other countries. Canada was a pioneer in peacekeeping operations and its Blue Helmets were among the most capable and effective peacekeepers. Furthermore, Boutros-Ghali liked the idea of having at his side a representative of a Western country whose international policy had broad support in the world, even among Third World countries. So Baril went to New York to meet the secretary-general on 17 June 1992. It was his first visit to the American metropolis. Boutros-Ghali was immediately charmed by this man of forty-eight years of age. Bilingual and dynamic, Baril had an impressive record both in the Canadian army and with the UN. A few minutes after the interview, while waiting in a room next to the office of the secretary-general, Baril was informed by one of Boutros-Ghali's advisers that he had the job and that he was to assume his new duties as soon as possible. A few weeks later, at the end of July, he moved into the offices on the thirty-sixth floor.*

* * *

When he arrived at his office at 8:30 a.m., General Baril would deal with three major concerns: directing the missions in the field, building a solid

*Baril held the position until the summer of 1995.

staff that would allow the UN to better manage its peacekeeping operations, and furthering Boutros-Ghali's great plan of establishing an army at his service.

'In the morning,' he said, 'I talk with the military commanders of the major missions, such as those in the former Yugoslavia, Somalia, Mozambique, and Rwanda. The commanders brief me on the situation, and at the same time, they take the opportunity to ask me for things or complain about problems with the parties in the field, or certain Blue Helmet contingents, or the UN in New York. This is their chance to pass along messages to the UN bureaucrats and get things off their chests.'[9]

After these discussions, at about 10 a.m., Baril would go to the office of Kofi Annan, who was then the senior civilian in charge of peacekeeping operations. There, with other civilian advisers such as Shashi Tharoor, they would go over all the missions. As a military adviser, Baril had to provide Annan with technical expertise on the operations of the missions and transmit messages from the commanders in the field. Annan would then meet with the secretary-general to give him a complete report on the civilian and military aspects of the peacekeeping missions. Baril would also give his opinion on the feasibility of projects devised by the civilians with the diplomats from the member states. Here friction could arise between civilian and military staff, try as they might to avoid it.

The worst headaches for the officers in the office of the military adviser occurred when the members of the Security Council decided to create a new peacekeeping mission or to send reinforcements to a mission already in operation. As soon as the resolution had passed, it would land on the desks of the civilian advisers, who were responsible for carrying it out. Kofi Annan would call General Baril to announce to him that the Security Council had decided to dispatch so many thousand more Blue Helmets to the former Yugoslavia, or to the border between Iraq and Kuwait, or to Rwanda. Most of the time, the situation was urgent. Baril and his officers would be tearing out their hair. Where could they find more troops, and how would they get them to the trouble spot? Did they have all the equipment required? What exactly was their mandate? There were usually dozens of questions, but very few answers.

Even if Baril managed to meet the demands of the Security Council quickly, he had very little room to manoeuvre. The civilians were always close by, making sure that certain political and diplomatic principles were respected. Sometimes, for example, the UN had to ensure that the military contingents deployed in the field in a peacekeeping mission equitably reflected the geographical diversity of the member countries. In other cases, the UN had to reject peacekeeping forces from countries that had too obvious a bias in the conflict. Everything depended on striking the right balance, which made the military adviser's task particularly complicated. Once the diplomatic negotiations were finished, Baril could state his point of view. He would give his opinion on the quality of the soldiers from the various countries and the state of preparedness of the contingents. He would always raise questions or offer answers with respect to the decisions passed by the Security Council. But if, for political reasons, it was decided that a particular country had to be part of a peacekeeping force, the office of the military adviser was forced to accept this decision whether or not the contingent possessed the military capabilities required. The country in question must not be allowed to lose face by having its offer refused for considerations which, in its eyes, were secondary. It was up to General Baril to find a role for the contingent and, if possible, supply it with equipment.

Once the political and diplomatic sparring was finished, Baril would set aside part of every day to assemble his staff. When he had arrived at the UN in July 1992, the office of the military adviser consisted of seven officers from as many countries. These officers provided continuity and maintained contact with the missions deployed in the four corners of the earth, and their number was barely sufficient. Baril did his arithmetic: to effectively manage a force that had increased from 11,000 Blue Helmets in 1991 to 50,000 in 1992 (and that would reach 76,600 by September 1994), he estimated that he would require a staff of more than one hundred. After discussion with the administrative officials, zealous guardians of the UN purse strings, he succeeded in getting his staff increased to forty-three officers in June 1993, and then to ninety-nine in summer 1994. However, only twenty-three of these officers were permanent employees of the UN, which led to problems.[10]

The seventy-six other officers worked on contract for periods ranging from six months to two years. They came from two dozen countries, and were loaned and paid by their countries of origin. There were no guarantees of their competence. They could be recalled by their respective governments at any time, and the UN could also easily remove them. Given these circumstances it was not easy to build a cohesive staff. Some officers would come in late, leave the office whenever they felt like it, and work according to their mood and availability. Moreover, their loyalty was not always above suspicion; some officers had been sent to the military adviser's office so that they could provide their governments with privileged information. 'Don't forget who pays your salary,' they would be told before leaving for New York. Such officers had two masters to serve, the one paying their salary and the one that had hired them.

Baril did the best he could in this situation. But his objective was to build up an independent staff. 'We have to be able to choose the officers who work for our office solely on the basis of competence,' stated the Canadian general. 'To attract them, we have to offer them permanent positions paid for by the UN. And this would be to the advantage of the UN for a very simple reason: loyalty to the institution. Our mission is much more important than the national interest of any one country. When these officers work for the UN, the UN will be in a position to impose its authority, its responsibilities, and its discipline on them.'

In his attempt to create an independent and cohesive staff, Baril came up against the contradictions of the member states. Several countries that participated in peacekeeping operations were critical of the inadequate material and human resources provided to the missions and the ineffectiveness of the military adviser's office. But when Baril went to the administrative and financial authorities of the UN to ask for a budget increase, he faced these same countries, which had instructions not to increase UN spending.

After two years of effort, General Baril's office was better staffed, it was in constant contact with the missions, and it responded more quickly to requests from the Security Council and the Blue Helmets in the field. But there was still much to be done.

* * *

Secretary-General Boutros Boutros-Ghali had grandiose plans for the UN. He wanted to reform the institution from top to bottom. He wanted to provide it with diplomatic instruments and even an army, which would enable the organization to be more independent and more effective in dealing with the conflicts breaking out all over the world. This at least was what he hoped for at the beginning of 1993. But the UN is only the sum of its member states, jealous of their prerogatives and protective of their independence, while glad to have the instrument of the UN at their service. Boutros-Ghali had thus to try to reconcile the global responsibilities of the UN with respect for national sovereignty. Would he be able to convince the international community that the renewal of the Blue Helmets was the solution for the future?

In subsequent chapters of this book, readers will visit the peacekeeping missions and will be able to judge for themselves the organization and the effectiveness of those missions. They will also see how Boutros-Ghali attempted to impose a 'muscular' *Agenda for Peace* through certain military operations – and how the great powers prevented him from doing so. It is a fascinating story, and sometimes a disturbing one.

2

A Nobel Prize for Canada

On 2 November 1956, in the General Assembly Hall of the United Nations in New York City, Lester B. Pearson, Canadian Secretary of State for External Affairs, silently watched the international representatives take their turns at the podium. The atmosphere was extremely heavy. For three days, Israeli, French, and British soldiers had been attacking Egypt, trying to take control of the Suez Canal. Despite the opposition of almost the entire international community, it seemed impossible to end the hostilities. Even the United States was unable to convince its Israeli and European allies to stop fighting and withdraw from Egyptian territory. At the same time, another major occurrence was causing turmoil on the international scene. On the day before, 1 November, Hungary had declared its neutrality, denounced the Warsaw Pact, and asked the UN for help in preventing a Soviet invasion. But in the corridors of the UN, the diplomats had only one concern: to do everything possible to prevent the Suez crisis from further degenerating and threatening international stability.[1]

The situation was critical. For several years Egypt had been governed by Gamal Abdel Nasser, a charismatic leader who had promised his people he would take back the Suez Canal from France and the United Kingdom, which had managed it since 1888. The Egyptian leader also entertained international ambitions. A revolutionary, he had called on Arabs to join together to free themselves from Western neo-colonialism and fight against Israel. He stirred up the resentment of millions of Arabs against their ruling classes, who were more or less docile toward the former colonial powers and powerless to solve the Palestinian problem. With Josip Broz Tito of Yugoslavia and Jawaharlal Nehru of India, Nasser had founded the Non-aligned Movement of countries seeking to distance themselves from the politics of the East and West blocs.

But Nasser was isolated by his pan-Arabism and anti-Westernism. In spite of the signing in October 1954 of an Anglo-Egyptian treaty governing the evacuation of the Suez Canal Zone (which was completed in June 1956), the Egyptian leader had turned toward the Soviet Union. The Soviets had begun supplying him with arms, making the West increasingly nervous. Israeli leaders, for their part, were seriously considering attacking Egypt, which was encouraging the Palestinian guerilla fighters of Gaza to strike into Israel.

The West broke abruptly with Nasser. On 19 July 1956, the United States blocked financing for the Aswan Dam on the Nile, which the Egyptians wanted to build to modernize their agriculture. Eight days later, on 26 July, Nasser announced the nationalization of the Suez Canal Company. The Western world reacted with shock. In London, the British cried robbery and demanded that the UN intervene. The French, who had financial interests in the Suez Canal Company and who did not appreciate Egypt's support for the rebels of the Front National de Libération in Algeria, joined with the British. The French leaders spoke of the emergence in the Arab world of a new Hitler, who had to be stopped or else 'all Western positions in the Middle East and North Africa will be lost within the next twelve months.'[2]

An international conference of the principal users of the canal was organized in London in August to find a solution. The conference recommended the establishment of an international commission to manage the strategic waterway between Europe and Asia. Nasser refused to accept the recommendation, and in September France and the United Kingdom went to the United Nations Security Council demanding energetic action against a country that 'endanger[ed] the maintenance of international peace and security.'[3] On 12 October, the secretary-general of the UN, Dag Hammarskjold, published six principles that were to guide the parties in their quest for a solution to the problem. The situation appeared to be easing, and the Canadians and Americans believed that the parties could begin serious negotiations.

But this did not occur. The British and French leaders plotted secretly to have Nasser's head. British prime minister Anthony Eden and his French counterpart Guy Mollet met on 26 September and 16 October to discuss military intervention against Egypt. On 23 October, the British foreign secretary went to France to meet with French and Israeli leaders; there they ironed out the details of the operation that was to begin a few days later. The Israeli-French-British plan was to be carried out in two phases. First, Israel would attack Egypt in reprisal for Nasser's support of the Palestinian fighters, who were continuing their attacks on Israel. The Israeli troops would head toward the Canal. Then, a few hours after the invasion, France and the United Kingdom would deliver an ultimatum to the two parties, ordering them to withdraw from an area twenty kilometres wide on either side of the Suez Canal and imposing the deployment of a French and British force around the Canal and in the cities of Port Said, Ismailia, and Suez, whose mission would be to separate the warring parties and protect vessels using the waterway.[4]

Of course, Israel promised to respect the ultimatum, which in all probability, Egypt would refuse to do, leading the French and British force to intervene vigorously and to confront the Egyptian army. The other countries in the West were unaware of this plan, but the many diplomats suspected something. Since the nationalization of the Suez Canal, the French and British had been telling their allies that they would solve the problem quickly, by force if necessary. The Canadians and Americans had made it known that they would not appreciate such a solution.

On the morning of 29 October, Israeli troops entered the Sinai Desert. The next day, the European powers delivered the two-part ultimatum. Israel announced that it would respect it; Egypt refused. Everything went as planned. On 31 October, French and British aircraft bombed Egypt. The entire world held its breath. How would the Soviets, and more important the Americans, react?

In Moscow, the Soviet leaders raged against European imperialism and threatened the French and British capitals with nuclear attack. The leaders of the Third World joined their voices to that of the Soviet Union. The West was in confusion. Australia and New Zealand supported Britain, but Canada and the United States, who admittedly were not enthusiastic supporters of military intervention, were furious because Paris and London had not consulted them. American president Dwight Eisenhower, who was campaigning for the 6 November presidential election, was particularly incensed at having been kept in the dark. Angry, he decided to rush to the aid of Egypt.

In Ottawa, Canadian leaders felt betrayed. Most of them learned of the ultimatum from the newspapers. A loyal ally of the United Kingdom, Canada had been rudely ignored. Furthermore, British prime minister Anthony Eden had had the audacity to ask his Canadian counterpart, Louis Saint-Laurent, for Canada's assistance and support.[5] But Canada was no longer a British colony. Saint-Laurent and Pearson, his secretary of state for external affairs, wrote to inform Eden that Canada would not necessarily come to Britain's aid. In addition, the Canadian leaders denounced the Israeli invasion and the French and British intervention, stating that they had damaged the credibility of the UN's conflict resolution system, brought the Commonwealth to the brink of collapse, and seriously damaged American-British relations. Diplomacy must once again take precedence over war before it was too late, they insisted. And it was in New York that all the persuasive force of diplomacy would be deployed.

Before leaving for UN headquarters, Pearson told the cabinet that he would propose a plan to dispatch a police force to the Israeli-Egyptian border to enforce the ceasefire and would suggest that a conference be held to negotiate a global settlement in the Middle East. On 1 November, when he arrived in New York, the UN debate on the Suez crisis seemed to be at a stalemate. The eleven members of the UN Security Council (their number was increased to fifteen in 1965) had the power to examine and judge issues related to international peace and security. But France and the United Kingdom, both of which had a veto on the Security Council, had blocked all resolutions on the Suez Canal question. The matter was therefore put before the General Assembly, where all members of the UN could vote and where there was no right of veto. When Pearson arrived at the General Assembly at about 5 p.m., the United States was calling for the adoption of a resolution demanding an immediate ceasefire and the withdrawal of foreign troops. Pearson was not satisfied with this resolution. He would have liked it to include his two suggestions: the deployment of a police force and the organization of a conference on the problems in the Middle East. Pearson was seeking a solution that would allow the two European allies to save face while doing justice to the Egyptians. But it was too late. The Americans had started the debate in the forum of the UN, and there was no way another motion could be presented.[6]

Pearson, the man with the famous bow-tie, took notes as he listened to the increasingly hard-line and sometimes hysterical speeches on the Suez crisis. He did not say a single word during that long session, which ended in the early hours of the morning on 3 November. The American motion was finally adopted at about 4:30 a.m., by sixty-four votes to five, with six abstentions, including Canada. The Americans were perplexed by the Canadian attitude. But Pearson explained it.

He stated that Canada had abstained because it regretted that the resolution did not contain any provision 'authorizing the Secretary General to begin to make arrangements ... for a UN force large enough to keep these borders at peace while a political settlement is being worked out.'[7] Was Pearson's idea destined to fail? To think so would have been to underestimate the Canadian minister who had been at the centre of every major international diplomatic initiative since 1945.

* * *

Before the Suez crisis Pearson was already an accomplished, internationally renowned diplomat. In addition to having visited Egypt in 1915, he had twenty-eight years of diplomatic and political experience. He had served as Canadian ambassador to the United States in 1945–6, and then as assistant secretary of state for external affairs. In 1948, when his boss, Louis Saint-Laurent, became prime minister of Canada, Pearson had succeeded him as secretary of state for external affairs. That was the beginning of an extraordinary career. Pearson played a crucial role in drawing up the UN's plan for the partition of Palestine, which led in 1948 to the creation of the state of Israel and a Palestinian state, and quickly became respected and sought after in the world of international diplomacy. 'Mike,' as he was affectionately known, participated in the creation in 1949 of the North Atlantic Treaty Organization (NATO), the cornerstone of Western security at a time when the Cold War divided the world into two antagonistic blocs. Throughout the Korean War (1950–3), he advised the Americans to work in cooperation with the UN to resolve that conflict. At the beginning of the fifties, he supported the proposal of the first secretary-general of the UN, Trygve Lie, to create a permanent armed force serving that organization.[8] He took up this idea again at the time of the Suez crisis. While solidly pro-Western and pro-American, he did not hesitate to criticize American policy, most often through the discreet and effective channels of diplomacy. A defender of collective security, Pearson believed in a key role for the UN in the development of civilized rules that would make it possible to avoid war. When he addressed the UN in November 1956, he was poised to provide the world with the solution to the Suez crisis, a solution that would win him the Nobel Peace Prize.

After the adoption of the American resolution ordering a ceasefire in Egypt, Pearson tried to convince as many people as possible that his idea of deploying a peacekeeping force to oversee the withdrawal of Israeli, French, and British troops and monitor the Israeli-Egyptian border was essential to the solution of the Suez crisis. On 2 November, he met with the secretary-general of the UN, Dag Hammarskjold, the U.S. secretary of state John Foster Dulles, and diplomats from several countries. The British had already stated that they were not opposed to the establishment of a UN force, and Pearson wanted to take advantage of this opening. Dulles proved to be somewhat favourable to Pearson's idea, but Hammarskjold expressed doubts. He did not see where the troops would come from or where they would be deployed. Hammarskjold was afraid that the suggestion would incur the wrath of the Communist bloc and the Third World, which he felt would accuse the UN of wanting to salvage the honour of the French and the British.

Despite Hammarskjold's misgivings, Pearson decided to attempt to get his proposal adopted. He discussed his peace plan at length with two assistants to the secretary-general of the UN, Andrew Cordier and Ralph Bunche, winner of the 1950 Nobel Peace Prize for his work in the negotiation of a ceasefire agreement between Israel and the Arab countries after the first Arab-Israeli war in 1948. On the morning of 3 November Pearson went to Ottawa to get the green light from the cabinet. Some hours later he returned to the UN, where the debate on the Suez crisis resumed at about 7 p.m. At about midnight, after several hours of negotiations with the American and British delegations and intense consultations between Paris, Washington, London, and Ottawa, Pearson introduced his motion. Time was short, since the French and the British were threatening to land their troops in the area of the canal. According to Pearson's plan, a ceasefire would be declared and within forty-eight hours the secretary-general of the UN would submit a plan for the establishment of a UN force in the Middle East. At roughly 2 a.m. on 4 November the General Assembly adopted the Canadian plan by a vote of fifty-seven to zero, with nineteen abstentions. Israel accepted the ceasefire on 5 November, and France and the United Kingdom did so the next day. On 7 November, following the presentation of a report by the secretary-general, the General Assembly passed a new resolution to create the UN Emergency Force (UNEF) under the command of a Canadian officer, Major-General E.L.M. Burns, who was at the time commanding the United Nations Truce Supervision Organization (UNTSO) in the Middle East. The Suez crisis, a political and diplomatic fiasco for France and the United Kingdom, was over.[9]

Officials at the UN were enthusiastic, but also very worried about the establishment of this new force. They felt that the UN would finally be able to play its role as guardian of the peace as envisioned in the Charter. But the establishment of a force to serve the UN created problems for these bureaucrats. In 1948, the UN had indeed, under UNTSO, sent military observers to monitor the truce between Israel and the Arab countries, and in 1949, it had sent observers to monitor the truce between India and Pakistan, who had gone to war over Kashmir. But this time, it was a matter of establishing an international force of several thousand soldiers to be deployed in a specific area between two countries. 'The employment by the UN of armed forces instead of unarmed individual observers required new principles and rules, as well as command, staff and logistical arrangements,' wrote Brian Urquhart, biographer of Ralph Bunche and himself a former head of peacekeeping operations for the UN.[10]

In spite of the difficulties and the novelty of the concept of peacekeeping forces, the UN did not lose a minute in equipping and deploying some six thousand soldiers from Denmark, Norway, Finland, Sweden, Colombia, India, Yugoslavia, and Canada. The first troops were in the field by 15 November. One of the initial concerns of the UN diplomats was to make sure that the UN troops did not look like those of the countries that had attacked Egypt. Many of the contingents, including Canada's, wore British-style uniforms. It was therefore necessary to find a distinctive way of identifying the UN soldiers. 'A UN-blue beret seemed to be the answer, but it was impossible to procure enough berets in time. American plastic helmet-liners, however, were available in quantity in Europe, and were ready, spray-painted UN blue, in time for the first UNEF detachments to wear on their entry into Egypt,' writes Urquhart.[11] The Blue Helmets were born. They were to become a symbol throughout the world.

* * *

Paradoxically, even though Pearson had contributed to the creation of the first contingent of Blue Helmets, Egypt fiercely opposed the participation of Canadian soldiers in it. Nasser was reluctant to accept the presence of forces from allies of France and the United Kingdom – Canada, Denmark, and Norway. Furthermore, he argued that the uniforms of the Canadians looked too much like those of the British and that people might not understand their presence in Egyptian territory. He feared that the Blue Helmets would be attacked.

Pearson was outraged. He had given his best to finding a compromise acceptable to all the parties in the Suez crisis. Canada had said it was ready to participate in the UN operation. And at home, the Liberal government, and especially Pearson himself, were under fire from the Conservative Party and the English-language press, both of which accused them of betraying the 'mother countries' and siding with Nasser. Canada's honour had to be saved. At the UN, the Egyptian position aroused concern. Hammarskjold shared Pearson's annoyance. He pressured Nasser, who finally accepted a compromise formula: instead of sending an infantry battalion, Canada would send administrative and logistical personnel into the field. This was a substantial contribution, since the Canadian contingent would number a thousand soldiers out of the six thousand projected.

Pearson was to receive another reward. On 14 October 1957, now serving as Liberal critic for external affairs on the Opposition benches in Ottawa, he received an unforgettable telephone call. A Canadian Press journalist announced that the Nobel committee had awarded him the Nobel Peace Prize for his work during the events of 1956.[12] The committee stated that 'the Suez crisis was a victory for the UN and for the man who contributed more than anyone else to save the world at that time.'[13]

* * *

The strict set of rules drawn up by the UN for the establishment and deployment of the United Nations Emergency Force (UNEF) became the example for subsequent UN peacekeeping missions. First, the Blue Helmets were deployed in a buffer zone, with the consent of the parties, with the role of enforcing an accepted ceasefire. Second, the Blue Helmets could not take sides in the conflict and could not to use their weapons except in self-defence. Third, the composition of the force had to exclude the great powers and reflect the geographic and political diversity of the UN. Fourth, the Blue Helmets had to arrive in the field with military equipment and food for at least ten days, enough time for the UN to organize supplies. Finally, the host country and the UN had to negotiate a legal agreement on the rights and duties of the Blue Helmets in the field. These were the basic elements in the establishment of the first-generation peacekeeping missions, the traditional missions set up to settle conflicts between two or more countries. With the exception of a mission in West Irian (related to decolonization), the thirteen operations that were set up prior to the end of the Cold War, between 1948 and 1988, were all what are now described as 'traditional' peacekeeping operations. 'They were largely military in composition and in functions, entrusted to maintain calm on the front lines while giving the peacemakers time to negotiate a settlement of the dispute.'[14]

Of course, some UN peacekeeping missions met with failure. But there have also been notable successes. In 1967, Nasser ordered the withdrawal of UNEF troops, provoking the third Arab-Israeli war, in which fifteen

Blue Helmets lost their lives. Another mission, UNEF II, was established in October 1973 after the fourth Arab-Israeli war. The Blue Helmets withdrew in 1979 after a peace accord was signed between Israel and Egypt.

The third UN peacekeeping mission, subsequent to the Suez crisis and an observation mission in Lebanon in 1958, was sent to the Congo in the summer of 1960 after the collapse of public order and the secession of the province of Katanga. This was the first UN intervention in an internal conflict. It was also the first time the Blue Helmets used force to carry out their mandate. This mission, the United Nations Operation in the Congo (ONUC), was the largest one until those deployed in 1992 in Somalia, Cambodia, and the former Yugoslavia. Some twenty thousand soldiers and six thousand civilians from thirty-four countries took part in its operations, which lasted four years. Its mandate was very complex: to ensure the withdrawal of Belgian forces; to assist the government in maintaining law and order; to maintain the territorial integrity and political independence of the Congo; to prevent civil war; and to expel mercenaries. In spite of the deaths of 234 Blue Helmets and of the secretary-general of the UN, Dag Hammarskjold, who was killed in an airplane accident in September 1961, the mission succeeded in fulfilling its mandate.

All other missions established up to 1988, including those in Yemen, the Dominican Republic, Cyprus, the Golan Heights, and southern Lebanon, were of the traditional type.

Between 1988 and 1994, taking advantage of the end of the Cold War and the alignment of the Soviet Union with Western positions, the UN established twenty peacekeeping missions, of which only half a dozen were of the traditional type. The other missions constituted what UN officials call 'second-generation' operations. 'As new conflicts take place within nations rather than between them, the United Nations today deals with civil wars, secessions, partitions, ethnic clashes and tribal struggles ... Complicated military tasks must be complemented by measures to strengthen institutions, encourage political participation, protect human rights, organize elections and promote economic and social development.'[15] This is the reason for the creation of multi-role missions in Namibia, El Salvador, Cambodia, Somalia, Georgia, Rwanda, Mozambique, Angola, and Western Sahara.

Concurrently with this profound change in the nature of peacekeeping operations, the UN decided to make more frequent use of Chapter VII of its Charter, which authorizes the use of force to fulfil UN mandates or to restore international peace and security. It even decided, in the case of Somalia, not to obtain the consent of the parties to its intervention. In the corridors of the UN in New York, it was rumoured that the use of force in Somalia might well 'represent the emergence of a third generation of peacekeeping operations.'[16] As we will see in the following chapters, the results in Somalia did not live up to the UN's hopes.

Pearson certainly never foresaw that his Blue Helmets, lightly armed soldier-diplomats in the service of peace, would one day be transformed into warriors for peace. In the chapters that follow we will examine what has become of Pearson's dream. Some people believe that there has been a change for the better; for others, the dream has become a nightmare.

Part Two:
The Peacekeeping Missions

3

The Soldier-Diplomat

On the terrace of his house, the mukhtar – the chief – of the village of Ramadiyah in southern Lebanon was entertaining his favourite Blue Helmet, Lieutenant-Colonel Sam Saumatua, commander of the battalion of Fijian soldiers deployed in the region to maintain some semblance of peace. A little old man, stooped but lively, wearing a white keffiyeh with a double black ring, the mukhtar was in a particularly good mood. Just opposite his home, the Fijians were helping a team of local workers rebuild a school that would soon be attended by a hundred students. The building was almost finished, and the workers took a short break to greet the officer.

The mukhtar shouted at Saumatua in Arabic, saying there was more work to be done in the village. The good-natured Fijian officer smiled a wide, white-toothed smile, said a few words in broken Arabic, and burst into laughter, setting off general hilarity. The dark-skinned Fijian giant, two metres tall, with typical Melanesian features, was an object both of curiosity, and of admiration in this multi-ethnic region of Lebanon, where Christians, Druzes, and Moslems live in a state of constant tension. Saumatua was no stranger here. The UN had a force of Blue Helmets from ten countries in southern Lebanon to help the Lebanese government re-establish its authority. Part of the territory was occupied by the Israelis, and Lebanese factions were involved in a bitter struggle for control of the rest. The Fijians were the first troops to be deployed in southern Lebanon in 1978, and since then they have done their best to fulfil their difficult mandate. Saumatua was on his fourth one-year assignment, which was unusual for a Blue Helmet. Most military personnel serving the UN did tours of duty of six to twelve months at a mission, and rarely went back. But the UN mission in southern Lebanon was one of the longest-standing, and the Fijian army was tiny, with only eight battalions, four of which were assigned to peacekeeping missions. In addition to the battalion serving in Lebanon, there was another in the Sinai, where a mission that was not under UN control monitored the peace between Israel and Egypt. Consequently each battalion went back to the Middle East every other year. (By comparison, a Canadian battalion in a peacekeeping mission only served six months every three or four years.) This was an extremely difficult rotation for the soldiers from the Pacific islands, and their commanding officers made no secret of the fact that the Fijian army was plagued by significant social and military problems: breakdown of couples and families, alcoholism, inadequate training, etc.

Replying to the chief, Saumatua said that his soldiers could not rebuild the entire village and that other villages were also asking for their help. The chief provided coffee, water, and fruit for the guests and continued to try to persuade the officer to change his mind. But the Fijian remained firm. After complimenting the chief on the beautiful flowers surrounding his house and the order that prevailed in his village, Saumatua put an end to the conversation, which had gone on for an hour. He had several visits to make before returning to the headquarters of his battalion in the village of Qana. I climbed into his white jeep with the UN logo and we headed toward a small camp of Fijian Blue Helmets where the lieutenant-colonel wanted to stop.

On our arrival in Qana, Saumatua pointed to the tower standing in the middle of the camp.

'Go take a look,' he said. 'Afterwards I'll tell you why I didn't give in to the mukhtar of Ramadiyah's demands.'[1]

In the tower, a Fijian Blue Helmet surveyed the horizon through binoculars. The weather was excellent, permitting the soldier to see clearly as far as the coast some ten kilometres away. But it was not the beach he was looking at today. He scrutinized the area surrounding the camp, which had been buzzing with activity for some weeks. The Lebanese were rebuilding the area which, at the end of July 1993, had been subjected by the Israeli air force, artillery, and navy to two weeks of the heaviest bombardment since 1982. In retaliation for continuing raids into northern Israel by Lebanese – in particular, the pro-Iranian Hezbollah – and Palestinian guerilla groups, the Israeli forces had hit dozens of targets throughout southern Lebanon. The damage was enormous. Many villages were levelled, some 10,000 homes were destroyed, and more than 200,000 people left their villages to flee north toward the Lebanese cities of Tyre, Sidon, and even Beirut. The Israeli army called the operation

'Accountability,' and its objective was precisely to cause an exodus of the population toward the major Lebanese centres in order to force the Beirut government to convince the Hezbollah to stop its attacks on Israel. Israeli fire was therefore aimed directly at the centres of the Shi'ite villages where, according to the Israeli officers, the Hezbollah terrorists were entrenched. On 27 July alone, some 5,000 shells fell on the villages of southern Lebanon.[2] This rain of fire, according to Israel, was intended to make the population exert pressure on Beirut and to weaken the Hezbollah, which would thus lose its local base. The Israeli strategy was not a complete success. Lebanese soldiers took advantage of the attack to extend the influence of the Lebanese government to several villages in southern Lebanon, but the Hezbollah remained powerful and the attacks against Israel and its militia in the security zone, although less frequent, continued. (They were still going on in 1997.) The Israeli government retaliated for each attack.

The Fijian sector was left relatively unscathed by Operation Accountability. Homes were destroyed in several villages, but this was nothing compared with the Ghanaian sector, located just to the north. The Israeli bombardment barely missed the headquarters of the Ghanaian battalion in the village of Al Qaranis. During the raids, recounted one Ghanaian soldier, the inhabitants of the village and the surrounding area fled to the UN camp for protection and food. Thousands of them climbed the rocky road up the hill to the headquarters. Overwhelmed, the Ghanaians were not able to accommodate them all. Hundreds took refuge in the open area in the centre of the camp; others congregated outside along the barbed wire and waited out the storm in makeshift shelters. The Ghanaians did what they could to relieve their misery.

The Fijians cared for the wounded, and since the end of the shelling they had been working on rebuilding several villages. This was a very delicate undertaking, as Saumatua explained. 'You see, as in the rest of southern Lebanon, there are different Moslem Shi'ite factions fighting bitterly for control of this sector. If my soldiers help one village to the detriment of another, I'll be accused of favouring one faction over the others. I have to remain outside all that.'

The Fijian Blue Helmets and those from the nine other countries represented in the United Nations Interim Force in Lebanon (UNIFIL) were in a hornets' nest. From 1975 to 1991 Lebanon had been ravaged by a long civil war that had turned it into a patchwork of more or less independent communities, and the south, where the Blue Helmets were stationed, was a microcosm of all the problems that had beset Lebanon for so long. This territory was at the mercy of several militias who were engaged in a bloody struggle for control.

Southern Lebanon was divided into several enclaves. After a first invasion in 1978, Israel had established a 'security zone,' a fifteen-kilometre band of Lebanese territory along the border, to protect itself against attacks from Palestinian and Islamic guerillas. This zone, populated by Shi'ites and Christians, was administered and patrolled by a Christian militia financed entirely by the Israeli army. In the centre of southern Lebanon, the Moslem guerilla groups Amal and Hezbollah vied for the allegiance of a population that was 80 per cent Shi'ite. In the north, in the Sidon region, a large population of Palestinian refugees had subsisted in camps since 1948. Its fighters infiltrated the border area to attack villages in Israel, and provided men and supplies to the Hezbollah in its fight against the Lebanese state, which was trying to re-establish its authority over the whole territory. The 5,200 Blue Helmets who arrived in the region in 1978 at the request of the Lebanese government patrolled the whole territory, with the exception of the security zone. The mandate of UNIFIL was 'to confirm the withdrawal of Israeli forces from southern Lebanon, to restore international peace and security and to assist the Government of Lebanon in ensuring the return of its effective authority in the area.'[3] The Blue Helmets soon realized that this vague mandate was impossible to fulfil in an area that was disputed by so many groups and within which the legal government in Beirut was incapable of exercising the slightest authority. As early as 1979, Kurt Waldheim, then secretary-general of the UN, pointed out that peacekeeping operations ran the risk of enormous problems when they were organized in emergency situations and their objectives and mandate were ambiguous or controversial and based on less than realistic hypotheses. He cited the example of UNIFIL.[4]

To add to the confusion and danger, the headquarters of UNIFIL were in Naqoura, a small coastal village located inside the security zone, which the Blue Helmets were not allowed to patrol. The installations had been shelled several times and the mission's communications lines had been cut.

In this imbroglio, Lieutenant-Colonel Saumatua was the embodiment of Pearson's description of the Blue Helmets as soldier-diplomats who would 'be frequently called upon to exert a mediatory rather than a military influence [and] required to display unusual self-restraint, often under severe provocation ... In many cases,' Pearson believed, 'an explosive situation can be brought under control through coolness, good

humour and common sense.'[5] Saumatua and his Fijian soldiers and the
Blue Helmets of the nine other contingents possessed all these qualities.
Since 1978, they had faced every insult, every humiliation, and every kind
of attack, including the most lethal. By 1994, UNIFIL had lost two hundred Blue Helmets, seventy-six of them killed by direct fire or in mine or
bomb explosions.[6]

In this part of the world, none of the rival groups – Israelis, Christians,
and Moslem and Palestinian guerilla groups – respected the UN peacekeepers. The factions were engaged in a brutal game that involved shooting at each other while hiding behind the Blue Helmets, who rarely shot
back. With rare exceptions, the scenario was always the same: a group of
armed rebels – Hezbollah or Palestinian gunmen – infiltrated the zone
patrolled by UNIFIL and fired Katyusha rockets into the security zone
controlled by the pro-Israeli militia, or at villages in northern Israel.
Retaliation would come within minutes: the soldiers of the militia and the
Israeli army would attack with mortars and missiles, and sometimes with
planes, aiming at the source of the firing. A UN post was never far away,
and frequently it was hit.

Using a network of road checkpoints, the Blue Helmets often managed
to prevent the guerrillas from penetrating the UNIFIL zone to attack the
Israeli forces and local militia. They also had a mandate to search vehicles, confiscate weapons, and arrest any men attempting to enter the
UN-controlled areas who did not belong to the legal Lebanese forces.
Sometimes, the fighters ignored the checkpoints and smashed through
the barriers. And sometimes they took the Blue Helmets hostage for a few
hours, long enough to attack their targets and disappear into the countryside.[7] But usually the commandos intercepted by the Blue Helmets
withdrew and tried to get through some other way. They often succeeded,
since the zone under UNIFIL jurisdiction was too large and the terrain
too hilly for the Blue Helmets to be able to control the comings and
goings of the inhabitants or the militiamen, who did not wear any official
uniforms.

Nor did the Israelis have any compunction about humiliating or attacking the soldiers of UNIFIL. When Israeli troops invaded Lebanon in
1982, they gave the Blue Helmets thirty minutes' warning. UNIFIL checkpoints were destroyed and Blue Helmets were wounded by Israeli fire.
When the Israelis returned the fire of the Lebanese commandos, it was
not unusual for their shells to land on UNIFIL positions. For example, on
27 December 1993, Israeli soldiers fired a shell at Norwegians they had
mistaken for 'Moslem guerrillas.'[8] The Israeli prime minister apologized,

of course, but the incident, which was not the first of its kind, underscored how little the UN forces mattered to the factions fighting in this region.

* * *

The Fijians are good soldiers and good Blue Helmets. Oddly enough, Fiji has a long military tradition, which distinguishes it from the other nations of the South Pacific, with the exception of Australia and New Zealand. It is the only country in the region that maintains armed forces and that has taken part in three wars: both world wars and the war against Communist guerillas in Malaysia in the 1950s. In southern Lebanon the Fijians have earned themselves a reputation as very aggressive soldiers who do not hesitate to bend UN rules in order to prevent the illegal Lebanese militias from penetrating their patrol zone. In contrast to more passive soldiers who adhere to the letter of the UN's orders, this contingent was not afraid to take the initiative. The Fijians were given a mandate suited to their strengths: they controlled the routes of infiltration into southern Lebanon, in the most dangerous area of the country.

But the Fijian Blue Helmets have had to pay a price for their initiative, especially at the end of the 1970s, when the PLO controlled a good part of southern Lebanon. In 1978 and 1979, several Fijians were killed, either in reprisal for killing Palestinian fighters or because they prevented PLO guerillas from penetrating further south. And in early June 1994, two Fijian Blue Helmets were killed in a firefight with members of the Hezbollah who were attempting to enter the UNIFIL zone southeast of the city of Tyre. By 1994, the death toll had reached twenty-nine.[9]

Why has Fiji maintained a contingent in this region for so long? Brigadier-General Jeremaia M. Waqanisau, military adviser to the Fiji mission at UN headquarters, who has done seven long stints in southern Lebanon, in the Sinai Peninsula, and in New York since 1978, answered this question.[10] The Fijian soldiers who go abroad acquire training and technical information that they would not receive if they stayed at home working in an under-equipped army. Joint manoeuvres with other contingents allow them to learn in the field. In addition, the bonds the officers form with their foreign counterparts and the opportunities they may have to command soldiers from other countries improve their military training and increase their chances for promotion.

While Fiji's participation in peacekeeping missions has allowed its soldiers to distinguish themselves internationally, it is above all a matter of money. Fiji, like many other countries in the Third World, gains considerable financial advantages from providing soldiers for the UN. These soldiers constitute a 'renewable natural resource' that costs the producers little but brings in a considerable return on the international market. Let us look at the figures.

As a member of the UN, each country has to contribute to the general finances of the organization and to the expenses incurred for activities such as peacekeeping missions, whether or not the country participates. The dues are set according to criteria of economic power. Thus, the United States pays 31.7 per cent of the expenses related to peacekeeping,* while Canada contributes 3.1 per cent.[11] Fiji and Ghana, two Third World participants in UNIFIL that I will use as examples, each contribute 0.002 per cent of the costs of the missions. This means that, for the one-year period from the beginning to the end of 1993, for UN peacekeeping operations that cost a total of just over $3 billion, the United States spent close to U.S.$800 million, Canada spent about $75 million, and Fiji and Ghana each spent U.S.$45,000.[12]

Except in the rare cases where the Security Council requires the countries responsible for a peacekeeping mission to completely finance their own participation, the UN reimburses the participating countries according to norms that apply to all. Thus, each government providing troops receives about U.S.$1,048 a month for each soldier. This amount includes a basic allocation, a daily rate, and allowances for clothing and wear on equipment.[13] In addition, the UN pays the bills for rations and for transportation of troops. It is very difficult to know exactly how much money the participating countries receive from the UN, because the organization refuses to publish the amounts it reimburses to each country. It is certain, however, that most of the Third World countries make substantial profits from their participation in peacekeeping missions, while Western countries lose money. Let us examine this more closely, again using the examples of Fiji and Ghana.

In 1993, the Fiji government provided 659 soldiers to UNIFIL for a period of twelve months, and received the sum of U.S.$1,048 per soldier per month, or about $8.1 million. The Fijian army also maintained a contingent of 350 soldiers with the Multinational Force and Observers (MFO) in the Sinai, which was not under UN jurisdiction. The MFO reimbursed the Fijian government according to UN rates, representing about U.S.$4.4 million in 1993. These are significant sums, considering

---

*The U.S. unilaterally changed its contribution to 25 per cent in 1996.

that Fiji's military budget for that year was an estimated $26 million. Of course, the Fijian army had to pay its soldiers, but their monthly salaries ranged from U.S.$150 to $500 according to rank. The same was true for Ghana. In 1992–3, roughly two thousand Ghanaian soldiers were deployed in Cambodia and in southern Lebanon. For that period alone, the government of Ghana would have received about $25 million, while its military budget for 1992 was an estimated $47 million. In addition, the contingents from these countries often arrive with no military equipment and are supplied by other, richer, countries or by the UN, which absorb the costs for its purchase or lease.

The reimbursements from the United Nations are often very slow to reach the participating countries, and many countries of the Third World or the former East bloc wait for the cheque from the UN to pay their soldiers deployed abroad. For example, in 1993, a battalion of nine hundred Nigerian soldiers was deployed in Croatia as part of the United Nations Protection Force in the former Yugoslavia (UNPROFOR). Toward the end of his tour, in August 1993, an officer from the battalion went to Zagreb to meet the deputy commander of UNPROFOR, Canadian Major-General Robert Gaudreau.

'I remember it very well,' said the Canadian officer. 'The Nigerian soldier came to my office with tears in his eyes. His men had been in Croatia for a year. They had endured the rigours of winter without complaining. But they hadn't been paid for six months. The officer asked me to help him before a riot broke out. So I asked the administrative staff of UNPROFOR to pay the soldiers and send the bill to UN headquarters in New York.'[14]

For the Western countries, the system is completely different. They are reimbursed at the same rate, but the cost of the salaries and upkeep of their soldiers is higher. In Canada, for example, in 1993, the average salary of a soldier or non-commissioned officer was about Cdn$3,000 a month, in addition to isolation pay, fringe benefits, transportation, and maintenance of military equipment. According to the Department of National Defence, the Canadian contribution to peacekeeping missions in 1992–3 – both UN-controlled and non-UN-controlled operations – cost the country Cdn$100 million, of which only $69 million was reimbursed by the UN.[15] However, the Department of National Defence estimates that its real costs included an additional $834 million for the salaries and expenses of the troops, abroad and on their bases in Canada.

According to a study by William J. Durch, one of the most prominent American experts on peacekeeping, it costs countries that provide troops an average of about U.S.$2,300 a month to maintain a soldier, 'so the average contributor absorb[s] about 59% of the actual costs of keeping its troops in the field.' But this average covers a wide gap between rich countries and poor ones. Durch goes on to say that the actual costs vary 'by 2000 dollars in either direction, from as little as 280 per month to as much as 4400. The lowest-cost contributor is thus reimbursed roughly 3.5 times as much as it spends, and the highest-cost contributor a bit less than one-fourth of its costs.' He concludes that 'the fixed reimbursement system functions, in effect, to redistribute resources to developing countries' militaries, but without requiring that surpluses be invested in, say, equipment or training that could be useful to the UN at a future date.'[16]

The financial and military benefits of participation in peacekeeping missions have led many countries of the Third World and the former East bloc to offer their services to the UN on a massive scale. For example, in 1982, ten of the twenty-five participating countries were from the Third World or the East bloc; in 1989, these countries made up twenty-seven of the forty-six participating countries; five years later, in September 1994, their number reached forty-eight out of seventy-three participating countries. The number of soldiers from the Third World and the former Communist bloc grew from 3,200 (out of 10,500) in 1982 to 45,500 (out of 76,600) in 1994.[17]

The civilian and military planners of the peacekeeping operations in New York and in the various missions throughout the world are not exactly delighted with the eagerness of these countries to offer their services to the UN. But no official wants to say this openly, and the UN must accept the soldiers provided. Moreover, a UN rule calls for an equitable geographic distribution of member countries when missions are formed. (An exception to this rule is the Cyprus mission, where, at the request of the local government, 'troops of colour' were excluded.)[18] The planners' misgivings have nothing to do with the skin colour of the soldiers, but rather with their training and discipline, the equipment with which they are supplied, and their professionalism. Too often, troops from Third World or former East bloc countries are below standard. Entire contingents have arrived in Namibia, Cambodia, the former Yugoslavia, or Somalia in a deplorable state from a material, financial, and human point of view. These contingents supplied no military equipment, received no pay, had no special training, and spoke none of the official languages used for communications within the missions. Some African or Asian units even landed in the former Yugoslavia in the middle of winter without warm clothing.

Such problems are likely to continue if the UN maintains its policy of setting up peacekeeping missions on an ad hoc basis and is unable to impose homogeneous training and equipment-purchasing programs. In the meantime, as we shall see in Chapter 11, the office of the military adviser to the secretary-general is working to correct these logistical deficiencies.

4

Cambodia: The Fairies around the Cradle

In the small village of Tuk Meas in southern Cambodia the deputy governor of the province of Kampot had been declaiming for half an hour on the benefits of the current government and the horrors of the previous regime, that of Pol Pot. The date was 15 April 1993. In a little more than a month, Cambodians were to take part in the first truly democratic election in their history, under the supervision of the UN. Standing on the small balcony of a former school, the deputy governor reminded his silent audience that the Khmer Rouge were back and that they would soon take over unless the villagers voted for the party in power. At his feet, several hundred Cambodians, mostly women, children, and old people, listless with the heat, listened indifferently. A few palm trees provided shade, but most of the crowd had their heads covered with the traditional pieces of checkered cloth sold in the markets, an essential part of Cambodian dress. Mopping the sweat from his forehead, the deputy governor finished his speech amid polite applause.

The French colonel Yves de Kermabon, sitting beside him, stood up to address the crowd. Choosing his words carefully, the officer, wearing a blue beret with the UN emblem, greeted everyone, particularly his soldiers. He had not come to Tuk Meas to take part in the electoral campaign, but to mark the reopening of a road that the French legionnaires had just finished repairing, a road originally built by France in 1927, when Cambodia was a French colony. While he spoke in French, some of the Cambodians talked among themselves, and others laughed and pointed their fingers at a tall legionnaire with a big black moustache. The crowd was beginning to disperse, and de Kermabon did not want to talk too long. Finishing his speech, he quickly descended the steps from the small balcony into the crowd, which surrounded him, applauding frantically, touching and speaking to him. With evident pleasure in 'pressing the flesh,' he shook hands and took babies in his arms. But the little celebration was soon over. The deputy governor of the province, escorted by his entourage, urged the colonel to come and cut the red ribbon in his company; impassive, de Kermabon complied. When the ceremony was over, he had to leave.

The helicopter was waiting near the old school with the rotor blades already turning. The Canadian pilot signalled us to hurry because the Cambodians were running toward the aircraft. Painted white, with a big UN logo on their sides, the helicopters always attracted a delighted crowd when they appeared in the Cambodian countryside. Children would approach as soon as they landed, and when they took off, the UN soldiers had to be very careful to keep the most daring ones at a distance.

During the six months it had been in Cambodia, the Blue Helmet battalion from the Foreign Legion – the French army corps made up primarily of foreign soldiers – had been very popular. The legionnaires had been deployed in sector six, a territory covering three provinces along the Gulf of Thailand, in the south of the country. After 150 years of soldiering in the service of France's interests abroad, the legionnaires were for the first time wearing the blue beret of the UN. Unlike the soldiers of traditional UN peacekeeping missions, they were not here to patrol a buffer zone and separate clearly identified belligerents, but to supervise elections. The task of the Blue Helmets in Cambodia was unique in the history of the UN, and the legionnaires accomplished it with their legendary warrior zeal. For the first time, the UN was taking charge of a territory and supervising all aspects of its reintegration into the international community after a quarter-century of war.

* * *

In spite of all its suffering, the Cambodian state had started out auspiciously.[1] In 1949, when it became independent, Cambodia maintained close ties with France but, through the skilful manoeuvring and the exceptional personality of its king, Norodom Sihanouk, it had avoided being drawn into the Vietnam conflict in which the French and then the Americans became entangled. In 1970, this policy of neutrality collapsed. A coup d'état installed a pro-American general, Lon Nol, in Phnom Penh. Sihanouk went into exile, organizing resistance from Beijing and allying himself with the Khmer Rouge although they had been fighting a guerilla war against his regime. Five years later, the Khmer Rouge overthrew General Lon Nol, made Sihanouk president, and established a bloody dictatorship. In forty-eight hours, they emptied the capital of its million inhabitants. For four years, the Khmer Rouge relentlessly persecuted supporters of the former regime and of Sihanouk – who had been made a prisoner in his presidential palace – and massacred Cambodia's entire political, intellectual, and religious elite. The goal of the Khmer Rouge was to create a 'new man,' and its leaders, under Pol Pot, relied on fifteen-year-old soldiers to renew the country. Initially allies of the Vietnamese who overthrew the pro-American regime in Saigon in April 1975, the Khmer Rouge turned against their former friends. Skirmishes escalated into open warfare, and Vietnam finally invaded Cambodia in December 1978. One month later, it installed a puppet regime in Cambodia. Sihanouk once again went into exile in Beijing, where he formed a government and allied himself again with Pol Pot's Khmer Rouge, this time to throw out the Vietnamese.

The UN became involved in the Cambodian problem in 1981, when it sponsored an international conference on Cambodia in New York on 13 July. However, Vietnam and the East bloc countries boycotted the event, and China opposed the exclusion of the Khmer Rouge as a condition for holding elections in Cambodia. In 1982, UN secretary-general Javier Perez de Cuellar appointed a special representative to promote dialogue among the different factions. Unfortunately, these talks dragged on for more than five years, as the political situation in Indochina did not permit any significant rapprochement.

Finally, in 1986, the Cambodian resistance coalition accepted the principle of a government of national unity with the Phnom Penh regime and gave Norodom Sihanouk a mandate to initiate negotiations with Prime Minister Hun Sen. The first meeting between the two men took place from 2 to 4 December 1987 in Fère-en-Tardenois, near Paris. Other meetings followed. At the same time, the countries of Southeast Asia offered their services in bringing together the Cambodian factions, which met in Djakarta in 1988 and in 1989. These diplomatic efforts led to a conference on Cambodia in Paris on 30 July 1989, attended by eighteen countries and the four Cambodian factions, and chaired by France and Indonesia. This conference ended in failure, but the dialogue continued. The five permanent members of the UN Security Council took back the diplomatic initiative; in a series of meetings in 1990, they endorsed an overall plan for settlement that was an improvement on one proposed by Australia in February and called for massive UN intervention. The Cambodian factions accepted this plan on 9 September 1990. Following further meetings at the beginning of 1991, the Paris Conference on Cambodia was reopened and on 23 October 1991 an international peace agreement was signed by the four Cambodian factions – the state of Cambodia, the Khmer Rouge, the royalists loyal to Sihanouk, and the republican Khmer People's National Liberation Front – and eighteen other countries.

The agreement formally recognized the Supreme National Council (SNC), formed in September 1990 and chaired by Norodom Sihanouk, as the legal transitional government of Cambodia. In addition, it authorized the establishment of the United Nations Transitional Authority in Cambodia (UNTAC), with a mandate to ensure the complete restoration of Cambodia's sovereignty and independence and in particular to organize general elections. During the transition period, from October 1991 to September 1993, the SNC delegated its powers to UNTAC, thus giving it full authority to run the country and implement the Paris agreement. The powers of UNTAC were the most substantial ever assumed by a UN peacekeeping mission.

The agreement included many obligations for the Cambodian factions, and UNTAC had to make sure they were respected. The four factions committed themselves to cooperate with the UN peacekeeping mission in organizing general elections; to allow UNTAC to control public institutions that could influence the elections, particularly five key ministries; to free prisoners of war and repatriate refugees and exiles; to allow the withdrawal of foreign forces and their weapons from Cambodian territory; to maintain a ceasefire; and finally, to confine their troops to designated locations and decommission their weapons, munitions, and equipment. UNTAC was also to set up a broad program to promote human rights and democracy and participate in the economic and social reconstruction of the country.

The UN invested enormous financial and human resources in carrying out this huge project of political, social, and economic rehabilitation. Created by a resolution of the Security Council on 28 February 1992, UNTAC was allocated a budget of some two billion dollars. It consisted of 15,000 armed Blue Helmets, 600 observers, 3,600 unarmed civilian police officers, 1,300 international employees, and 700 foreign volunteers to supervise the elections. In addition, UNTAC would hire 8,000 Cambodians in the field for the duration of the mission, and 50,000 during the elections.[2]

The purpose of these provisions was to create a stable, neutral political environment to ensure the smooth running of elections for the 120 members of the Constituent Assembly, to be held from 23 to 28 May 1993. The head of UNTAC was to proclaim the results if the elections were 'free and fair.' The Assembly would then approve a new constitution, transform itself into a legislative assembly, and agree to the formation of a new government. At that time, UNTAC would leave the country.

* * *

After leaving Tuk Meas, the helicopter landed in a small clearing where some fifteen legionnaires had set up camp. They were combat engineers, engaged in rebuilding a nearby bridge. Since the small unit moved every two weeks to do repair or construction work, everything in the camp was temporary and uncomfortable. Colonel de Kermabon visited his men to check on their morale, to find out about their relations with the local authorities and residents, and to identify any supply problems or disciplinary problems. He took the opportunity to examine each soldier's personnel file and distribute rewards and reprimands. The legionnaires, many of whom had chequered pasts, were no angels, and with soldiers from ten nationalities in such a small group, isolated from the rest of the battalion for weeks at a time, interpersonal relations were sometimes tense. De Kermabon warned photographer Robert Côté that some of the men refused to have any contact with foreigners, particularly with journalists. Robert walked around the camp with his camera, but several legionnaires signalled him not to take photos. He did not insist.

De Kermabon and his aides visited another site before returning to spend the night in the legionnaires' camp at Tuk Meas, where thirty-odd soldiers had set up their quarters in an enormous unused warehouse. They had built a bamboo terrace and arranged their cots side by side, with low partitions of straw or cloth to provide a little privacy. Some had even bought old pieces of furniture in the local market to hold their personal effects. Next to the warehouse, UNTAC had erected prefabricated houses for its civilian employees in the region. They were modern and clean, with screened windows, and each one contained two new beds and a few other pieces of furniture. A generator supplied electricity. But the UN personnel did not live there. All of them – enumerators, election volunteers, secretaries, observers, police officers – had decided instead to stay in town. In groups of four or six, they had rented big houses surrounded by palm trees and gardens, and hired Cambodians to cook and clean. It was more pleasant – and cheaper. Although UNTAC rented the prefabricated houses at a reasonable price, it was still less expensive to live in town. This allowed the UN personnel to keep a large part of their daily stipend, which varied from U.S.$110 to $145 according to the job and the length of their stay. Foreign civilians have good reason to knock on the UN's door to volunteer for the peacekeeping missions: the pay is good and it's in U.S. dollars.

When the inspection was completed, the non-commissioned officer in charge of the small camp invited the colonel and his entourage for a drink before dinner. At exactly seven o'clock, the legionnaires gathered on the terrace waiting for their commander. This was their break from the routine in this out-of-the-way corner of Cambodia, a chance to find out what was going on in the rest of the country and in France. De Kermabon moved from group to group, shaking hands and chatting with his men. Then he approached the group of officers and non-commissioned officers who were accompanying him. The conversation quickly moved to the everyday problems facing the French Blue Helmets.

As in all peacekeeping missions throughout the world, the French Blue Helmets in Cambodia were subjected to rigorous testing of their 'neutrality and impartiality'[3] by the factions in the field. To ingratiate themselves with the legionnaires, the factions often showed a willingness to cooperate, but in return they expected the Blue Helmets to close their eyes to certain things. If the UN soldiers did not cooperate fully, the factions did not hesitate to attack and even to kill. Many contingents in Cambodia had experienced this dangerous but unavoidable game.

'There's a representative of the government in Phnom Penh who regularly warns us to be careful, especially at night,' said the NCO commanding the camp, 'because the opposition parties and the Khmer Rouge want to attack us and provoke an incident.'[4]

'He wants to get us on his side,' remarked de Kermabon.

'Exactly,' replied the NCO. 'I told him I know the people in the opposition well, and they're asking to be protected from intimidation and attacks by government soldiers.'

'What do you do to protect them?' asked the colonel.

'I've increased the number of patrols accompanying the UN civilian police (CIVPOL),' replied the NCO. 'But the police are always late and some of them are very lazy or scared. I can't force them to do their work.'

'What do those CIVPOLs do all day, anyway?' exclaimed de Kermabon.

'That depends on the officer, sir. Some never leave their quarters. They're afraid of getting killed. Others look the other way. In any case, you know the reports they write are sent to the government for investigation. And after that? No one knows. But what worries me the most is the safety of the election volunteers. They're very vulnerable.'

'Have there been any attacks on them?' asked de Kermabon.

'No direct attacks, but everyone tries to intimidate them. As the elections get closer, the parties are trying to get control of the voters. The volunteers' work is becoming more difficult. Sometimes people prevent them from going into certain villages or tell them their houses will be burned down if they persist in reporting violations of the election code.'

'We'll take care of that,' said de Kermabon.

'It's not easy with the volunteers,' said the NCO. 'They want to be independent and they don't like to go around surrounded by soldiers. They say there are enough soldiers in this country. I understand them. We'll have to be discreet.'

'Dinner is served!' called a legionnaire wearing a chef's hat.

The legionnaires moved quickly to a long table. Before sitting down to the meal, they recited their traditional prayer, a bawdy little song entitled 'Le boudin' (The Blood Sausage), part of the Foreign Legion repertoire.

* * *

In Sihanoukville, a major port in southern Cambodia, Colonel de Kermabon's legionnaires had their headquarters in a dark concrete building in the centre of town. The road leading to the small building teemed with people. The Cambodians had set up shops and restaurants to take advantage of the influx of soldiers. These stalls were crammed full of all kinds of imported and local products: Thai cookies, Japanese noodles, Coca-Cola, local bread and cakes, cigarette lighters, pens, and so on. Next to the headquarters, a merchant had set up a dozen tables where the legionnaires came for a breakfast of tea and little cakes filled with strawberry jam.

In the map room upstairs, one of the colonel's aides, Major Jean-Claude Paniez, pointer in hand, was describing the deployment of the French forces in sector six. Cambodia was divided into eleven sectors, with a Blue Helmet infantry battalion based in each one. Paniez described how each battalion had to redeploy itself in its sector. The French had stretched their troops to the limit. In a territory stretching 250 kilometres from east to west, they had set up twenty-two camps, whereas the other battalions had chosen to distribute their soldiers in eight to fourteen camps. This type of deployment, which existed in most UN peacekeeping missions, had several advantages. It allowed the contingents to be visible to the local population, dissuading potential troublemakers; to provide regular patrols on the roads and in many villages; and to react quickly in any crisis. Paniez and his staff maintained contact with the commanders of the camps in the sector.

'Here, the Khmer Rouge are not a serious threat,' said Paniez. 'There are about 500 of them between Takeo and Kampot, in the eastern part of the sector. They're completely isolated from the bulk of the Khmer Rouge forces, which are concentrated along the Thai border and are harassing the Netherlands, Pakistan, Malaysia, and Bangladesh battalions. 'Things are hot for the Blue Helmets there.'[5]

But today Paniez had received some bad news. The evening before, a grenade had exploded near the Hotel Soriya, where foreigners stayed, injuring four people. That morning another grenade had been found, opposite the CIVPOL villa.

'The French sector has always been very calm,' explained Paniez. 'But in the past few weeks, the Khmer Rouge have become more reckless and the goons from the political parties are increasing the pressure on the voters, who are frightened and a little disoriented with twenty political parties running in the election. Up to now, the reports I've received have been of acts of intimidation against voters or party officers. But now with the grenades, it's starting to get serious.'

Paniez could not say whether these explosives were planted by the Khmer Rouge or by one of the three factions that claim to respect law and order in the region. But he suspected the government party of knowing something about it. After all, there were very few Khmer Rouge in the region, and in Sihanoukville, the opposition was gaining momentum. Paniez asked Lieutenant Nicolas Brengues to visit the headquarters of each of the parties, especially the Buddhist Liberal Democratic Party, the most vulnerable.

Brengues jumped into his jeep and grabbed the radio microphone. He tried to contact the CIVPOLs, whose job was to make the rounds of the offices of the twenty-seven political parties in the city. The Blue Helmets were supposed to accompany and protect them, since the CIVPOLs were not armed. But the Blue Helmets frequently made the rounds alone, since there were not enough CIVPOLs and sometimes they were too lazy or too scared to do the work.

'Ah!' cried Brengues, satisfied, turning off the radio. 'It's the Irishman and the Indonesian. They'll come with us. We can count on them. They're hard workers.'

The CIVPOLs had not acquired a good reputation in Cambodia. Eighty per cent of them were from Third World countries, and most were not properly trained to fulfil their mandate of enforcing human rights and democracy. As a woman in UNTAC's electoral component asked, 'How can police from dictatorial states, who are responsible for repressing opposition in their own countries, suddenly be transformed into protectors of the law?' In addition, the civilian police did not seem to understand the scope of the powers they had been given. They tended to write reports rather than to investigate crimes that had been committed. And their laxity seemed to be a general problem. Stories about CIVPOLs raping Cambodians, getting drunk, trafficking in UN equipment, or avoiding their responsibilities fuelled innumerable rumours during the mission. Moreover, UN officials in New York admitted in confidence that this first large-scale use of police in a peacekeeping mission was not a success. There was no comparison with the CIVPOLs deployed in Cyprus for twenty-five years. Those police, from Australia, Austria, Denmark, Sweden, and New Zealand, successfully carried out their mandate of investigating violations in the international security zone between the two communities on the island. Their success was due to their knowledge of the law and human rights.[6]

Brengues's jeep, followed by another one carrying four legionnaires, turned onto the main street to join the all-white jeep of the two CIVPOLs waiting at an intersection. The three vehicles then headed toward the headquarters of the Buddhist Party, located in a small two-storey building surrounded by trees and gardens. There was no gate to control access, and the doors of the offices were wide open. A few employees were filling boxes with election leaflets, while others arranged chairs for the meeting that evening. As soon as they saw the legionnaires and the two CIVPOLs, one of them went to get the person in charge and the others smiled broadly and kept repeating 'merci,' the only French word they knew. The official arrived and began telling Brengues and the two policemen what had happened the night before. Late at night, cars with loudspeakers had driven past the building shouting slogans against the Buddhist Party, accusing it of being infiltrated by the Khmer Rouge. Shots were fired in the air and the troublemakers promised that even stronger action would soon be taken against the 'traitors' and 'criminals' of Pol Pot's clique.

The policemen took notes while Brengues explained to the official that the commander of the French Blue Helmets was offering them round-the-clock protection by the UN. Two legionnaires would park their jeep in the street opposite the building to keep an eye on things until the situation calmed down.

'This is the work of the government party,' said the French officer. 'It accuses all the other parties of being in the pay of the Khmer Rouge. But we can't do anything about it. The CIVPOLs will write a report and ask for explanations from the civilian and military authorities of the town, who are in cahoots with the government.'

'You'll see where the report ends up,' he added, pointing to the waste water flowing slowly in an open sewer.

* * *

The French Blue Helmets controlled a comparatively calm sector. The Khmer Rouge were isolated and the three other factions had decided to play the electoral game in spite of a few violent incidents. But that did not fully explain the quietness of the area. The French, unlike some of the other Blue Helmet contingents in the country, had quickly imposed their authority when they arrived in this region. They accomplished this, first, by their very visible presence throughout their sector. Systematic patrolling of the towns and villages and their help in rebuilding bridges, schools, hospitals, and orphanages facilitated the establishment of what Colonel de Kermabon called 'the small peace of the rice paddy.' The legionnaires also had their own interpretation of something that is a cornerstone of the peacekeeping mission – the directive on the use of force.

When a mission is created without any explicit provision in its mandate with respect to the possibility of using weapons (Chapter VII of the Charter), the UN's manual of procedures emphasizes that the use of force is permitted only in self-defence and that it must occur in stages.[7] Ultimately, it is the commander in the field who has to judge whether the use of force is warranted. In Cambodia, the various contingents interpreted the UN guidelines in different ways. For example, the battalion of Japanese engineers, who did not patrol a sector and who stayed together in their headquarters in Takeo, had received instructions to use weapons only when absolutely necessary, shooting into the air to persuade the attacker to withdraw. Aside from the French and the Dutch, the other contingents had received similar instructions. But the legionnaires had been ordered not to wait until they were directly attacked before responding. The French contingent's tough policy was to let the factions, especially the Khmer Rouge, know that French Blue Helmets who felt threatened could use their weapons to dissuade or even neutralize an adversary. The Dutch applied the same policy. The French and the Dutch consequently avoided any losses during their stay in Cambodia. This was not the case for other battalions, such as the Bulgarians.

Throughout its stay in Cambodia, the Bulgarian contingent occupied a region north of the French sector that consisted of two provinces, Kompong Speu and Kandal, in which the Khmer Rouge were not particularly numerous. As soon as a contingent arrived on the territory of a particularly active peacekeeping mission, the factions in the region would test its reaction to attack and its firmness in applying its mandate in the field. The Bulgarians proved not to be up to the task, and the factions, particularly the Khmer Rouge, took full advantage of their weaknesses.

The Bulgarians had arrived in Cambodia in a lamentable psychological and financial state. The soldiers were fresh recruits, who had learned on arrival that they would be staying for eighteen months, without leave and without pay. Demoralized and poorly trained, the Bulgarians quickly gained a terrible reputation both in their own sector and throughout the country. They understood neither English nor French, they sold UN equipment on the black market for American dollars, and many of them spent the whole day drinking. They were so undisciplined and unruly that even their commanding officer could not get them to obey him. One day, infuriated by the disorder, the officer fired a shot over the heads of his men to make them listen.

Given the circumstances, the Bulgarian Blue Helmets showed little enthusiasm in applying their mandate. They rarely even left their camps for the patrols that were necessary for the visibility of the UN in the field, and they had little contact with the local population. When UNTAC redivided the sectors of the Blue Helmet contingents so that they corresponded to the administrative boundaries of the Cambodian provinces, the French took over northern Takeo province, which had formerly been under Bulgarian control. When they arrived in the region, the legionnaires were surprised to discover that the Bulgarian soldiers were practically unknown in the area. They had made no visits or patrols and had not set up a camp. The legionnaires had to start from scratch.

The Bulgarians paid dearly for their laxity. On 2 April 1993, there was a showdown between the Blue Helmets and the Khmer Rouge. In the evening, a Khmer Rouge commander and two soldiers had dinner with eleven Bulgarian Blue Helmets in the Phum Prek camp, in the province of Kompong Speu. Everything seemed to go well, but after the meal the commander left and came back with some fifteen soldiers, obviously looking for a fight. After heated discussion, the Khmer Rouge opened fire, hitting six Bulgarians. The final toll was three dead. On 5 and 19 April there were further attacks on Bulgarian camps, and more casualties.

UNTAC was never able to clarify the Khmer Rouge's motives for gunning down the Bulgarian soldiers in cold blood or attacking their contingent directly. In the area bordering Thailand, where the Khmer Rouge forces were most numerous, the Bangladeshi, Malaysians, and Indonesians were increasingly subjected to violent attacks as the election date in May 1993 drew near. But in Phnom Penh, many UN employees had their own ideas about why the Khmer Rouge were challenging the UN peacekeeping mission.

* * *

In the UNTAC headquarters in Phnom Penh, the soldiers were furious. For several weeks, the Khmer Rouge and government soldiers had been interrupting election meetings and attacking the offices of political parties. They no longer even hesitated to go after UN staff, civilian or military. The list of wounded and dead was growing, to the dismay of UN officials, who were looking for a scapegoat.

'This is the fault of that indecisive, incompetent, Machiavellian Japanese,' suggested a French officer, nervously pacing one of the small airconditioned cubicles that made up the headquarters. 'If he showed a little more firmness and less concern for diplomatic subtleties, the mission wouldn't be on the verge of collapse.'

'Yes,' replied an Indian officer, 'but the Australian didn't help him. The order was always no rough stuff with the factions. Well, now we're getting it!'

'That Japanese' was Yasushi Akashi, the civilian head of UNTAC, proconsul of the UN in Cambodia. 'The Australian' was Lieutenant-General John Sanderson, head of the military component of the mission, made up of some 16,000 Blue Helmets from thirty-two countries. The former was a diplomat, the latter a soldier. It was their job to run what was at the time the most important mission in the history of the UN. This was not easy, and they were showered with criticism.

The tasks of UNTAC, as we have seen, were numerous: to disarm the soldiers and confine them to designated locations; to monitor the administration of the factions; to repatriate refugees; to prepare the electoral list; to organize elections; to transfer power to the new government; to promote human rights; to help in the rebuilding of the country; and even to arrest, try, and imprison those responsible for political crimes. To carry out these tasks, the leaders of the mission in Cambodia were given broad powers and considerable human and material resources. They were in charge, at least on paper. In the field, the situation was very different, which explains the complex manoeuvring of the UNTAC leaders.

The four factions had signed the Paris agreement, but the Khmer Rouge, quickly followed by the other three, had decided not to give up its weapons. Pol Pot's men, convinced that there were still Vietnamese soldiers in Cambodia and that UNTAC did not control the Phnom Penh government, had sworn to sabotage the election. In this situation, the UNTAC leaders had two alternatives: either to apply the agreement by force, or to continue the process leading to the elections and ignore the troublemakers. Akashi and Sanderson chose the second option. There were two reasons for their decision. First, the mandate of UNTAC had not been adopted under Chapter VII of the UN Charter, which provides for the use of force. It was therefore impossible for them to enforce the agreement. Second, the Khmer Rouge controlled only 10 to 15 per cent of the territory and less than 10 per cent of the population. The rest of the country was clearly in the hands of the Phnom Penh government. Akashi and Sanderson quickly understood the advantage this situation gave them. It was no longer possible to influence the Khmer Rouge through their long-standing allies, China and Thailand, who seemed to have lost their influence over them, nor was it possible to subdue them without a bloodbath, which no one – especially not the Japanese and Australian governments – wanted. Fewer than 10 per cent of the voters would be unable to vote. The Phnom Penh government, under scrutiny by the international community, and believing it could win the election, was willing to proceed. The two leaders of UNTAC were counting on the cooperation of the government – and they were proven right.

Akashi denied that he was weak, and justified these concessions to the Khmer Rouge. From the luxurious former residence of the French governors in the middle of UNTAC headquarters, he ruled over Cambodia. Flexible and benevolent, like the man himself, his reign would be a short one: eighteen months.

Modest and courteous, Akashi came to greet his visitors in the anteroom of his office. For this Japanese diplomat of sixty-two, who had risen through the ranks at UN headquarters in New York, running a UN peacekeeping mission represented the crowning achievement of a long career. During his stay in Phnom Penh, he was dismissed as a narrow, indecisive, easily influenced bureaucrat. But what many saw as cowardice was in fact a quiet strength drawn from his profound conviction that Cambodia had received special attention from the international community and that this was the opportunity to re-establish peace. The fairies had gathered around the cradle as soon as the agreement for a global settlement was signed in Paris in October 1991. The five great powers and the states bordering Cambodia had agreed to put an end to the war in Cambodia. Three of the four factions within the country were determined to play by the rules and to give the peace process a chance. The only disruptive element was the Khmer Rouge faction, which was quickly isolated. Such an international consensus was rare and, although it was fragile, there was much reason for hope.

In addition, Akashi was convinced that the election would serve as a catalyst to enable Cambodia to regain its place on the international scene after twenty-five years of war, and allow it to establish a democratic system, however imperfect. This election had become his greatest obsession, and for good reason: it was the first time in the history of the UN that the institution was organizing and supervising an election.* Akashi wanted nothing to interfere with this unique mandate, even at the price of a little bending of the Paris agreements and a few stains on the honour of the Blue Helmets.

'I'm not satisfied with the way this mission is going,' he said in April 1993, a few weeks before the election. 'But we have to accept the reality in the field. There's no democratic tradition in this country and I'm having a lot of trouble convincing the factions to show respect for their opponents. But this election must go ahead. It is the best chance Cambodians have had in a very long time. The presence of the UN is therefore indispensable for the rebirth of this country.'[8]

There was one doubt in Akashi's mind: everything could collapse at the last minute if the Khmer Rouge succeeded in killing enough Blue Helmets to intimidate the troop-contributing countries. Too many casualties in the ranks of UNTAC could force the UN to postpone the election while it waited for the situation to calm down. The special envoy of the secretary-general was aware of this danger. And in fact, at the beginning of April, a Japanese election volunteer was killed in cold blood (it was later learned that the Khmer Rouge had nothing to do with this murder), provoking lively debate in Japan about its participation in the peacekeeping mission. Then the Bulgarian Blue Helmets were killed and the camps of several contingents were systematically shelled. Tension remained high right up until the election, on 23 May 1993; some countries lost patience and quietly demanded the return of their civilian and military personnel.

But Akashi did not falter, and the results of the election would justify the strategy of quiet diplomacy he had pursued for eighteen months.

---

*In Namibia, in 1989–90, all it had done was monitor the election organized by South Africa and the local political parties.

From 23 to 28 May 1993, in spite of torrential rains, some 4.2 million Cambodians (90 per cent of the registered voters) made their way to 1,400 fixed voting stations and 200 mobile teams to vote. After the election week, which was punctuated by a few insignificant incidents and marked by the participation of several hundred Khmer Rouge, the Japanese diplomat proclaimed that the election had taken place freely and equitably.[9] Tears in his eyes, savouring his triumph, Akashi left Cambodia on 26 September, having presided over the return to power of Norodom Sihanouk. This election represented a much-needed success for the UN and its secretary-general, because elsewhere – in Western Sahara, Somalia, and the former Yugoslavia – the peacekeeping missions were either making little progress or failing completely.

5

Sabotage and Betrayal in Western Sahara

The small Royal Air Maroc ATR-42 set down gently on the runway of the airport in Laayoune, the capital of Western Sahara, in West Africa, where Morocco was involved in a bitter struggle with the Polisario Front independence movement. The airplane taxied for a few moments and came to a stop in front of the terminal, where a long red carpet had been rolled out. An honour guard in full regalia was awaiting the order to salute under the warm late-February sun. Some Sahrawi and Moroccan dignitaries disembarked. They were returning from a visit to Rabat, where Morocco had been celebrating the anniversaries of two major events that took place on 26 February: the accession to the throne of King Hassan II in 1961 and, fifteen years later, the proclamation of Moroccan sovereignty over the Spanish Sahara. In 1993, the whole country celebrated this double anniversary, rallying around its monarch. The king was as attached to Western Sahara as to his throne. Hassan II had put so much energy into conquering this desert region that were he to lose it he would very likely not survive politically. Western Sahara was his possession, as everyone who went there quickly learned.

While the local authorities congratulated the dignitaries, I headed toward the passport control counter, where the official on duty was already waiting for me. The Royal Air Maroc plane was the only one to land in Laayoune that day and among its passengers were only two foreigners: myself and, to my surprise, another Quebecker, a businessman from the Beauce region who had been trying for a year to establish a business in this remote corner of the world. The inspector knew him and let him pass. For me, it would be more difficult.

'You're the journalist, aren't you?'

'Yes, as a matter of fact,' I said, taken aback. When I looked up, I noticed a huge portrait of the king on the wall, surveying the scene.

The inspector motioned me to an office where I had to fill out a detailed form concerning my visit to Western Sahara, naming the hotel where I was staying and reporting how much money I was carrying and the people I was planning to see. He explained that he would have to keep my passport for several days to run some checks on the purpose of my visit. Just as I was about to protest, the UN officer who was supposed to meet me and help me get through arrived. Captain Daniel Villeneuve, a Canadian, entered the office holding a pile of papers, which, after greeting me, he handed to the official.

'We have the authorizations for this journalist to travel throughout the territory,' said Villeneuve, who worked for the headquarters of the United Nations Mission for the Referendum in Western Sahara (MINURSO). 'This gentleman is a guest of the mission commander.'

'Ah! well,' replied the official, hurriedly returning my passport. 'Go ahead.'

I was over the first hurdle. Another lay just ahead. After dropping my bags off at the hotel, Villeneuve drove me to mission headquarters, where I had an appointment with the deputy commander. Two Moroccan policemen standing guard in front of MINURSO's buildings stopped us at the entrance. Villeneuve showed them the authorizations and the letters to the governor of the province, the governor of the city, and the military authorities. It was no use; the two policemen refused to let me pass. They demanded more authorizations. Villeneuve and I waited in the parking lot. Then, one of the policemen asked us to go into a nearby residence to see some other policemen. Again we were forced to wait while two policemen tried to contact their superiors by cellular telephone. After half an hour of talk, they got the green light.

'Welcome to MINURSO,' said Villeneuve. 'You have to understand these policemen. They're terrified. The Moroccans want to control everything here.'

From high in the sky, Western Sahara had looked like an uninhabited, inhospitable patch of desert, nothing but endless sand dunes. However, when the plane approached Laayoune, the city had appeared, spread out over a large area, with a few big buildings. The capital is a far cry from the small village of twenty years ago, a few thousand inhabitants huddled together under tents. Today Laayoune, with close to 100,000 inhabitants, has an ultra-modern airport, broad avenues lined with well-tended flowers and trees, and brand new residential neighbourhoods. In the centre of the city, the Moroccan government has built several new hotels and renovated the sumptuous Hotel Parador, a Spanish establishment with Moorish architecture. Two storeys tall, with walled gardens, a swimming pool, a bar, a magnificent restaurant, and rooms furnished with deep couches, the Parador is a pleasant place to stay. And this is where the principal staff of MINURSO headquarters lived.

But behind this façade out of the thousand-and-one nights lies a completely different reality. There was a reason Laayoune was modernized at such great expense. The Moroccan government wanted as many Moroccans as possible to move here so that it would not lose control of the territory when a referendum organized by the UN allowed the inhabitants to choose between independence and remaining part of the kingdom of Morocco. The reason the hotels are so luxurious in Laayoune was quite simply to please the foreigners – Blue Helmets included – who could not move around in the territory without being watched. And while the cuisine at the Parador was excellent, the telephone operator was incapable of making a connection for you, especially if you were a journalist.

Unlike many other territories where the UN has had peacekeeping operations, Western Sahara was very difficult to get into. Sometimes the authorities would simply stop a visitor who was a little too adventurous – such as Jarat Chopra, a Brown University academic researching peacekeeping issues for the Ford Foundation. Several times in 1992, when he was trying to enter the territory and meet with MINURSO officials, Chopra was harassed by the Moroccan authorities. His description of his stay in Western Sahara is Kafkaesque.[1] Since then, the Moroccans loosened the screws somewhat, but their basic strategy remained unchanged since the beginning of UN involvement in the Western Sahara question in 1987. Morocco used every means possible to prevent contact between journalists and the local population, and to keep the media from scrutinizing its activities in the territory. Even the UN was not spared; the first contingent of Blue Helmets who went to Western Sahara in September 1991 had a taste of this Moroccan medicine.

* * *

When Brigadier-General Armand Roy of the Canadian army agreed to take command of MINURSO in June 1991, he did not know what he was getting into. A few months earlier, Roy had succeeded in peacefully resolving the Oka crisis, which had arisen when Mohawk Indians put up barricades on a bridge and roads near Montreal. As commander of the 5th Canadian Mechanized Brigade, based in Valcartier near Quebec City, the general had maintained a siege around the Mohawk barricades for sixty-two days without a single shot being fired. His keen sense of diplomacy, his patience, and the coolheadedness of his soldiers earned him unanimous praise and helped breathe new life into the Canadian Armed Forces. Roy seemed to be the ideal candidate for the mission to Western Sahara, and the UN did not hesitate when the Canadian government proposed him for the job. But the problem of Western Sahara proved to be much tougher than the Mohawk situation; Roy found himself having to deal with the twists and turns of international diplomacy, systematic sabotage by the Moroccans, and betrayal by a close associate.

Washed by the Atlantic Ocean in the west, and bordered on the north and south by Morocco, Algeria, and Mauritania, Western Sahara is a vast desert territory of 270,000 square kilometres, inhabited by about 700,000 people, most of whom lived in towns and villages.[2] A former Spanish colony, Western Sahara first came to the attention of the UN in 1965, when the General Assembly called on Spain to recognize the Sahrawi people's right to self-determination. For ten years, Madrid ignored this request, while Morocco and Mauritania staked claims to the territory.

In 1974 events moved quickly in the region. The UN asked the International Court of Justice (ICJ) for an opinion on the legal status of the territory and the territorial claims of Morocco and Mauritania. It also sent a fact-finding mission to determine the local population's wishes regarding the future of Western Sahara. One year later, the mission concluded that the inhabitants wanted independence, and on 16 October 1975, the ICJ rejected the Moroccan and Mauritanian claims and confirmed the Sahrawis' right to self-determination. The next day, in the famous 'Green March,' King Hassan sent 300,000 Moroccans to conquer Western Sahara. With its leader Franco on his deathbed, Spain had other things to worry about. It did not want to fight the Moroccans over this patch of desert, so it capitulated and negotiated an agreement to partition the territory between Morocco and Mauritania, which lost no time in occupying it. On 28 February 1976, the Spanish troops left their former colony.

The same day, the Polisario Front, a Sahrawi organization that had been fighting for independence for several years, proclaimed the Saharan Arab Democratic Republic (SADR), which was immediately recognized by Algeria and Libya. A war began between the Sahrawi guerrillas and the Moroccan and Mauritanian forces, which continued for twelve years. The Polisario Front forced the Mauritanians to withdraw and the Moroccans to build a wall of sand more than 2,000 kilometres long to contain its attacks. Although Morocco sent more than 100,000 soldiers to Western Sahara, it was unable to defeat the Polisario Front, which had considerable diplomatic and military support.*

Finally, in August 1988, after many attempts at international mediation, Morocco and the Polisario Front accepted a UN proposal to declare a ceasefire and organize a referendum for the population to choose between independence and integration into Morocco. Both parties were exhausted, but Morocco felt the tide turning in its favour. The Moroccans had not been able to destroy the Polisario Front, but the thousands of settlers they had brought into the territory had changed the demography, and they hoped that this would affect the outcome of the referendum. On 29 April 1991, the UN Security Council established MINURSO, and a few weeks later, the secretary-general, Javier Perez de Cuellar, set 6 September 1991 as the beginning of the ceasefire and the deployment of the MINURSO forces to monitor it.

In May 1991, in Quebec City, Armand Roy received a call from the commander of the Canadian army, Lieutenant-General Ken Forster, informing him that his name had been submitted to the UN for the post of military commander of MINURSO.[3] Forster explained that the secretary-general, the parties involved, and the members of the Security Council would study his record, and that if they raised no objections, his appointment would immediately be made public. Commanders of contingents are never notified in advance. On 25 May as planned, the UN announced Roy's appointment. 'In fact,' said the general, 'I found out I had been chosen when I read the newspaper on May 26.'

In July, after leaving his post as commander at Valcartier, Roy went to New York for a series of meetings with the secretary-general and the members of the Office of Peace-keeping Operations. There he met the civilian head of MINURSO, Johannes Manz, the Swiss diplomat in charge of the Western Sahara file since 1990, who had been appointed special representative of the secretary-general.

At the UN, Roy familiarized himself with the facts of the Western Sahara situation and with MINURSO's ambitious mandate. According to the 1988 proposal and the resolution of 29 April 1991, MINURSO was to monitor a ceasefire throughout the territory of Western Sahara, verify the

---

*The SADR was admitted to the Organization of African Unity in 1985. Some eighty countries recognized the republic.

reduction of Moroccan troops, monitor the confinement of Moroccan and Polisario Front troops to designated locations, ensure the release of prisoners of war, repatriate refugees, identify and register voters, and organize a referendum on the political status of the territory and proclaim the results.[4] This was a task unlike any other the UN had tackled. In order to carry it out, the UN sent two technical assessment missions, both commanded by Canadians. The first mission, led by Brigadier-General Terry Liston, arrived in the field at the end of 1987. In his report to the secretary-general, Liston proposed that the UN deploy between 15,000 and 25,000 observers, soldiers, and civilian employees to fulfil the mandate. This plan was overly ambitious and the UN backtracked. A second mission, led by Lieutenant-Colonel Alain Forand, visited the region in July and August 1990. Forand recommended that the UN deploy 2,600 observers and soldiers, a contingent of 300 police officers, and 1,000 civilian employees.[5] This was still too ambitious and definitely too costly for the UN. Finally, on 8 May 1991, the office of Perez de Cuellar's military adviser revised Forand's plan. The mission would consist of 1,700 soldiers, 300 police officers, and 1,000 civilian employees. Roy would have to carry out his mandate with the resources the UN gave him.

'General Liston's first plan was impressive,' said Forand. 'The number of soldiers reflected the situation in the field. The UN had to protect the access routes, the movement of refugees, the election process, the voting stations – on a territory as big as the United Kingdom. My proposal was more modest because I had to take into consideration the financial aspects of the mission. We had to do as much with less.'

In addition to having to live with logistical constraints, Roy realized that he was not fully in charge of his staff or his associates. For the first time in the history of peacekeeping operations, the 'Big Five' of the Security Council – the United States, the Soviet Union, France, the United Kingdom, and China – had decided to participate in a mission. But they had set their own conditions. They demanded key positions on the MINURSO staff, which meant there would be five colonels working with the general. Roy found jobs for them: one chief of staff, one military adviser, and three sector heads. But Roy was anxious to have Forand, who knew the situation well and had established good relations with the Polisario Front, with him on the mission. The position of liaison officer with the independence movement was therefore created; the officer would be based in Tindouf, in Algeria, where tens of thousands of Sahrawi refugees had been living since 1976.

In New York since July, Roy and his team were becoming impatient.

The political talks seemed interminable and the date of the ceasefire and deployment was fast approaching. Finally, in mid-August, they went to Morocco, Algeria, and Western Sahara to meet with their future negotiating partners and make certain everyone understood the meaning of the UN mission. Roy went to Rabat and Algiers, while his technical team got ready to go to Laayoune to prepare for the deployment of the first observers. The Morocco visit went badly. Appointments were repeatedly postponed, and the Moroccans did everything possible to hinder General Roy's movements. The technical mission could not get to Laayoune, while the general was a virtual prisoner in his hotel room. Morocco was imposing conditions before authorizing the deployment of the force; among other things, it was demanding that the problem of the criteria for eligibility of voters in the referendum be settled. To put pressure on the UN, Morocco prevented the unloading of the Blue Helmets' logistical equipment, which was sitting on ships in the Agadir harbour.

Perez de Cuellar was embarrassed. As the official date of the ceasefire drew near, his personnel were virtual prisoners and the Moroccan authorities were thumbing their noses at him. The secretary-general and the leaders of MINURSO looked at three options: delaying the deployment of the mission and risking failure, circumventing the Moroccans' objections and fully deploying the mission, or proceeding immediately with a limited deployment. They choose the third option.

* * *

On 4 September, the secretary-general of the UN announced that a hundred observers would leave for Western Sahara in the next forty-eight hours. Caught off guard, Morocco invited the observers to travel through its territory. After his experience in the gilded hotels of Rabat, Roy quickly understood the danger behind this invitation. Going to Morocco was out of the question. They had to land directly in Western Sahara. Roy turned to the United States, which had agreed to deploy some fifteen observers and which had had very close ties with King Hassan for thirty years. He asked the Pentagon to supply the UN with a military airplane. The Americans agreed, and the airplane took off from Washington without authorization from Morocco to land in Laayoune.

On 5 September, at about 11 a.m., the airplane approached the capital of Western Sahara. It circled the airport several times without receiving permission to land. Roy had foreseen this possibility, and planned that if the plane could not land, it would head to the Canary Islands until the

Moroccans' attitude changed. But the Americans did not see things this way. Alerted by radio messages from the pilot, the authorities in Washington immediately put pressure on Rabat, and the airplane landed in Laayoune, where the local governor received the members of the delegation with full honours.

After the formalities, Roy realized that he did not have his entire staff with him. Several observers, who had come from all over the world, were being held prisoner in Rabat; the Moroccan authorities refused to let them continue on to Laayoune. But it was urgent that they get there, because the observers had to be deployed quickly to monitor the ceasefire which was to take effect the next day (6 September). Roy asked the political authorities of the UN to put pressure on Morocco. In the meantime, since many of the observers had travelled with him, he started deploying them in the field. Using obsolete vehicles belonging to the Moroccan army, the first observers arrived at their makeshift camp on the very day of the ceasefire. By 15 September there were a hundred of them at the ten sites chosen by the UN; a month later there were two hundred.

In order to act as liaison with the Polisario Front on the day the ceasefire was to begin, Forand left Canada on 5 September for Tindouf by way of Amsterdam, Frankfurt, Geneva, and Algiers. In the Algerian capital, he realized he did not have his luggage, and he met a British officer who was to work with him. He also met the technician responsible for the operation of the INMARSAT communication system, which allowed the members of the mission to communicate with each other and with UN headquarters without going through the Moroccan communication network. This system was used on all peacekeeping missions. Forand, his two colleagues, and three representatives of the Algerian Ministry of Foreign Affairs arrived in Tindouf three days later. Forand would remain with the Polisario Front until April 1992.

The observers' task was complicated by the refusal of the Moroccan authorities to allow the UN to take delivery of its equipment in the port of Agadir. The headquarters staff of the force was housed in hotels in Laayoune, including the luxurious Parador. Conditions were dramatically different at the observation sites on both the Moroccan and the Sahrawi sides. Some of the observers were living in stables, without sanitary facilities, and their vehicles and radios did not work. The food was supplied by the local authorities. Heat and bad weather made the work difficult, and several camps were actually destroyed by the December rains.

Roy did everything in his power to boost the morale of his troops. He regularly visited the observation sites and tried to supplement their supplies with purchases from the markets of Laayoune. But it was not enough. The general was losing patience. His men seemed to be more concerned with trivial everyday matters than with their task of observation, which they were unable to carry out for lack of equipment. Several observers fell ill and had to be evacuated. Week after week, the Canadian general asked the UN for the release of his equipment in the Agadir harbour. The answer was always evasive. In Washington, some senators were worried about the health of the American observers. In January 1992, the Senate Committee on Foreign Relations sent an investigator to the region who published a report that was devastating for Morocco and the UN. The report concluded that unless the Blue Helmets' living conditions improved quickly and Morocco ended its systematic obstruction, the mission would soon fail. The American senators were ready to recommend the withdrawal of their observers.[6]

At his headquarters in Laayoune, Roy tried to find out why he was getting such vague answers to his questions to the UN. The special representative of the secretary-general, Johannes Manz, the civilian head of the mission, who worked in New York, was too busy with the political aspects of the mission to worry about its material problems. He suggested that Roy address his concerns to his assistant, Zia Rizvi. When Roy made his requests to Rizvi, he quickly discovered that the Pakistani diplomat was in close contact with the Moroccans, keeping them informed of everything that happened on the mission. He was also intervening directly at UN headquarters to keep Roy from getting the equipment and supplies the mission needed. Officially, Rizvi was claiming that the mission must not spend too much money and that certain equipment was not essential. But it was public knowledge at the UN that he did not share Roy's and Manz's views on the referendum in Western Sahara. Rizvi favoured a 'Moroccan solution.'

While Roy was struggling to improve living conditions for the Blue Helmets in the far reaches of Western Sahara, the operation was stalled diplomatically. Manz knew the issues well, and he knew that the main bone of contention between Morocco and the Polisario Front was the electoral list; whoever controlled it would be sure to win the referendum planned for January 1992. Morocco and the Polisario Front had agreed to accept the census of 1974 as the basis for voter eligibility. An Identification Commission was to be set up to define the criteria for adding voters and completing the 1974 list. Already in the summer of 1991, Morocco had claimed that the list was incomplete, and that thousands of Western Sahara residents who were outside the country at the time of the Spanish census had had the right to vote since 1976. In fact, Morocco had brought tens of thousands of Moroccans into Western Sahara and it wanted some 120,000 additional voters registered.[7]

Morocco's demand was unacceptable to the Polisario Front, but Rabat could count on staunch allies to get its position adopted. Morocco's special relationship with the United States and France and its participation in the 1990–1 Gulf War as part of the multinational coalition played in its favour. There were negotiations between Morocco and Secretary-General Perez de Cuellar – from which Johannes Manz was excluded – and Rabat managed to impose its point of view on Perez de Cuellar, whose mandate as secretary-general was to end in December 1991. The secretary-general informed Roy and Manz of his decision to broaden the eligibility criteria for voters and wrote a report to this effect for the Security Council. Furious, Manz tendered his resignation.

Perez de Cuellar's successor, Boutros Boutros-Ghali, inherited the question in January 1992. In the field, the UN was convinced that the mission had been sabotaged by Rizvi: the new secretary-general discreetly obtained the Pakistani diplomat's resignation in February 1992.[8] Roy became *persona non grata* in Rabat, and Hassan II tried to get him recalled to Canada. But the UN refused to yield to the pressure and kept Roy in his position until April 1992.

After Roy's departure there was little change in the situation in the field. Morocco continued to obstruct the process, convinced that time was on its side. And in fact, after the defection of its minister of external affairs to the Moroccan camp in August 1992, the Polisario Front was in complete disarray. In addition, the independence movement could no longer count on the staunch support of Algeria, which was destabilized by a deep political and economic crisis.

The referendum was postponed several times. It is now expected to be held at the end of 1998, thanks to the diplomatic efforts of former American secretary of state James Baker, who acted as mediator between the two parties. In September 1997, Morocco and the Polisario Front agreed on the number of voters.[9]

* * *

While waiting for Morocco, the Polisario Front, and the UN to settle their disagreements, the Blue Helmets continued to patrol the desert. In March 1993, in Mahbas, the most easterly UN site of the Western Sahara territory, a few kilometres from the Moroccan, Algerian, and Mauritanian borders, I met Major Simon Lang, the British officer commanding the site. He provided detailed information on the camp and the surrounding area and on the work done by the observers based there. There were some fifteen of them, from Canada, China, Kenya, and several other countries.

The tiny camp consisted of five big Weatherhaven shelters made for use in the Canadian North. These huge white tents, wind-resistant and equipped with heating and air-conditioning, were welcome in the Sahara, where temperatures could reach 0°C in winter and easily as high as 45°C in summer. Two of these shelters served as canteen, bathroom, and meeting room for the observers. The camp was surrounded by a high wire fence, beyond which there was nothing but sand. The nearest camp of Moroccan soldiers was at least ten kilometres away.

In this isolated outpost far from the capital, life was not always pleasant. Sandstorms sometimes made it impossible to go outside, and the observers struggled to amuse themselves. Everyday activities often gave rise to frictions that poisoned the atmosphere, because some of the observers were from countries where they were accorded a degree of respect unknown in the West. Some officers balked at doing cleaning chores or guard duty, tasks that would fall to subordinates in any army. But here all the observers were equal – at least in principle. The camp commander had to exercise great tact and be able to command respect to break the monotony and prevent quarrelling. His main concern was to keep his men busy with responsibilities for managing the camp, patrolling the territory, and maintaining relations with the local authorities.

Lang unfolded a small map of Western Sahara on the hood of his white UN Jeep and indicated the area his team had to monitor: 10,000 square kilometres of flat desert terrain to the north and mountains to the south. Mahbas was situated in Moroccan-controlled territory a few kilometres within the wall of sand. On the other side of the wall was Sahrawi territory.

The Blue Helmets made a minimum of two patrols daily, each consisting of two vehicles carrying two officers. The area was divided into ten sectors, which had to be patrolled weekly. Each group of observers visited a different sector every week. They also instituted twenty-four-hour patrols, in which the observers would spend the night on watch at a specific location to make sure the Moroccans were not moving military equipment without authorization or increasing the troops they had stationed there.

The jeep advanced slowly along the paved road. At each turn Lang made sure the road ahead had been cleared of mines. A few months before, a few kilometres from Mahbas, a vehicle had been blown up by an anti-tank mine, seriously injuring a Blue Helmet. For increased safety, there was a heavy metal covering on the floors of the UN vehicles, but it provided only limited protection. In spite of repeated requests by the UN, neither Morocco nor the Polisario Front would provide the Blue Helmets with a list of the mined areas of Western Sahara. 'There have been mines buried in this territory for sixteen years,' said Lang with a sigh. 'I don't think they know where they are anymore.'[10]

Kilometre after kilometre from the Mahbas site, there was nothing but desert. Then, suddenly, the headquarters of a Moroccan mechanized brigade appeared before us, a huge fort with small towers. Within it we could see officers' quarters and troop transporters and other trucks. Lang could only enter the fort with the express authorization of the commander. Generally, the UN officers would present themselves at the entrance and the Moroccan officers would come out and drink mint tea and talk with them. We drove on a few kilometres farther, with the road becoming worse and worse and the sun beating down mercilessly. We came to the first camp of Moroccan soldiers. It consisted of rows of barracks built of earth and stones, without water or electricity, and with sand getting in everywhere. Each building held about a hundred soldiers, who slept on the ground. These deplorable living conditions were a far cry from those enjoyed by the officers. But Lang pointed out that most of the soldiers were conscripts who came from poor areas and were only stationed there for six months or a year. A few hundred metres away, we stopped at a very busy water point. Huge tanker trucks came here to fill up from the thin stream of water. The Moroccan soldier in charge of monitoring the site received us in his tiny guardhouse, which was barely large enough to contain all of us. In halting French he offered us mint tea. He himself would not have any, since it was Ramadan. Lang asked how he was and if he needed anything.

'I come to see this guy regularly,' said Lang. 'He's in a privileged position here. He doesn't live packed in with the other soldiers.' Lang kept in contact with the soldier, talking to him about everything and nothing, and always managing to obtain some information that helped him understand the Moroccans better.

From the beginning, Morocco had been less than frank. According to the UN plan, when the ceasefire took effect each party was supposed to declare the number of soldiers and the amount of military equipment it had in Western Sahara and identify the locations of its troops. The Polisario Front complied with the plan, but the Moroccans always refused to give details on their forces. In addition, they imposed numerous restrictions on the movements of the Blue Helmets. The result was that the Blue Helmets were reduced to noting observations made during their difficult ground or aerial patrols. The work of analysing the data was complex. Lacking solid information, the Blue Helmets estimated that there were between 65,000 and 150,000 Moroccan soldiers in Western Sahara.

'With the information we've gathered, we've managed to sketch a fairly accurate picture of their units in order to monitor their withdrawal when the peace plan goes into effect,' explained Lang. 'We can't allow ourselves to be neutralized by harassment and irritations.'

* * *

A few kilometres east of Mahbas, in Algerian territory, the ten Blue Helmets living in Tindouf were having a slightly easier time. With an energy born of despair, the Polisario Front was cooperating fully. The independence movement no longer had anything to lose.

The Tindouf camp was also located in the middle of the desert, but it was not isolated. There were tens of thousands of Sahrawi refugees in this region, living in tents while waiting to return home. The ten Blue Helmets lived in a modern Algerian army camp built for a whole battalion in the mid-1980s, when Algeria was preparing for armed conflict with Morocco over Western Sahara. Now that Algeria was facing a crumbling economy and a threat to political stability from Islamic fundamentalist terrorism, Algiers had lost its pro-Polisario fervour and, like the Sahrawis, was waiting for the UN referendum.

In one of the buildings of the camp, a Russian colonel spent his days in the TV room watching videos. Wearing a jogging suit, he was stretched out on a sofa. 'He always dresses like that,' said one of the Blue Helmets with exasperation.

'There's nothing to do here,' retorted the Russian. 'Yesterday there was a huge sandstorm. Impossible to go out.' This colonel was not held in very high regard by his colleagues. As in many peacekeeping missions, the men in positions of responsibility were not necessarily the most competent. In assigning these positions, the UN had to maintain a delicate balance among the troop-contributing countries, doing the best it could with the soldiers they provided. The colonel rarely left the building and he did not like to mix with the local population. He was in Tindouf because there was no room for him at MINURSO headquarters in Laayoune. His one desire was to go home.

The Russian colonel told Canadian captain Raymond Ouellette that he could take me to see the Sahrawi leaders, and indicated that he had signed the papers authorizing my visit to the refugee camps. There would be no problem moving around here, since the Polisario Front had every interest in gaining as much sympathy as possible.

In his jeep with the UN colours, Ouellette sped toward one of the refugee camps, grumbling about the Russian colonel and some of the officers, who spent their time playing video games while he was always on the road patrolling. But Ouellette enjoyed what he was doing. The last thing he wanted was to twiddle his thumbs waiting to be transferred to Laayoune or repatriated to Canada at the end of his one-year tour in Western Sahara.

The jeep stopped in front of a group of small, low houses. A Sahrawi was waiting to guide us through narrow streets to a house where we had an appointment to meet some leaders of the Polisario Front. Two leaders of the independence movement were already there, in a room that was dark but well furnished, containing several large sofas, a beautiful bookshelf, a television, a cassette player, and a telephone. They welcomed me warmly.

Emhamed Khadad, a member of the Polisario national secretariat, was the more talkative of the two. He spoke non-stop and with a good deal of assurance – possibly too much. 'The Sahrawis will vote for independence if they have the opportunity to participate in a truly democratic consultation,' he declared.[11] 'If that doesn't happen, we will take up the armed struggle again.' Khadad cited his organization's military exploits against the Moroccans over the previous decade, and listed the Polisario Front's diplomatic and political supporters. He brandished the UN texts on the organization of the referendum.

The head of the Polisario army, Mohamed Louali, sat silently on another sofa through almost the entire interview. He must have known that his troops were becoming exhausted and that every day that passed strengthened the Moroccans' military and diplomatic position. Like Khadad, though, he made a few pat pronouncements on the strength of the Polisario Front. 'We will know how to deal with our enemies if the war resumes,' he declared. But war with what and with whom? The Polisario Front had no more weapons, since its usual suppliers, Algeria and Libya, now had other problems to deal with. Morocco occupied practically all of Western Sahara, while the Polisario Front held only a few hectares of desert. In the camps, the cause had lost its attraction after seventeen years of fighting. Sahrawis, including several traditional chiefs, were defecting to the Moroccan side by the hundreds. Cracks were even showing in the government of the Saharan Arab Democratic Republic. In August 1992, the minister of foreign affairs had gone over to the Moroccans, and to show his gratitude, King Hassan II had appointed him ambassador-at-large. Since then, he had constantly been criticizing the organization, weakening the Polisario Front's diplomatic position in the world.

'Individuals don't count,' said Khadad. 'The defections have not led to the departure of large numbers of soldiers or common people to Morocco or to the part of Western Sahara controlled by the enemy. We still have hope.'

Khadad and Louali were placing a lot of faith in the UN peace process. Indeed, it was their only hope. They were friendly to the Blue Helmets and made every effort possible to make their lives easier and to show them that the Polisario Front was respecting the ceasefire and indeed the UN resolutions on Western Sahara. But their hearts were no longer in it. No one cared about this quiet desert people who got no live coverage on CNN. There was no fighting here; there were no children dying of hunger; no hospitals were being bombed. The Sahrawis were the Palestinians of western Africa. Like the Palestinians, they had been living in crowded refugee camps for a long time. And like them, they clung to the UN bureaucracy in the hope that one day the world would come to their aid.

6

The New Warriors

Somalia is a big country at the eastern edge of the African continent, located in a region that, because of its shape, is called the Horn of Africa. Washed by the Indian Ocean and the Gulf of Aden, its eastern tip seems to be reaching northward toward the Arabian Peninsula. On the west, Somalia borders on Djibouti, Ethiopia, and Kenya. Home to a population of some eight million, it has a huge desert in the south, while the north is greener, with a more hospitable climate. Somalia is one of the poorest countries in the world. Its geographic location on the route of the oil tankers made it highly coveted by the Soviets and the Americans during the Cold War, but after the collapse of the East bloc Somalia was completely abandoned. Its old allies left only one legacy, a mountain of weapons, and the groups that began fighting for power in 1988 used them with brutal determination.

When fighting first broke out in Somalia in the late 1980s, the country had been governed for twenty years by a complex, scheming character, General Mohamed Siyad Barre. Over the course of two decades, Siyad Barre had made Somalia his personal fiefdom, in which his family and his clan divided up the power and foreign aid among themselves. When he became president in 1969, Siyad Barre established a socialist regime and appealed for Soviet aid to counterbalance the influence of his long-standing enemy, pro-American Ethiopia. But the alliance with Moscow was short-lived. In 1974, the Ethiopian emperor was overthrown by a Communist revolution, and Soviet and Cuban military advisers soon arrived in Ethiopia. The Somalis, who were involved in a dispute with Ethiopia over the Ogaden province, did not appreciate their allies becoming so friendly with their enemies, and they invaded the disputed province. Aided by Soviet and Cuban soldiers, the Ethiopians fought back, and in 1977 they prevented the Ogaden from falling into Somali hands. Moscow and Havana had chosen their camp. So Siyad Barre invited the Americans, who had been thrown out of Ethiopia, to come to Somalia. They accepted.

The alliance with the Americans, however, did not help Siyad Barre to consolidate his power. The president had lost support within the Somali population after his defeat in the Ogaden. To foil his enemies, Siyad Barre increasingly played on the system of clan alliances – the old basis of power in the region – which he had actually attempted to break up at the beginning of his reign. A rebellion broke out among clans that controlled vast regions of the country. Between 1988 and 1990, the clans of the north, centre, and south of the country took control of those regions. Siyad Barre was left in control of nothing but the capital, Mogadishu, and an insurrection broke out there in December 1990. A month later, the president fled the capital, which was being looted by armed gangs. Those who drove Siyad Barre out did not, however, form a united front: no sooner had they rid themselves of the old regime than they began quarrelling among themselves. For two years, Mogadishu and the central and southern regions of Somalia were plunged into bloody fighting among clans and opposition movements. Entire towns were destroyed. As Somalia sank into civil war, the population began to suffer.

By the end of 1991, the international community was concerned about the Somalis' situation. It was difficult to intervene, since Somalia was a sovereign member state of the UN. But it was obvious that there was no government in control of the country: the north had declared independence, while the capital was split in two. As the fighting continued, the secretary-general of the UN, Javier Perez de Cuellar, announced in December 1991 that he was sending a representative to the region to attempt to bring the factions together.

On 23 January 1992, following the presentation of a report on the situation, the Security Council adopted a resolution calling on all parties to accept a ceasefire and asking the UN to speed up its humanitarian aid program. In April, after a ceasefire agreement was accepted by the leaders of the two major factions – the interim president, Ali Mahdi, and the head of the United Somali Congress, General Mohamed Farah Aidid – the Security Council authorized the creation of the United Nations Operation in Somalia (UNOSOM I) to enforce the agreement, and accepted the appointment of Mohamed Shanoun, an Algerian diplomat who knew Somalia well, as special representative of the secretary-general. The resolution authorized the sending of fifty observers to monitor the ceasefire and a security force to protect the humanitarian aid arriving by ship and plane. In a report presented to the Security Council in April 1992, the new secretary-general, Boutros Boutros-Ghali, stated that the situation in the country was critical and that about five million Somalis required emergency food and medical aid.[1]

In spite of these decisions, fighting and looting continued in Somalia. The UN's slowness in deploying some five hundred Blue Helmets – who arrived five months after the resolution was voted – allowed the various factions to hold the humanitarian organizations to ransom and intimidate UN personnel already in the country. Mohamed Shanoun sharply criticized the humanitarian organizations associated with the UN for their slow response in coming to Somalia's aid. He also had a few choice words for 'UN employees who demand guarantees about their working conditions before they leave.'[2] In August, Boutros-Ghali again alerted the Security Council that the situation was deteriorating. In another report, he spoke of the famine ravaging the central and southern regions of the country and the unsafe conditions that hampered the work of the humanitarian organizations.[3] The Security Council then authorized an increase from 500 to 4,200 Blue Helmets.[4]

By November, the situation in the country had become desperate. The five hundred Pakistani Blue Helmets protecting the Mogadishu airport were fired on. The special representative, Mohamed Shanoun, resigned dramatically; he had been attacked for having too openly criticized UN activities in Somalia. In fact, he had been unable to see eye to eye with Boutros-Ghali on political and military strategy in Somalia.[5] UN efforts to bring the warlords together were unsuccessful, and every day Western television was filled with intolerable images of emaciated Somalis dying of hunger while the militias stole the food shipments arriving in the port of Mogadishu. Finally, the Blue Helmets who were supposed to provide back-up support to the Pakistanis could not be deployed – the Somali factions would not let them enter the country. In a letter to the Security Council on 27 November, Boutros-Ghali expressed frustration, but also his determination to see the UN intervene more energetically. He held General Aidid responsible for the situation. At the end of his letter, he said that it 'might become necessary to review the basic premises and principles of the United Nations effort in Somalia.'[6] The secretary-general was already planning military intervention.

For several weeks, in fact, Boutros-Ghali and his advisers had been toying with the idea of more forceful UN intervention in Somalia. Two things were required for this: a commitment from the United States, and the consent of the members of the Security Council to invoke Chapter VII of the UN Charter, which authorized the use of armed force. Until now, the Blue Helmets had always been sent on missions under Chapter VI. They were responsible for *peacekeeping*, with the consent of the parties, and used their weapons only in self-defence. In Somalia Boutros-Ghali wanted to go further, and to test the reaction of the members of the Security Council to the views he had expressed on the use of force in his *Agenda for Peace* in June 1992. Boutros-Ghali envisioned military intervention without the consent of the parties in order to provide security for the work of the humanitarian organizations. It was a matter of creating a climate of security in the country in which the distribution of relief to the Somalis would become possible. To fulfil this mission, the secretary-general needed to transform his Blue Helmets into well-armed warriors.

The military intervention that the secretary-general was planning involved a second innovation: Boutros-Ghali wanted the UN to take command of the forces that would be sent to Somalia under Chapter VII.[7] For the first time, the UN would lead a *peace-enforcement* mission. During the Gulf War in 1990–1, the multinational coalition had been under United States command and operated with the permission of the UN. Boutros-Ghali now wanted to go one step further to assert the independence of the UN in relation to the great powers. The idea of entrusting command of the forces entirely to the UN was a bold one – and it met with a categorical refusal by the United States.

American president George Bush, having lost the presidential election on 3 November 1992, wanted to go down in history as dramatically as possible when he left the presidency. The success scored against the Iraqi forces in the Gulf War was not enough for him. Somalia provided an opportunity. Like all Americans, he was disturbed by the images of the famine raging there, and he calculated that he could save the Somalis and give his image a boost at the same time. Bush therefore enthusiastically welcomed Boutros-Ghali's suggestion that the United States spearhead a coalition that would land in Somalia. However, he set two conditions that Boutros-Ghali found difficult to accept: that the United States lead the coalition, and that the American forces withdraw quickly.

The secretary-general was not pleased, but he had no choice. Who but the United States could undertake such a rescue operation? Boutros-Ghali reluctantly accepted. On 3 December 1992, pressured by the United States and France, the thirteen other members of the Security Council adopted Resolution 794 authorizing the formation of a coalition to come to the aid of the Somalis. The only concession the U.S. made to Boutros-Ghali's demands was with respect to the leadership of the coalition: there would be coordination between the UN and the military forces under U.S. command. Thus the Unified Task Force in Somalia (UNITAF) was born. The small UNOSOM I force deployed in Mogadishu would remain in the background as its leaders prepared for the transition from UNITAF to UNOSOM II to take place on 4 May 1993.

The participation of the United States persuaded many other countries to follow suit. Some 38,000 soldiers from twenty-two countries took part in Operation Restore Hope. Canada sent 2,300 soldiers, including 750 deployed at Belet Uen. These soldiers – who were not, strictly speaking, Blue Helmets since they were not under UN authority – had the right to enforce peace through war. The actions of the Americans and Canadians in Somalia must be understood within this context.

* * *

The huge camp of the multinational force at the Mogadishu airport was slowly waking up. At dawn, military cargo planes from Nairobi, Kenya, had begun landing, and the roar was deafening. They were loaded with food for the starving population or supplies for the thousands of UNITAF soldiers. Every five minutes, an airplane would land or take off. It was impossible to sleep in the tents near the landing strips.

When the UN decided to send a multinational force to Somalia, planners for UNITAF visited the country before the troops were deployed. Their plans were to deploy half of the soldiers in the central and southern regions of the country, where fighting and famine were ravaging the population, and the other half – soldiers specialized in logistics and transportation, and headquarters personnel – in an accessible location. The UNITAF planners did not have to do much research to decide where the latter group should be stationed: the airport was the obvious choice. The runways were in good condition and the airport was located on the ocean, so the UNITAF supply ships could deliver military equipment. It was certainly the most secure place in Mogadishu, which was still being terrorized by armed gangs, and also the most secure in Somalia. To avoid making the airport a ghetto cut off from the Somali population, however, UNITAF established its headquarters in the buildings of the former American embassy in the centre of Mogadishu.

The soldiers were beginning to busy themselves around their respective camps. It was the end of February 1993; the rainy season was over and the weather was good in spite of the humidity. There were at least 10,000 soldiers throughout the airport site. Each contingent's camp reflected the circumstances of the country it came from. The Canadians had set up their tents between the post guarding the entrance to the airport on the north and a hill of earth and sand that hid the sea on the east. They controlled part of the activities at the airport. Their Canadians' neighbours were a diverse group. To the south were the Zimbabwean and the Norwegian contingents. The Zimbabweans lived in total privation, without toilets or showers. They spent their days asking the Western soldiers for music cassettes, toothbrushes, or bottled water, and their commander complained that he had nothing to do. Next to them, the Norwegians had erected a miniature Scandinavian village with immaculate tents, clean streets, and well-wrapped garbage.

To the west of the Canadian installations, across the road separating the camps from the airport itself, the three small tents of the Botswana contingent were squeezed between the Australian and New Zealand camps. The Botswanans didn't complain, as they benefited from the generosity of those two contingents, which provided food, beer, and consumer products otherwise unavailable to them. Further south, the Turks, Swedes, Moroccans, Kuwaitis, and others were well set up, and on some evenings the aroma of Moroccan couscous whetted the appetites of the other contingents. The American, French, and Italian units had established their quarters on the hill facing the sea. What contrasts there were among all these different contingents from all over the world! When they were not on a patrol or a special mission, the Marines would exercise, while the Italians washed and hung up their laundry and talked endlessly in an atmosphere of dolce farniente. The French soldiers lay on their cots, reading quietly. War seemed so far away.

The multinational force lived in isolation. The soldiers traded currency or possessions, they organized video nights, and, when permitted, invited each other for meals to sample the different cuisines. The Canadians were instructed to eat only rations, or food brought in by the Canadian planes. This was a matter of safety; food poisoning, always a possibility, could confine soldiers to bed for days. But the Moroccans did not care. They devoured their couscous with fresh meat.

Mogadishu was like Beirut, only worse. Getting there required an armoured vehicle, a steel helmet, and bullet-proof vest. It was the world of the Mad Maxes, or 'technicals,' vehicles with guns mounted on them, crammed with armed young Somalis who chewed khat leaves all day long, which made them irritable and irrational. Fighting between rival clans in

1991 and 1992 had completely destroyed the city, reducing the superb Italian-style villas and other buildings – Italy was the former colonial power – to ruins. Not a single neighbourhood had escaped the fury of the fighters, who looted everything, even electrical wire and underground cables.

Everywhere in Mogadishu, the contrasts were striking. In this devastated city, on the cliff road leading to the seashore, a magnificent restaurant with large sparkling clean windows offered exorbitantly priced dishes to the UN officials and the few privileged Somalis who had access to dollars and an escort to get there. The Indian Ocean Bar and Beach Club overlooking the beach lapped gently by the waves of the Indian Ocean, seemed unreal, given the ruin and desolation which lay all around it. A handful of Somalis had set up housekeeping in the neighbouring buildings. As the women searched for something to eat, children smiled and played in the debris and the broken glass. There were few men in sight; they must have been meeting somewhere to prepare for the next clash between rival groups.

In the heart of the capital, near the green line dividing the city into two territories – the south controlled by the militias of General Mohamed Aidid, the north by those of President Ali Mahdi – was a ghostly zone where the Catholic cathedral, hotels, and other buildings had been reduced to dust. A few kilometres away stood the UNITAF headquarters. In this strange place, you might believe yourself to be in the middle of a science fiction film. Bristling with antennas, the huge headquarters housed the offices of UNITAF and several foreign contingents. A small city had grown up around it, its inhabitants seeking safety by crowding close to the barbed wire surrounding this haven of peace. These refugees had built hundreds of huts out of branches, rags, and trash recovered from the garbage cans of the soldiers of Operation Restore Hope. The inhabitants of the shacks were often Somalis who worked for the multinational force and received good salaries. The others had to rely on the humanitarian organizations, which brought daily meals. Close to the headquarters, dozens of women and children accosted visitors, trying to sell statuettes, wooden canes, and necklaces.

Within, the headquarters was an oasis of tranquillity. Some soldiers jogged, while others lounged under the trees. Some of the contingents had air-conditioned shelters, where the soldiers worked night and day to provide satellite communication in this city which had no telephone system. The soldiers could buy chocolate, gum, potato chips, t-shirts, paper, or newspapers. In the centre, the former American embassy housed the offices of the UNITAF leaders. Here they planned the military operations of the multinational force and made preparations for the political negotiations among the Somali factions. It was also here that Operation Restore Hope turned into a nightmare for the coalition and for many Somalis.

* * *

On 8 December 1992, only five days after the adoption of the UN resolution on intervention in Somalia, the first American soldiers landed on the beaches of Mogadishu. They were greeted by a swarm of American journalists and star correspondents, who had been given advance notice of the landing. Television viewers throughout the world watched the soldiers' arrival live. The U.S.-UN humanitarian intervention began like a major Hollywood production.

Although there was much criticism of this transformation of Operation Restore Hope into a media event, the Somalis did not complain – at least not at first. The coalition soldiers re-established order and security in Mogadishu and in the central and southern regions of the country. The militias, with their menacing 'technicals,' disappeared from the streets and roads. Humanitarian aid was unloaded in the harbour of the capital in complete safety, and convoys began once more to travel back and forth across the country. In a few months, the starving babies who had troubled the world's conscience disappeared, replaced by happy little children. Roads were repaired, hospitals and schools rebuilt, and vaccination programs for people and livestock re-established. The humanitarian operation was a success. However, certain incidents occurred that, at the time, were swept under the rug. When it came to light that deadly acts had been committed, investigations were instituted by the UN and three of the participating countries, Canada, Belgium, and Italy. (This will be discussed further in the next chapter.)

But the aim of Operation Restore Hope was not merely to fill the stomachs and dress the wounds of the Somalis; it was also to restore the country's institutions and establish a stable political order, by force if necessary. At least that was what Boutros Boutros-Ghali believed.

Before the intervention of the UNITAF coalition, the secretary-general's many reports on Somalia emphasized two objectives that had to be met in order to re-establish order and security in the country. The factions must be induced to enter into a process of political negotiation leading to national reconciliation, and the militias and the population had to be disarmed. The latter objective was a veritable obsession for

Boutros-Ghali, because the country was flooded with arms – every Somali had a weapon. The prevalence of arms threatened both Somali society and the workers of the humanitarian organizations. As early as 21 April 1992, Boutros-Ghali wrote that 'there is a pressing need to recover the enormous number of small and medium-sized arms which are already in the hands of the civilian population throughout Somalia, and particularly in Mogadishu.'[8] A few months later, in July, he raised the question again, proposing the innovative idea that the UN consider 'the feasibility of an "arms for food" exchange programme, bearing in mind that this would require military personnel adequately armed and equipped for this task.'[9] The secretary-general made this recommendation on the basis of a traditional peacekeeping operation, that is, one having the consent of the parties. As the situation in Somalia deteriorated – people were dying of hunger, and the few Blue Helmets deployed on the ground could not even leave their bunkers – Boutros-Ghali wanted to take more forceful action. So the UNITAF coalition was established, with permission to use force. Less than two weeks after the American landing in Somalia, Boutros-Ghali met with President Bush; brandishing Chapter VII of the UN Charter on the use of armed force, he asked that UNITAF fulfil two conditions that would allow the national reconciliation process to go forward and yield concrete results: neutralization of the factions' heavy weapons, and disarmament, by force, of the irregular militias and gangs.[10] However, Bush refused to agree to this, reiterating that the UNITAF mission was strictly humanitarian.

* * *

In addition to the coalition's humanitarian mission, there were subtle and complicated political negotiations to reach a peace agreement among the many parties involved in Somalia. The UN, UNITAF, the Americans, and the Somali factions were involved in a dangerous, explosive game. Through most of 1992, Boutros-Ghali and his special representatives in Somalia were the only parties acting as intermediaries among the Somali factions. Meetings took place in various African capitals, but the results were disastrous. The UN was unable to command respect, and the factions ignored the resolutions that were passed. Moreover, a personal vendetta emerged between Boutros-Ghali and one of the most powerful Somali warlords, General Aidid. In his reports to the Security Council, Boutros-Ghali regularly condemned the Somali leader, accusing him of sabotaging the negotiations and dragging his feet in responding to UN offers.[11] This infuriated Aidid, although all observers recognized that it was he who was primarily responsible for the civil war in Somalia. In August 1992, Aidid refused to accept the deployment of the Blue Helmets, and in November, when it became obvious that the UN was planning armed intervention, he threatened to attack the Pakistani battalion already in the field. However, the Somali general did not oppose American intervention, secretly hoping that the United States would support his faction.

The power struggle between Aidid and Boutros-Ghali came to a head when the secretary-general attempted to visit Mogadishu on 3 January 1993. A crowd of the general's supporters stoned the UN bunker and prevented Boutros-Ghali from going there. They accused the UN of interfering in Somali affairs and asked for help from President Bush, the 'saver of the Somali nation.'[12] Aidid hated the secretary-general, whom he accused of having had a close relationship with former Somali president Siyad Barre in the 1980s, when Boutros-Ghali was Egypt's minister of state for foreign affairs and Aidid was an opponent of Siyad Barre. The Somali warlord demanded the exclusion of the UN from the political negotiations among the Somali factions. He stated that the UN did 'not understand Somalia's intricate political problems' and that its approach to re-establishing peace was 'too meddling, too divisive and too secretive to produce any positive results for the betterment of Somalia.'[13] Boutros-Ghali would remember the humiliation he suffered, and he would have his revenge. But he would have to bide his time, because the Americans had entered the fray.

As soon as they arrived in Mogadishu, the Americans took control of the city and the political process. Having initially agreed reluctantly to Boutros-Ghali's objective of disarming the Somali militias by force, they backed off and allowed the militias to do as they pleased as long as they did not attack the coalition soldiers directly. Politically, the Americans short-circuited UN efforts. There were several persons speaking on behalf of the international community on the Somalia question: the secretary-general of the UN and his special representative; the military commander of UNITAF, an American general; and the special representative of the United States, Robert Oakley. Each had his own strategy, all of them very different. The UN wanted to impose its vision of things and asked UNITAF to be firm with the faction leaders, especially Aidid. The UNITAF commander thought in terms of his soldiers' safety and stated – not unreasonably – that his mandate was to ensure that the humanitarian aid reached its goal and to prepare the transition to the new UN mission,

UNOSOM II, which was to take over in May 1993. As for Oakley, who knew Somalia well, having served there as ambassador in 1983 and 1984, he sought a way to get the factions to sign an agreement so that the American forces could be brought home without bloodshed. A clash was inevitable, because the faction leaders were fomenting conflict among the coalition forces. Ali Mahdi's clan, supported by a dozen other factions, demanded the immediate application of the UN line. Aidid's clan shrewdly courted the Americans, who let themselves be led along. The UN was constantly ignored, and the political negotiations took place in the American embassy in Mogadishu.

Aidid quickly understood two things: in the spring of 1993, the Americans wanted to withdraw quickly, and they were not prepared to sacrifice their soldiers' lives in a showdown with the factions. Aidid still hoped for U.S. support, but the Americans were thinking only of getting out. They pressed the UN to take over the UNITAF mission and turn it into UNOSOM II, which would allow them to withdraw most of their forces from Somalia. Boutros-Ghali accepted reluctantly, warning the international community of the consequences. In a report presented to the Security Council on 3 March 1993, on the transition between the two missions, he said that when UNITAF withdrew, the situation in Somalia would be very unstable, explaining that disarmament of the factions and gangs had not been completed and that UNOSOM II would have to finish the task, using force if necessary.[14] A confrontation was brewing.

On 4 May 1993 the American troops began withdrawing and the UNITAF commander transferred his powers to the commander of UNOSOM II, the Turkish general Çevik Bir. But the Americans did not withdraw completely from Somalia. They left a contingent of 4,000 soldiers, including a quick reaction force not under UN command. In addition, the Turkish general's second-in-command was an American officer, Major General Thomas Montgomery, who was also the commander of the quick reaction force. Finally, the new special representative of the secretary-general was an American admiral, Jonathan Howe. With the departure of President Bush in January 1993, the United States had again changed its policy in Somalia. The new Clinton administration yielded to Boutros-Ghali's pressures for an American presence and, more important, for the application of the UN's more forceful plan. On 26 March, when Resolution 814 on the new mandate of UNOSOM II was adopted, the American ambassador, Madeleine Albright, expressed Washington's enthusiasm for UN activism and hailed this decision as a first, in that it would involve the UN and the United States in completely rebuilding the Somali state. All the other delegations around the Security Council table expressed the same blissful optimism; even China, which was normally averse to supporting missions in which force was authorized, shared in the enthusiasm. They would soon change their tune.

Howe did not possess Oakley's familiarity with Somalia. He was a military man who had planned operations such as the one leading to the capture of General Manuel Noriega in Panama in December 1989. He shared Boutros-Ghali's opinions on what should be done about the factions, especially that of General Aidid. As for the Somali warlord, he was disappointed by the Americans; he had thought they would support his bid for power. The return of the UN and Boutros-Ghali to the scene enraged him. Aidid called for the withdrawal of the UN troops and began a vigorous campaign against the Blue Helmets. Tension mounted daily.

Admiral Howe was not intimidated. He ordered the soldiers of UNO-SOM II to continue their patrols and to seize the weapons of factions that refused to respect the agreements signed during the previous negotiations. On 5 June 1993, a detachment of Pakistani Blue Helmets was inspecting several ammunition dumps belonging to General Aidid's supporters. One of these dumps was located near the facilities of Radio-Mogadishu; the radio station, Aidid's property, had been broadcasting anti-UNOSOM II messages for several weeks. The Aidid supporters harassed the Blue Helmets, accusing them of trying to destroy the station. In other parts of the capital, there were armed attacks against the Pakistani soldiers. In fighting around a feeding station and on October 21 Avenue, twenty-five Pakistani soldiers were killed. The bodies of several of them were horribly mutilated by enraged Somalis. UN headquarters in New York was in an uproar.

An emergency meeting of the Security Council was called the next day to study a report on the massacre by the secretary-general. In it, Boutros-Ghali accused General Aidid of being responsible for a 'premeditated act,' the objective of which was to intimidate UNOSOM II.[15] The fifteen members of the Council, still in a state of shock, adopted a resolution ordering the arrest of General Aidid and his accomplices.[16] The Somali general condemned the resolution, protested his innocence, and called for an international inquiry. Mogadishu erupted. For three days, units from the American quick reaction force and Blue Helmets from several countries attacked ammunition dumps and buildings belonging to Aidid's supporters. Admiral Howe put a $25,000 reward on the Somali general's head. On 13 June, Pakistani Blue Helmets fired into a crowd, killing some twenty Somalis and setting in motion a spiral of violence. For four months, fighting continued between UN forces and Aidid supporters.

Pressed by Boutros-Ghali and Admiral Howe and, disgusted by the methods used by Aidid in attacking the Blue Helmets, President Clinton agreed to take part in the manhunt for the general.[17] Boutros-Ghali had stated in a report presented to the Security Council that 'civilian crowds, including women and children, were used by General Aidid and his supporters as human shields to screen attacks on UNOSOM II fixed guard posts and strong points.'[18] The use of this tactic was confirmed in accounts by several journalists and observers on the ground.[19] In August, Washington dispatched a contingent of Rangers with a mandate to capture the Somali leader. However, the warlord, who knew the streets of Mogadishu like the back of his hand, thwarted all attempts at capture. The UN never succeeded in arresting him.

The bitter U.S.-UN attacks against the supporters of General Aidid began to worry many contingents of UNOSOM II. Several governments discreetly informed the UN that they had sent their contingents to Somalia on a humanitarian mission, not to wage war. It was the Italians who were most troubled by the deaths of the dozens of civilians caught in the crossfire between the Blue Helmets and Aidid's soldiers. The commander of the Italian contingent complained that he had not been consulted about the military operations and announced that his soldiers would no longer take part in the attacks.[20] In Rome, the Italian minister of defence, Fabio Fabbri, asked for the suspension of military operations, stating that the Italian contingent had been sent to Somalia for peacekeeping and humanitarian aid operations as defined by a UN resolution, and not to carry out actions aimed at enforcing peace through combat.[21] But the Italian minister was wrong: the UN reminded him that the UNOSOM II mission was operating under Chapter VII of the Charter, which authorized the use of armed force. Boutros-Ghali demanded that the Italians obey the orders of the force commander in Somalia. Rome refused, and Fabbri further inflamed the situation by denouncing the UN again, declaring that the Italians were not used to massacres, that they preferred dialogue, and that they didn't like 'Rambos.'[22] The UN responded by asking for the immediate recall of the Italian commander in Mogadishu.[23] UNOSOM II was in complete disarray. Meanwhile, General Aidid was still at large, thumbing his nose at the UN force and granting interviews to journalists.

To re-establish unity within the force deployed in Somalia, the UN made peace with Italy and agreed to deploy the Italian units that were in Mogadishu elsewhere in the country. But Boutros-Ghali was deeply upset, and he took the opportunity to emphasize that unity of command was imperative in a mission. However, the command of UNOSOM II was divided between two sources of authority: the UN secretary-general and the Pentagon, represented in Somalia by General Montgomery and Admiral Howe. Boutros-Ghali dealt with this problem in a report to the Security Council in which he indirectly criticized the Italian contingent for failing to obey the orders of the UNOSOM commander while at the same time expressing agreement with the Italian complaint regarding the lack of consultation within the mission.[24]

* * *

In September 1993, television images of Somalis killed by American soldiers and accounts of the dissension within UNOSOM II were beginning to influence American policy. Public opinion was questioning the actions of the American soldiers in Somalia, and some members of Congress and senators were demanding the withdrawal of the troops. The war the UN was waging against General Aidid had resulted in dozens of deaths in the UN forces, including those of several Americans. At the end of September, the House of Representatives passed a resolution requiring President Clinton to get authorization from Congress to keep the American contingent in Somalia until 15 November.[25] At the same time, the American state department discreetly informed Boutros-Ghali that American troops should not be used to patrol Mogadishu. The Americans wanted to dispel the impression that their contingent had become just another clan in Somalia. They insisted that the UN stop persecuting Aidid and recommended a political solution. Boutros-Ghali had no intention of yielding, and reminded the Americans that not so long ago they had been on his side.[26]

In New York, the United States and the UN attempted to harmonize their political strategy in Somalia; in the field, the American military was preparing a raid against General Aidid's supporters, which would turn out to be catastrophic. The state department was apparently not informed of the attack. On 3 October at 4:15 a.m., Rangers from the quick reaction force launched an assault on a building in the centre of Mogadishu and captured about twenty Somalis, including several top officials in Aidid's militia. The battle lasted about fifteen hours. During the operation, two helicopters were shot down by the general's supporters and eighteen American soldiers were killed. There were television cameras at the scene, and a few hours after the attack, Western networks broadcast horrific images of maddened Somalis dragging the naked corpse of an American soldier through the streets. Then a soldier being held hostage by Aidid's supporters appeared, his face swollen, and said that he was being well treated. This brought back for Americans the harrowing images of hostages in Teheran in 1980 and Beirut in the 1980s.

In Washington, American political and military leaders, with President Clinton in the forefront, unleashed their fury against the UN. They accused Boutros-Ghali of carrying out his own personal agenda in Somalia and dragging the United States into military operations against its will. Clinton announced that American troops would be withdrawn from Somalia on 31 March 1994, and he sent Robert Oakley back to Mogadishu on a mission to resume political negotiations with the Somali factions. Oakley was even ordered to bypass the UN in the field if necessary to carry out his mission. President Clinton himself directly attacked the UN, stating that its aggressive policy against General Aidid 'never should have been allowed to supplant the political process that was ongoing when we were in effective control, up through last May.'[27] He even suggested that his officials in Washington had not been informed of the raid because the state department had been seeking a political solution to the conflict with General Aidid. He repeated this claim on 12 May 1994, during an audience in the White House with the families of the soldiers killed during the operation.[28] Boutros-Ghali was again publicly humiliated. But the Americans had approved the secretary-general's policy change regarding the Somali warlord in May 1993, Boutros-Ghali replied bitterly to Clinton. In a report to the Security Council on the situation in Somalia, he asserted that 'the planning and execution of the Ranger operation of 3 October 1993 was decided by United States commanders and carried out by United States forces that were deployed to support the UNOSOM II mandate, but were not under United Nations command and authority. Not until the rescue phase of the victims did a multilateral operation take shape.'[29]

In Mogadishu, Oakley met with emissaries of Aidid and supported the general's demand for the establishment of an international commission of inquiry on the massacre of the twenty-five Pakistanis on 5 June. The American representative obtained a truce to allow the withdrawal of American troops.

At the UN, things moved quickly. On 16 November, the Security Council adopted a resolution to create a commission of inquiry on the events of 5 June and 'pending completion of the report of the Commission, suspend the arrest actions'[30] against Aidid and his lieutenants. Curiously, that report, which was submitted to the secretary-general at the beginning of March 1994, was not made public. The author obtained a copy thanks to the UN correspondent for the newspaper *Le Monde*, Afsané Bassir Pour.

The eighty-page report was not gentle with the UN. Its authors criticized the command and control procedures of the Somalia mission and stated that General Aidid was justified in saying that the Pakistani soldiers had received orders to neutralize his radio station. The commission concluded that the leadership of the UNOSOM II mission had been divided on the question but that there had indeed been a plan to destroy the station. According to the report, General Aidid was responsible for the massacre of the Pakistanis, but this atrocity was not premeditated. Examining the events of 3 October that resulted in the death of eighteen American soldiers and several hundred Somalis, the commission pointed out that the operation was led by the Rangers, who did not seem to have received authorization from UNOSOM II. Thus, the commission felt that General Aidid had the right to defend himself. Analysing the UN's political and military strategy in Somalia, the report concluded that forcible disarmament of the Somalis had 'proven unattainable' and that this policy should be abandoned. In conclusion, the commission submitted a list of recommendations on peacekeeping missions, emphasizing that in future the UN 'should refrain from undertaking further peace enforcement actions within the internal conflicts of states' and that force should not be used except 'as the ultimate means after all peaceful remedies have been exhausted.'[31]

Strangely enough, on the eve of the U.S.-UN landing in Somalia on 8 December 1992, the American ambassador to Kenya, Smith Hempstone, Jr, had warned that the Americans were walking into a quagmire. In a cautionary diplomatic dispatch to the State Department, Hempstone wrote, 'Somalis, as the Italians and British have discovered to their discomfiture, are natural born guerrillas. They will mine the roads. They will lay ambushes. They will launch hit and run attacks. They will not be able to prevent convoys from getting through. But they will inflict – and take – casualties.' Speaking of the warlords, the diplomat warned the Americans, 'The warlords will fade away and wait us out. Then when we leave, they will go back and the burden will fall on the UN peacekeepers.'[32] This was precisely what happened.

* * *

After a particularly violent year for the UN in Somalia, in March 1994 UNOSOM II received a new mandate that emphasized a return to the mission's humanitarian goals and peaceful means. The force of Blue Helmets, which now consisted of 18,000 Asian and African soldiers, remained in the country until the spring of 1995, with a mission to protect the main ports and airports as well as roads vital to the distribution of humanitarian aid. As for the national reconciliation process, the UN supported it as best it could with the means available.

On the thorny question of the use of force, Boutros-Ghali drew the same conclusions as the commission of inquiry. The new mandate was to remain within the framework of Chapter VII of the Charter, but the secretary-general had given up the idea of disarming the factions by force. He wrote, 'Under that option, UNOSOM II would not use coercive methods but would rely on the cooperation of the Somali parties.'[33] Somalia subsequently sank more deeply into chaos, but the UN had learned a lesson. The great adventure of the new warriors of peace was over.

7

Murder in Somalia

The column of a hundred Canadian soldiers, bare-chested and bare-headed, advanced jerkily along the road to Belet Uen. The heat was overwhelming. The soldiers were shouting. With each step, they raised huge clouds of fine dust, which clung to their bodies, their hair, and their clothing. The soldiers were exercising before getting on with the day's tasks; they were anxious to keep in shape even in this distant corner of the Horn of Africa where, at mid-morning, the temperature had already reached 40°C. Along the road, gaunt Somalis wearing brightly coloured robes watched the scene with surprise and amusement. They did not seem to understand why these white men from across the world insisted on running day after day, for several weeks now, in the hottest season of the year, between December and February.

An officer gave an order and the soldiers dispersed. In small groups, they returned slowly to the camp. Some went to lie down, while others had to go on guard duty, clean up the camp, or prepare their vehicles and load their equipment for a patrol to a distant village.

'These soldiers have been in Somalia for almost two months now,' explained a Canadian officer. 'The living conditions here aren't very pleasant, and they're already starting to get restless. You have to keep them busy all the time or some rascal will get into mischief. They're paratroopers, after all.'[1]

These soldiers were members of the notorious Canadian Airborne Regiment based in Petawawa, Ontario. According to the myth surrounding them, they were the most formidable and best-trained Canadian military unit. Some people saw them as violent killers, while others admired them as the cutting edge of the infantry, a unit that was always on alert, ready to be deployed anywhere on the globe with a few hours' notice.

There was no doubt that the members of the Airborne were impressive soldiers, specially trained to carry out daredevil missions in conditions of intense cold or suffocating heat. According to the pamphlet published by the regiment, its role was to 'provide a quick reaction force in support of national security, North American defence and international peacekeeping.'[2] Its tasks were many: to destroy or capture strategic positions held by the enemy, to take control of or build runways, to help soldiers or civilians in vulnerable positions, and so on. The Airborne was in a sense the Canadian equivalent of the French Foreign Legion; it was assigned jobs that ordinary soldiers could not always undertake.

These elite soldiers knew that they were a special group. They underwent rigorous military and physical training that made some of them into potential Rambos. There was a cult of the body in the Airborne: being in shape physically was essential for these soldiers, and they regularly engaged in demanding athletic activities and military exercises in which they tested themselves and each other.

At two o'clock, a group of soldiers started a jogging exercise inside the boundaries of the camp, following a very precise course that snaked through the tents and equipment depots. They would run for half an hour under the blazing sun.

'I don't get it,' exclaimed an American soldier who was spending a few days in the Canadian camp. 'Jogging in 50°C heat is nuts. These soldiers are really gung ho.'

Aggressiveness was a quality sought by the leaders of the Airborne Regiment. Without it, their special missions, which were often carried out under conditions of extreme stress, would be impossible. These soldiers had to be ready for anything, any time of the day or night. But in Somalia, this quality became a disadvantage. The aggressiveness of the Canadian soldiers combined with the aggressiveness of the desperate Somalis, who had been sorely tested by four years of civil war and famine, led to a series of deadly incidents that sullied the regiment and tarnished Canada's reputation as a peacekeeper.

* * *

When the Canadian soldiers arrived in Belet Uen on 28 December 1992, all they knew about Somalia was that a horrible civil war had ravaged the country, that there was no government, and that hundreds of thousands of people were dying of hunger in several isolated regions.

The soldiers of the regiment had been ready to go to Africa since September 1991, but their final destination had changed. They were originally supposed to be deployed as part of MINURSO in Western Sahara, to maintain order during the referendum on the political status of that territory. But the referendum was put forward, and when the UN asked for troops for Somalia in August 1992, Canada offered the regiment. The Airborne troops were initially supposed to go to the Bossasso region in the north of the country in autumn 1992, but the establishment of UNITAF led to a change of plans. The leaders of the U.S.-UN coalition decided to limit their intervention to the central and southern regions of the country, which were most affected by the war and famine. UNITAF's zone of operation was then divided into seven sectors: two in the north, controlled by the Canadians and the Italians; two in the centre, controlled by the French and the Americans; two in the south, controlled by the Australians and the Belgians; and finally, Mogadishu, the capital, which the Americans would be responsible for, along with some twenty other countries, most of them from the Third World.

The arrival of the Canadians in Somalia was not as spectacular as the Americans' landing on the country's shores. On 28 December, when the Canadian soldiers took over the Belet Uen airport, there were no TV cameras there to record the event. They arrived alone in that sandy desert where the temperature had already reached 50°C. In four days they set up a camp southwest of the city, across the Shebelle River. There the soldiers lived for several weeks with no armoured vehicles, no water for washing, and no tents or cots. Essential equipment and vehicles began to arrive toward mid-January, and the camp was finished at the end of February.

The task of the Canadian soldiers in this sector of 30,000 square kilometres was the same as that of the other contingents: to ensure security for the ground communication lines, protect towns and villages, escort humanitarian aid convoys, identify mined areas, seize heavy weapons and establish a registry of small arms in urban areas, re-establish local police service, build bridges and schools, help local authorities re-establish order, and finally, act as mediators between the factions.

The Canadian camp was situated a few kilometres from Belet Uen on a large, very flat piece of land three kilometres long. It was divided into five smaller camps belonging to the five units of the regiment. The regiment commander and the officers were housed at the north end of the camp. In spite of fierce winds, it was a suitable spot, because the terrain of sand and pebbles was hard enough to support the tents and keep the vehicles from getting stuck. The soldiers of 1 Commando and 3 Commando were housed in the centre of the camp, in an area covered with very fine sand. With the slightest gust of wind, the sand got into everything. The soldiers had to gulp down their food if they did not want it generously sprinkled with sand. A helicopter unit was located further south, and 2 Commando was at the gates of the huge camp.

The military intelligence office of the Belet Uen camp looked more like a flea market than a centre for processing secret information. Sergeant Tim Power's tent, which was open on all sides to let in air, was cluttered with piles of paper, rolls of tape, and other articles. In the centre was a big table with drawers full of scissors, pencils, jars of glue, and rulers. Power was in charge of collating information brought by the soldiers from their patrols. On the basis of this information, he advised the camp headquarters on the soldiers' future patrols.

On a makeshift wall, Power had pinned up an aerial photograph of Belet Uen that the Americans had kindly provided. It showed the neighbourhoods of the city, the river running through it, and the Bailey bridge built by the Canadians to link the two sides. Power pointed out the neighbourhoods controlled by the various clans. When there was a demonstration against one of the clans or against the presence of the Canadian troops, Power could tell the commander which streets and roads the demonstrators would take and which houses might be used as hiding places or shelters. The commander could then prevent the situation from degenerating by blocking the roads and sealing off the neighbourhood until things calmed down.

While the soldiers keeping watch over Belet Uen had this information to rely on, those patrolling the countryside sometimes as far as the Ethiopian border, where the Canadian sector ended, were less fortunate. Power had no aerial photographs of the territory assigned to the Canadians outside of Belet Uen. At first, these soldiers did not even have maps of the entire Canadian sector. In mid-January, when a military unit went to an area near the Ethiopian border, its soldiers had to map all the roads and dirt tracks, and especially the minefields.

Finally, in early February, the UNITAF authorities came up with the bright idea of sending the contingents maps of Somalia. What they sent, Power explained, were some old Russian maps the Americans had reprinted with corrections to some of the details. The maps were detailed and accurate, but each one showed only part of the territory. To make a complete map, Power cut up several and pasted them together. Once the new map was covered with a sheet of plastic to protect it from water, sun, and sand, it could be used to prevent patrols from getting lost in the rocky, inhospitable desert.

* * *

Lieutenant-Colonel Carol Mathieu pulled on his boots while his aide-de-camp prepared breakfast. This giant, with his low voice and cowboy bearing, commanded the 750 soldiers of the Canadian Airborne Regiment and ruled the whole Belet Uen region, where he had imposed his authority in a few weeks. The elders called him the military governor. Mathieu smiled, visibly flattered.

'I'm not here to govern the region,' he said, swallowing his rations. 'I have a mandate from UNITAF that mainly involves helping the humanitarian organizations do their work in a secure environment. So I have to make sure my soldiers dissuade groups or even looters from taking our equipment.'[3]

Mathieu explained that before the arrival of the Canadian contingent, Belet Uen was controlled by 'leeches.' Because of the high incidence of theft, looting, thuggery, and extortion, the personnel of the humanitarian organizations were armed and they were forced by the warlords to hire Somali armed guards to protect them. These protective measures were not always effective, and they were very costly for the NGOs.

'The Red Cross was paying 150 Somalis to provide security for the landing strip in Belet Uen,' said Mathieu. 'The warlord controlling the area demanded landing fees. Everything had to be paid for. The NGOs were running out of money, and their personnel were reluctant to go on missions outside the city. Three weeks after our arrival, the leeches were gone.' Under the protection of the Canadian soldiers, a Red Cross convoy ventured into the countryside for the first time in a year. Mathieu also made sure that the jobs reserved for Somalis and paid for by UNITAF or the NGOs were distributed equitably among the clans.

The lieutenant-colonel, supported by local authorities, also imposed strict rules against carrying weapons in the sector: no one was allowed to be armed, and the patrols of the various factions had to show identification to the Canadian soldiers. The officer was not joking about the weapons. His clan had the power, and UNITAF's rules of engagement allowed him to use it. And his soldiers did use it, both on their patrols and to neutralize Somalis who sneaked into the camp to steal.

* * *

When the soldiers of the regiment set up camp in their sector, Lieuten-ant-Colonel Mathieu divided up the tasks among the three commandos. He gave 1 Commando the mission of patrolling the territory west of the Shebelle River, which stretched to the Ethiopian border; 3 Commando was to provide security in a large territory east of the Shebelle River; and 2 Commando was to provide security for the city of Belet Uen and its immediate area.[4] The zeal with which 2 Commando did its job was so remarkable that the local population called it 'the clan that never sleeps.'

Monitoring Belet Uen and the surrounding area proved to be the Canadians' most arduous and most controversial task. With some 100,000 residents and refugees, the city was divided into neighbourhoods con-trolled by rival clans. The Bailey bridge across the Shebelle River allowed the inhabitants to go from one neighbourhood to another. The different clans had been fighting for control of the bridge before the arrival of the Canadian soldiers, who had rebuilt it and made it neutral territory. A pla-toon of soldiers stood guard there throughout the contingent's tour of duty (from December 1992 to June 1993).

During my stay in Belet Uen, I spent several hours at the Bailey bridge. There, on 20 February, I met Captain Michael Sox, the leader of a pla-toon from 2 Commando. Several of his soldiers were guarding the two ends of the bridge or conducting patrols in the streets of the city.

Sox was nervous. He had just learned that a group of demonstrators wanted to cross the bridge to a neighbourhood run by a rival clan. Mathieu had given him very strict orders not to let the troublemakers pass. Sox had good reason to be concerned; three days earlier, a similar demonstration had turned into a clash with the Canadian soldiers, and the soldiers had lost their composure and fired toward the demonstra-tors, killing a young Somali. That was the first incident the contingent was involved in. There would be other, more serious ones.

Sox gave the order to let the Somalis cross the bridge a few at a time and to search anyone who looked suspicious, as well as all cars that wanted to cross. The tension was palpable, and the soldiers on guard held their weapons at the ready. Some of the soldiers, who had been on duty for two days, were asleep on the ground while their comrades relieved them.

Suddenly, while I was talking with Sox, a Somali of about twenty years old approached me and in laboured English complained of mistreatment of the Somalis by the Canadian soldiers. Glancing nervously around him, he stated that the Canadians were killing his friends. He held out slips of paper with short sentences in English written on them denouncing the soldiers and their leader, Lieutenant-Colonel Mathieu. 'We were waiting the Canadian troops for peace and humanity but they bring to dead and worry,' read one of the messages.

The young Somali immediately ran off and disappeared into the crowd waiting to cross the bridge. Sox shrugged. 'We get this kind of letter every day. Some people seem to be interested in getting us out of this city,' he said.[5]

The young captain did not have to use force that day. The demonstrators gathered at the bridge dispersed after a few minutes of discussion. But there would be another time; Sox would soon have a rendezvous with violence.

A month later, on the evening of 16 March, Michael Sox entered the perimeter of the 2 Commando camp dragging a sixteen-year-old Somali named Shidane Arone, bound and trembling. The youth had been captured in a former American camp across from the Canadian camp. He was suspected of trying to enter the Canadian camp to steal. This was the beginning of one of the most sordid episodes involving Canadian soldiers abroad, one that would unleash a political storm in Canada. There would be an official inquiry into the actions of the Canadian Airborne Regiment, and eight soldiers, including Mathieu, would be charged and court-martialled.

According to testimony given in several trials that took place on the base at Petawawa, Ontario, between February and June 1994, Michael Sox delivered his prisoner to a soldier, who took the young Somali into a bunker that was being used as a munitions depot. There two soldiers, Elvin Kyle Brown and Clayton Matchee, beat and tortured the Somali for several hours. Some fifteen other soldiers witnessed the Somali's ordeal without intervening. Brown, who was subsequently sentenced to five years in prison for murder and discharged from the army, claimed that Sox had ordered them to beat the prisoner. Sox was convicted of negligent performance of duty.

Exhausted by the blows from fists, feet, and sticks, Arone lost consciousness after screaming 'Canada! Canada! Canada!' The soldier who later found him sounded the alarm, but it was too late – taken to a medical unit, he was declared dead as a result of his injuries. Two days later, Matchee was arrested and detained, and a few hours later, he was found hanging in his cell. He was not dead, but in a deep coma. Matchee was transported to an Ottawa hospital; a year later, he was declared unfit for trial.

In Canada, the murder of Arone, the 17 February incident on the Bailey bridge, and the deaths of two other Somalis on 4 and 17 March sparked fierce controversy. The opposition accused the minister of defence, Kim Campbell, who aspired to become prime minister, of negligence in the performance of her duties for failing to make the matter public quickly enough. Indeed, while the latter three incidents were reported in newspaper articles, Arone's murder was not revealed in the press until the beginning of April. However, a press release on it had been issued on 18 March by the UNITAF information office in Mogadishu.

It took close to a month before the minister responded with measures to get at the truth about these events. On 27 April, Campbell announced the establishment of a board of inquiry on the activities of the Airborne Regiment in Somalia.[6] In May, September, and November 1993 and September 1994, charges were laid against eight soldiers and officers, including the commander, Mathieu. In December 1993, another officer, Captain Michel Rainville, was charged – and later acquitted – in connection with the death on 4 March of a Somali who had attempted to enter the Canadian compound in Belet Uen and had refused to surrender when spotted by the soldiers. The soldiers fired and the Somali was killed. He was taken to the hospital, where the staff observed that he had wounds to the abdomen, head, and neck.[7] According to a Canadian military physician who was there, the Somali, who was lying on the ground, had been finished off with a bullet in the neck and another in the head.[8]

* * *

The Board of Inquiry on the Canadian Airborne Regiment and the trials of soldiers brought to light disturbing information about the management of military units of the Canadian Armed Forces and the confusion that existed among the decision makers about a UN mission that was operating under different rules than those that governed traditional peacekeeping missions. The Board of Inquiry's report, which was made public on 31 August 1993, revealed that even before the regiment's departure for Somalia, there was a group of 'rebel' soldiers in 2 Commando who defied military authorities, threatened superior officers, destroyed equipment, and damaged property, and that some soldiers displayed racist behaviour.[9] Internal investigations had failed to unmask the guilty parties because of the wall of silence put up by the soldiers. Discipline was so bad in this unit that the former commander of the regiment 'had recommended that the whole of 2 Commando not be deployed to Somalia,'[10] a suggestion that was ignored. That commander lost his position, five soldiers were excluded from the contingent sent to Somalia, and the disciplinary problem was left for the new commander of the regiment – Lieutenant-Colonel Mathieu – and the commander of 2 Commando.

The report painted an unattractive picture of 2 Commando and its pranks, and made it clear that the officers and non-commissioned officers had been perfectly aware of the behaviour of the soldiers in the unit when they were deployed to Somalia to maintain security in Belet Uen. Because of the nature of their mission, these soldiers were in constant contact with the local people; among other things, they were responsible for guarding arrested Somalis.[11]

To understand the soldiers' attitude to the Somalis when there were demonstrations or arrests, the board examined the rules of engagement (ROE), 'those orders which govern the use of force to achieve the mission.'[12] Since the mission had been adopted under Chapter VII of the UN Charter, which authorizes the use of force, the board took the view, in the cases where Canadian soldiers had fired on demonstrators (17 February) or on an armed Somali (17 March), that 'the application of force was within the limitations imposed by the ROE.'[13] However, the board considered that there were still ambiguities with regard to the use of force against looters on 4 March, and that the rules established by Canada with regard to looters were not clear enough. But the Board of Inquiry did not look into the suspicious death of a Somali on 4 March or the murder of Shidane Arone on 16 March, because it did not want to interfere with the ongoing judicial process.

The courts martial held in Petawawa between February and June 1994 revealed that Lieutenant-Colonel Mathieu and some of his officers had ordered the use of force contrary to the rules of engagement established by the Department of National Defence. According to information in the search warrants for the residence and office of Lieutenant-Colonel Mathieu, six officers of the Airborne Regiment stated that they had received the order to fire on sight at anyone attempting to enter the Canadian compound in Belet Uen, whether armed or not.[14] But the rules supposedly governing their conduct restricted the use of force to self-defence or the protection of humanitarian aid workers and civilians.

The Board of Inquiry found that the rules of engagement were not clear: 'There was confusion regarding the application of ROE depending on whether an intruder was attempting entry, has successfully penetrated the camp to steal items or equipment, was departing with or without vital items such as weapons or munitions.'[15] But those rules had nevertheless been violated by Lieutenant-Colonel Mathieu. As Major Anthony Seward, one of the soldiers convicted in the Arone case, wrote in his diary, the commander of the regiment permitted his men to fire on – and kill – looters.[16]

The sentences handed down in the courts martial have been severely criticized. Private Brown was sentenced to five years in prison but was freed after a few months. Other soldiers were given reprimands or demoted. Most were acquitted. While the trials were going on, in 1994, the media published allegations of attempts by senior political and military officials to cover up certain aspects of the Somalia affair. In response to the public outcry, the minister of defence, David Collenette, ordered the creation of a civilian commission of inquiry on the deployment of the Canadian forces in Somalia, chaired by Justice Gilles Letourneau. The commission was given a mandate to look into the actions and decisions of the Department of National Defence before, during, and after the deployment of troops in Somalia. It was supposed to focus specifically on leadership in the Canadian Armed Forces and the accusations of concealment and destruction of evidence. After a rather slow start, the Letourneau Commission began its hearings in September 1995, and heard testimony from more than one hundred witnesses. Throughout the inquiry, Justice Letourneau complained about the slowness of the Department of National Defence in handing over important documents and the refusal of certain military witnesses to cooperate. The commission also heard sensational revelations. The most controversial concerned the falsification of documents on Somalia, and led to the resignation of the chief of defence staff, General Jean Boyle. In January 1997, just as the commission was about to begin hearing testimony on the role of senior political and military officials, the minister of defence, Doug Young, ordered it to end its work on 31 March and directed Justice Letourneau to submit his report by 30 June 1997 at the latest.

On 2 July, the Commission of Inquiry published its report. Some 1,600 pages long, the report was damning. The commission concluded that the Somalia mission had been poorly planned, that the troops were poorly trained, that there were discipline problems within the Canadian Airborne Regiment before and during its tour of duty in Somalia, that there were failures of leadership among the commanders, and that some senior officers had attempted to conceal the truth about the Canadian soldiers' misdeeds. Even more disturbing, the commission found that its work had been slowed down by a strategy of calculated deception on the part of certain military witnesses, and that by imposing a time limit on its work, the government had prevented it from fully investigating the accusations of cover-ups within the Department of National Defence itself. The commission was able, however, to make 160 recommendations for the reform of the Canadian Armed Forces.[17]

The Canadian soldiers were not the only ones in the UN mission in Somalia to be accused of crimes or brutality against Somalis. As we have seen in the preceding chapter, the American forces killed or wounded Somali civilians or soldiers in several operations against one of the clan chiefs, General Mohamed Farah Aidid. The methods and the weapons used by the Americans were criticized by humanitarian organizations and even by certain member states of the coalition. The Belgian contingent was also accused of war crimes within months of its arrival in the Kismayo region in the south of the country, where it was stationed from January to December 1993. In a report published in London in July 1993, testimony by several Somalis, the organization African Rights claimed that the Belgian troops were responsible for the deaths of between two and five hundred Somalis. While the organization recognized that the majority of these deaths had occurred in combat, it emphasized that in twenty-six cases Somalis were tortured to death or executed in cold blood.[18] In confirmation of these accusations, paratroopers returning to Belgium confessed on the radio that some soldiers had beaten or killed Somalis. One soldier even talked about a Walloon sharpshooter who had collected some thirty 'trophies.'[19] The Belgian government reacted by undertaking an investigation of its soldiers' actions.

The Belgian soldiers' responsibilities, like those of the Canadian contingent, were to maintain order, assist the humanitarian organizations, repair schools, and re-establish a local police force. However, from January to April, the soldiers witnessed very violent clashes among the various militias fighting for control of the city of Kismayo. They were regularly harassed and were sometimes the direct targets of rifle fire or grenades. Each time, the soldiers fired back, causing deaths among the Somalis.

After questioning 120 witnesses, examining complaints by Somalis, and studying the military records of the contingent, the Belgian Board of Inquiry rejected the accusations against the soldiers. In its report, the board stated that it had received no formal complaints of abusive use of force, although there had been 'a few cases of unacceptable behaviour,' and that force had been used only where necessary, and then applied 'gradually and proportionately.' The report further stated that while the board could not exclude the possibility that there were cases of unacceptable behaviour unknown to it, it nevertheless felt there could only be a very limited number of such cases, and that the accusations by African Rights and the statements of the ex-paratroopers on the program on BRT-Radio did not reflect reality.[20] Some fifteen Belgian soldiers were tried for acts of sadism in 1995, but none were found guilty. However, the publication in March 1997 of photographs showing soldiers holding a Somali over a fire revived the affair.

In June 1997, another scandal broke out, this time in Italy, where soldiers were accused of the torture, rape, and murder of Somalis. An official commission of inquiry confirmed that there had been cases of torture but declared that they were isolated incidents.[21]

In the past, the UN rarely had to deal with lack of discipline among its Blue Helmets. Such incidents were rare because of the small number of UN soldiers deployed in the world and the nature of the missions. Most Blue Helmets worked in a relatively peaceful environment. Supply problems were also very rare. In recent years, the activities of the UN have changed. In 1993–4, ten out of seventeen missions were deployed in countries in which there was fierce fighting. In September 1994, the number of Blue Helmets had reached 76,600 and living conditions in some missions were extremely difficult.

In addition to the charges of violence against Somalis by American, Canadian, Belgian, and Italian Blue Helmets, the UN had to respond to accusations against its soldiers in the former Yugoslavia and Mozambique. In certain regions of Croatia and Bosnia, Blue Helmets were accused of trafficking in cigarettes, coffee, alcohol, and fuel, as well as procurement,[22] and in Mozambique, members of ONUMOZ were accused of abusing child prostitutes.[23] The UN conducted investigations in all these cases, but it could not punish the guilty; they were sent back to their home countries, and disciplinary measures had to be taken by those countries.

The incidents described in this chapter are only the tip of the iceberg. In my travels to several peacekeeping missions, I met many Blue Helmets who told me about misconduct that had never been investigated: the frequent use of force and weapons, sexual harassment, black marketeering in all kinds of goods, theft of UN equipment, and so on. One of the most serious accusations concerned Blue Helmet involvement in trafficking in diamonds in the Cafunto region of Angola in 1992. With the country in the midst of a civil war, soldiers whose mission was to monitor a ceasefire and see that the parties respected their political and military commitments took advantage of their position to fill their pockets with diamonds.[24]

Since the countries supplying the troops are responsible for the discipline of the Blue Helmets, the UN will certainly not be able in future to impose sanctions on soldiers placed under its command. However, it could require the troop-contributing countries to publicly punish guilty soldiers. In this regard, the prosecution of the Canadian soldiers constituted a precedent.

8

The Unhappy Warriors

Bosnia could have been a land of dreams. A small, mountainous country, it is like a Switzerland in the Balkans, except that there are no snow-covered peaks, only mountains worn by time, looming over deep valleys containing little villages dotted with the minarets of mosques or the spires or domes of Catholic or Orthodox churches. Some of these villages are barely visible from the main road, and can only be reached by a steep, narrow path through a field, impassible by car. Sometimes the main road – of gravel and dirt – passes through one of these idyllic villages, so calm, so beautiful, so peaceful that you want to stop to take in the wild, magnificent landscape. That, however, is where the dream ends. The village is empty. Houses have been gutted by fire. If it is a Moslem village, the minaret of the mosque is in ruins; if it is Catholic or Orthodox, shelling has ravaged the façade or the dome of the church.

The armoured jeep carrying the two monitors from the European Community was going twenty kilometres per hour. The road was too rough and the jeep too heavy to go any faster. But they had to hurry, because they were transporting medicine for the hospital for the mentally handicapped in Drin, near Fojnica, whose patients – all children – had been abandoned by the staff, frightened away by fierce fighting between Moslems and Croats.

'Before going there,' explained French captain Philippe Sidos, 'we'll go see the Canadian soldiers in Visoko to make sure the road is free and there's no fighting. According to the information I got yesterday, the road was closed by a Croat warlord who's set himself up in the village of Otigosce, blocking access to the hospital. I'm not sure we'll be able to get through.'[1]

Sidos was dressed completely in white, as was his driver; so too were the local interpreter and a Dutch monitor who followed in another jeep. They belonged to the group of monitors sent to the former Yugoslavia by the European Community in 1991, during the breakup of the federation, to help maintain calm and bring aid to the population, although they could not stop the war. They were the White Helmets of Europe, and they worked in close cooperation with the Blue Helmets of the UN who had arrived there a year later. The White Helmets came from the various countries of the European Community and three other countries, including Canada.

In Visoko, a small town thirty kilometres northwest of Sarajevo, Sidos went to the Canadian communications centre, which was located on the base that housed the hundreds of Blue Helmets of the Canadian battalion in Bosnia. There was an atmosphere of great excitement that day, 31 July 1993. Fighting between Croats and Moslems was reported throughout central Bosnia, and the Serbs were continuing to shell Sarajevo. The centre had to maintain constant contact with every Blue Helmet contingent patrolling in the region or providing protection for humanitarian convoys to Sarajevo and other cities and towns. Sidos spoke to the officer in charge of the centre.

'I want to go to Fojnica to bring medicine. Is it possible to get through?'

'I'm trying to establish communication with a Blue Helmet patrol in the region,' replied the officer. 'There isn't any fighting, but I'm not sure the Croat commander will let you through. He's been threatening us and demanding that our soldiers at the hospital in Drin hand over the director to him. He says she's a criminal. I sent a message that it was out of the question.'

'So we won't be able to get through,' said Sidos, 'unless you provide an escort.'

'Impossible,' replied the officer. 'I don't have anyone to spare now. My men are all out. You'll have to go there without us.'

Sidos thought for a moment. He considered postponing the visit until the next day, when the Canadians could provide an escort. But he did not want to let the Croat warlord intimidate him. If no one went to try to talk with him, the warlord would harden his position and prevent all contact with the Drin hospital.

'Sidos,' said the Canadian officer, 'I've just received a message. You can go meet the Croat warlord. He's waiting for you. What's more, I think I'll be able to send two Blue Helmets who'll be in the area then. Tell me what time you expect to be in Otigosce?'

'It should take about ninety minutes to do the thirty kilometres. So tell your soldiers to be there about two in the afternoon. Okay?'

'Perfect,' replied the officer.

The White Helmets' two white jeeps set out again for Otigosce. The village, clearly indicated on Sidos's detailed map, was not easy to reach. The roads were narrow and often blocked by trees felled by Moslems or Croats. We also had to go through checkpoints set up by one or another of the factions. When the jeeps arrived at one of these checkpoints the drivers would stop, but they did not open the car doors; the passengers showed their papers through the windows, and the soldiers would let them pass. That was the rule that had been accepted by the three Bosnian factions. Moslems, Croats, and Serbs respected it because they knew the monitors were not carrying any weapons and their jeeps were too small to hide soldiers from any of the factions. But this was not the case for the Blue Helmets, who were armed and drove trucks. The local militias systematically searched the UN vehicles.

At last we arrived in Otigosce, a small village clinging to a hill overlooking a magnificent verdant valley. From there, the Croat soldiers could shoot at anything that moved, and that is exactly what they did.

Sidos, his Dutch companion, and the interpreter asked to see the leader. One of the men led us to a brick house whose walls were protected from shrapnel by rows of long planks. We went in and were motioned to sit down at a table. We were told the chief was lying down. About fifteen men were lounging around in the big room. They did not look very reassuring in their untidy military uniforms, and some had obviously not slept for several days. They smoked cigarette after cigarette.

On one side there was a bedroom. From it emerged Branko Stanic, the undisputed ruler in this part of central Bosnia. Stanic shook hands with us. He was a tall man with a shaven head and short beard, his face softened by his blue eyes. He spoke quietly. At first glance, Stanic did not look very formidable. This was not true of some of his men, who watched us in silence, machine guns on their thighs. One of the soldiers sitting behind his chief looked like Rambo with his tattoos, long hair, headband, and dark glasses. He later asked Robert Côté, a Canadian photographer who had come with us, to take a picture of him giving the fascist salute.

Stanic was not a typical warlord. Three months earlier he had been living quietly in Vienna, where he had moved about ten years before. His family, which lived in the vicinity of Otigosce, had pressed him to return home to save the Croats, who were on the verge of being driven out by the Bosnian army, the majority of which consisted of Moslems. Seeing himself as a saviour, Stanic had abandoned everything, trading his job as an insurance salesman for the role of angel of death.

'I'm thirty-three years old, the age of Christ,' he said laughing. 'And I'm not afraid to die.'[2]

Sidos began a discussion that would last close to an hour, trying to convince Stanic not to block shipments of humanitarian aid, which contravened the local ceasefire agreements the factions had signed with the Blue Helmets in Bosnia. The French monitor stressed that the leaders of his faction had approved these agreements in Geneva.

'Those agreements don't exist here. I make the law. I've already been too patient. The relief won't go through, and I'll attack tomorrow. The Turks must leave the region,' he declared, referring to the Moslem residents of Bosnia.

Stanic claimed that the UN had betrayed him. On 30 June, the commander of the Blue Helmets in Bosnia, General Philippe Morillon, had come to the region and had praised the moderation of the Croats and Moslems who had signed a local peace agreement. That agreement was supposed to make the town of Fojnica a combat-free zone and, Stanic said, it stated that anyone attacking the town would be identified as the aggressor by the UN.

'The agreement lasted less than 48 hours,' recalled the Croat warlord. 'The Moslem forces attacked Fojnica and drove out the Croats, who were the majority. So where is General Morillon now? What is the UN waiting for to identify the aggressors and punish them? Where are the UN observers who are supposed to investigate the "ethnic cleansing" the Moslems have carried out against the Croats?'

Sidos took notes. He would report on it, he said. The warlord shrugged contemptuously. The French monitor asked him what was happening with the Moslem prisoners he was holding in the village and suggested they be placed under UN protection and then exchanged.

Stanic did not take him up on the offer. 'We have prisoners who are Moslem soldiers, but the other side won't get them,' he replied sarcastically. 'We'll keep them.'

'I would like to remind him about the Geneva Convention on prisoners of war,' Sidos said to us in French, 'but I think it would be useless. We're not getting anywhere.'

'Speak English,' demanded Stanic.

Sidos changed the subject. He asked the Croat leader to allow supplies into the hospital in Drin, arguing that the children could die, and asked if he could visit the hospital for mentally handicapped adults in Bakovici.

But Stanic was furious with the director of the children's hospital in Drin. He accused her of letting Croat patients die and claimed that she had falsely accused the Croat staff members of abandoning the hospital, where 70 per cent of the children were Moslem. No one was able to give an objective account of this complicated, obscure situation. According to the Canadian soldiers, the two hospitals – in Drin and Bakovici – had been abandoned when they discovered them in the middle of July 1993, their staffs apparently having fled in panic from the violence of the fighting between Croats and Moslems, leaving the patients to fend for themselves. The Canadians said they had found some children dead and others who had received no care for three or four days. About thirty Canadian and British Blue Helmets were now at the hospital caring for 220 mentally handicapped children. It was exhausting work for which none of them were trained. As for the 450 mentally handicapped adults in Bakovici, it would take several weeks before relief reached them. The hospital was shelled in November 1993, and many patients died.

Sidos suggested that this was surely not the time to judge the hospital director. He insisted that the lives of the patients were the important thing, and asked the leader to promise to let several aid vehicles through, as well as some of the staff, who had taken refuge in Fojnica.

'We'll see,' said Stanic. 'I'm not sure my soldiers will respect my orders. In any case, today you can go through.'

Stanic said he wanted to show us something. Leaving the bunker, we headed toward a barn from which you could look out over a big valley. Far in the distance, plumes of white smoke rose in the sky. A village was burning.

'Those Moslem villages behind that mountain,' he said pointing toward the horizon, 'I'm going to level them tomorrow. I'm at the end of my patience. I made a mistake by agreeing to peace at any price. Now we're paying for our weakness because many of our villages have been occupied by the Moslems.'

While Stanic allowed himself to be photographed with his principal lieutenants, the two Blue Helmets arrived. They would take over from the European Community monitors and try to convince the Croat to soften his position. One of them was French and the other was an unfriendly-looking New Zealander wearing an Indiana Jones hat.

'You haven't brought the most conciliatory one,' remarked Sidos to the French officer, referring to the New Zealander, who seemed to have a reputation for being tough.

'Don't worry, I'll keep an eye on him,' said the officer. 'But we have to show these Croats we're not chicken, that we're as tough as them.'

We left Otigosce for Zenica, a big Moslem town north of Sarajevo. The two white European Community jeeps drove through the village of Gojevici. On the Croat side, the houses were in perfect condition. On the Moslem side, they had all been burned down.

'Now we'll go back to headquarters so I can write my daily report,' said Sidos. 'I'll describe how a village changed hands or a zone was or will be cleared of its inhabitants. My report will be nothing but a litany of human tragedies. I'll document one of the most terrible aspects of the war in Bosnia, the "ethnic cleansing" – and I won't be able to do anything about it.'

Sidos had not seen the worst horrors of the civil war in Bosnia; he had been in Zenica for two months and this region was calmer than other parts of the country. But many Blue Helmets had witnessed the tragic consequences of this war – rapes, massacres, deliberate shelling of civilians, concentration camps, and mass expulsions of one ethnic group by another – powerless to stop them. Some had even participated indirectly in these tragedies, as had the British Blue Helmets trapped between Croats, Moslems, and Serbs in the centre of Bosnia.

Forty kilometres southwest of Zenica, a company of the British battalion in Bosnia was guarding Gornji Vakuf, a key town on the road to the Croat port of Split. Control of that road was vital for everyone – the UN contingents needed it to bring in supplies and the humanitarian convoys used it – and the Croat and Moslem troops were fighting over it. The British troops were there to keep it open. On 2 August 1993, the day I was there, the road to Split had been closed for three days because of intense fighting between the Croats and Moslems. The Moslems were trying to gain as much territory as possible to the south before the peace negotiations, which were taking place in Geneva, reached an agreement that would freeze the status quo. The Croats, who now controlled all of southwest Bosnia, were resisting and even attempting to penetrate toward the Croat towns of Vitez and Kiseljak, which were hemmed in by Moslem Bosnia. Gornji Vakuf was on the front line.

The British had set up camp in a modern factory built by a Scandinavian industrial group a few years earlier. The building was spacious and equipped with toilets, showers, and central heating. The camp was located outside the town and the soldiers could easily control access to it. However, it was sandwiched between the centre of the town, held by the Moslems, and the mountains, where the Croats had brought in tanks and mortars.

On the roof of the camp, British soldiers were using binoculars to observe the Croat forces, which had been firing on Moslem positions for three days. The shells passed within metres of the camp, which shook with every explosion. Sometimes automatic-weapon fire from snipers in the woods around the base would rip through the air and the soldiers would have to take cover for a few minutes. The bullets often hit the windows of the British camp and sometimes lodged in the wall just above the soldiers' beds.

'It's been like this since January,' said a British soldier with a sigh. 'They fight for a few days, then there's a truce for a few hours, and then it starts again. In six months, neither the Croats nor the Moslems have really gained any ground.' He said that here in Gornji Vakuf he would see lines of Croat refugees from the north fleeing to the south, the region controlled by Croat forces hostile to the Bosnian central government. 'Here, it's the Moslems who are driving the others out to expand their territory,' he said. 'But these same Moslems were driven out of their towns and villages by the Serbs further north. Go to Bugojno, you'll see.'

Before arriving in Bugojno, a medium-size town north of Gornji Vakuf, the jeep driven by Canadian officer Major Peter Havenstein, a European Community White Helmet, crossed a region controlled by the Moslems. Everything seemed calm; peasants were working in the fields and women were weeding their gardens. Then, a few hundred metres from the town, a house was burning. Half a dozen people holding bundles and suitcases watched the flames destroy their property. Havenstein told me that they were Croats being subjected to intimidation by the Moslems. They were among the last remaining Croats, who had refused to leave the town in the exodus a few weeks before.

'I'll go to the town hall to ask for an explanation,' he said. 'The Moslem authorities promised us they would protect anyone who wanted to stay.'[3]

Obviously, the authorities had not kept their promise. Before the fighting began in this region of central Bosnia, Bugojno was a peaceful town where, to all appearances, Moslems and Croats lived in harmony. Then, suddenly, in June 1993, fighting had begun, triggered by fear and suspicion when the Moslems became aware that further south the Croats had broken their alliance with the Moslems, driving them from their villages and turning the Moslem neighbourhoods of Mostar, the capital of the region, into a killing field. How could they continue to trust these Croats who were living among them? At the same time, the Croats of Bugojno told themselves that if they did not act immediately, they would suffer the same fate as the Moslems of Mostar. The deadly spiral of violence had begun. Who had fired first, no one really knew. But the result was that the Moslems now controlled a town in which they had once made up 42 per cent and the Croats 35 per cent of 45,000 inhabitants. Now there were no more than 3,000 Croats; the rest had fled to Gornji Vakuf and the Croat territories further south.

But the Moslem authorities in Bugojno also had their problems. Thousands of Moslem refugees were converging on the town, fleeing from northern Bosnia, a region ravaged and terrorized by the Serb militias, where the Moslems suffered terribly. In the opinion of the European Community monitors and the British Blue Helmets, the Moslems in Bugojno never engaged in systematic killing of Croats; they aimed rather to drive them from their homes and their neighbourhoods. A 'clean "ethnic cleansing,"' as one British soldier put it. In contrast, the Serbs in northern and eastern Bosnia had shown no respect for anything; the 'ethnic cleansing' of the regions they controlled was accompanied by rape, slaughters, looting, and humiliation that horrified the most impartial observers.

Stories of the Serb atrocities fill hundreds of pages of official reports by the UN and its commission of inquiry on human rights violations in the former Yugoslavia, reports by non-governmental organizations, and memoirs written by Blue Helmets who wanted to share their experiences in the field. Bob Stewart is one of the latter.

A lieutenant-colonel in the British army, Stewart commanded the first battalion of British Blue Helmets deployed in central Bosnia, which was there from November 1992 to May 1993. His memoirs are eloquent testimony to the powerlessness of the Blue Helmets to contain the war or protect civilians from attacks and 'ethnic cleansing.' The Serbs of Bosnia began 'cleansing' the north and east of the republic immediately after international recognition of Bosnian independence in April 1992. The Serb militias first occupied the towns, villages, and countryside to force the Moslems to 'voluntarily' leave their homes. Moslems were constantly threatened and intimidated until they gave in and agreed to sign a declaration that they were voluntarily abandoning their homes. The Serbs then sent them to the centre of the republic or let them go to the major Moslem towns of Sarajevo, Zepa, Tuzla, Zenica, and Srebrenica. But thousands of Moslems clung to their land, and the Serbs began to lose patience. As early as the summer and fall of 1992, they began killing and raping to force the Moslems to leave. The massacres had an immediate effect; tens of thousands of Bosnian Moslems fled in turmoil to central and southern Bosnia, clogging the roads and swelling the population of the towns and villages that took them in.

Stewart relates that the fall of the Moslem bastion of Jajce in November 1992 sent some 20,000 Moslems into exile. The refugees filed past his headquarters in Vitez, about fifty kilometres to the south. Some of them had been walking for days. Many were heading towards Zenica. All Stewart and his Blue Helmets could do was count the people and report to the UN. In March 1993, however, they were forced to become involved. The Serbs had agreed to allow a group of about 2,000 Moslems they were holding to go to territory controlled by the Bosnian government. The two parties invited Stewart to supervise the population transfer, which was to take place not far from the town of Turbe. The British officer accepted, but the transfer was difficult. The Serbs forced the refugees, who were mostly women, children, and old people, to walk in bitter cold across a buffer zone several kilometres wide while they shot over their heads in the direction of the Blue Helmets. Stewart realized then that he was taking part in 'ethnic cleansing' under the flag of the UN. Later he wrote in his memoir: 'True, we have been instrumental in ethnic cleansing, but it would have happened anyway. Probably we made it less painful than it might have been and, possibly, by being quick about it, we saved lives.'[4]

This was not the only time the Blue Helmets, for humanitarian reasons, collaborated with the ethnic policy of the Serbs. The story of the enclave of Srebrenica is another good example.

The small town of Srebrenica was besieged and shelled daily by the Serbs for close to nine months before it made headlines around the world in March 1993, thanks to the courage of French general Philippe Morillon. The flood of Moslem refugees had swelled the population from 6,000 to 60,000, and no relief convoys were able to get through the Serb lines to bring supplies. On 13 March, General Morillon, commander of the UN forces in Bosnia, decided to establish a base in Srebrenica to force the Serbs to open a humanitarian corridor to the town. A television team was on the scene, and the entire world watched as the French soldier, perched on a tank, declared that he would not abandon the town. The Serb militia gave in, and a week later the general left the town. But the Serbs knew that the aid trucks entering the town would not leave empty. The Moslem inhabitants of the town were so exhausted by months of deprivation and shelling that thousands of them were demanding to leave while the road was open. The UN agreed to organize the transport of some 10,000 persons to the town of Tuzla. The departures took place in complete panic, and dozens of people were trampled to death or suffocated in overloaded trucks.

This was far from the end of the UN's problems. The Bosnian authorities of Srebrenica and Tuzla refused to authorize any more departures, on the pretext that they contributed to emptying Srebrenica and played into the hands of the Serbs. The UN responded by accusing the Bosnian authorities of using the civilians as human shields against the Serbs. The UN officials also defended themselves by stating that their priority was protecting civilians and that 'such evacuations are not ethnic cleansing but an attempt to save lives.'[5]

Srebrenica finally fell to the Serbs. On 11 July 1995, a few months before a general peace agreement was signed, the Serb forces captured the enclave. The Moslem authorities in Sarajevo did not lift a finger to defend the town, while the Dutch Blue Helmets were unable to resist the attack or to protect the population from the fury of the Serb soldiers. According to UN reports, several thousand men were massacred, while thousands of others are still missing.

* * *

To understand how the Blue Helmets came to participate indirectly in the 'ethnic cleansing' of Bosnia and certain regions of Croatia, we need to look briefly at the situation in the former Yugoslavia and examine the mandates the UN gave their troops in the Balkans.

The Yugoslav federation began to fall apart in 1990 under the combined weight of the nationalist demands of the Slovenes and the Croats and Serb territorial ambitions. The economic collapse of the country and the paralysis of the League of Communists of Yugoslavia, which had governed Yugoslavia since 1945, had allowed the leaders of the republics to make policy as they pleased. The Slovenes and Croats demanded greater autonomy, while the Serbs, who were in control of the federal army, realizing that the country was breaking up, launched an aggressive policy of annexing territories with Serb populations in the rest of Yugoslavia. In the summer of 1990, Kosovo and Voivodine lost their status as autonomous provinces and came under Serb administration. During the same period, nationalist governments were elected in Slovenia and Croatia, and the Serbs in Croatia were demanding autonomy for their regions. Aided by the presence of the federal army, which was Serb-dominated, the Serbs in the region of Knin, in Croatia, revolted in September 1990. Their movement grew and spread to other Serb regions of Croatia in the spring of 1991. On 28 February, the Serb Autonomous Region of Krajina declared independence from Croatia, and on 12 May 1991, its inhabitants voted to merge the Serb territories with Serbia. Slovenia and Croatia, after holding referendums, proclaimed their independence on 25 June 1991. The war in the former Yugoslavia began when the Serb-dominated federal government refused to recognize the legality of these declarations. The war did not last long in Slovenia, a very homogeneous territory. Its army inflicted a humiliating defeat on the Serbs, forcing the federal army to withdraw from Slovenia on 18 July, after only a few weeks of fighting.

In Croatia, the situation was very different. The federal army openly supported the Serbs, who had boycotted the referendum on independence and held their own consultation, in which they voted to join Serbia. Fighting between the Serbs and Croats lasted more than eight months and was so fierce that it led to the exodus of Serbs to Serbia and of Croats to the territories controlled by the Croat government in Zagreb. The UN estimated that more than 10,000 persons were killed in the fighting and 500,000 became refugees. Finally, in March 1992, the Serbs and the Croats declared a ceasefire and accepted the deployment of a UN force in the Serb-controlled zones, the first units of which arrived in April.

The fighting was temporarily over in Croatia, but it started up again farther south with incredible ferocity. In Bosnia, the multi-ethnic leaders of the republic – Croats, Moslems, and Serbs – watched in horror as Yugoslavia fell apart, keenly aware that their territory was next on the list of Serb claims. They attempted to maintain unity, but their success was short-lived, because, as one of the most knowledgeable French experts on the Yugoslav question wrote, 'it [was] very difficult for Bosnia to escape the principle laid down by the government of [Slobodan] Milosevic: to unite all Serbs in a single state.'[6] In September 1991, the Serbs of Bosnia, who made up 34 per cent of the population, had established three 'Serb autonomous regions,' in the north, the southeast, and the east of the republic. Then, in October 1991, with the parliament deserted by its Serb members, the Bosnian government, led by Alija Izetbegovic, adopted two resolutions on Bosnian sovereignty and withdrawal from the Yugoslav federation. In January 1992, the three Serb autonomous regions responded by uniting to form the Serb Republic of Bosnia, which wanted to remain part of 'Yugoslavia.'

Izetbegovic called for recognition of Bosnia by the international community. But the European Community demanded that a proper referendum be held first. This took place on 29 February 1992, without the participation of the Serbs. The Moslems and Croats voted in favour of Bosnian independence, which was recognized internationally in April. The Serbs reacted immediately by shelling Sarajevo, the Bosnian capital, and systematically expelling Croats and Moslems from territories the Serbs controlled or wanted to appropriate. The Serb strategy of 'ethnic cleansing' was extremely effective, and on 6 November 1992, the United Nations Special Rapporteur on human rights in the former Yugoslavia, former Polish prime minister Tadeusz Mazowiecki, wrote that 'that goal, to a large extent, has already been achieved.'[7] Using rape, massacre, expulsion, and concentration camps, the Serbs gained control of 70 per cent of Bosnian territory.

While the Serbs were consolidating their positions, the fragile alliance between the Moslems and the Croats was disintegrating. On 3 July 1992, the Croats, who constituted the majority in the southwest of the republic – western Herzegovina – proclaimed the Republic of Herceg-Bosnia. They chose Mostar as the capital, and decided to empty the city of its Moslem inhabitants. Trapped between the Serbs and the Croats, the Bosnian Moslems were reduced to a territory that in early 1994 covered about 20 per cent of the former Bosnia. But the situation changed drastically in March 1994 when the Moslems and the Croats signed a political agreement to end the fighting between them. Fighting between the Serbs and the Moslems continued for another year.

In the spring and summer of 1995, the Croat armed forces went on the offensive in Croatia and recaptured two of the three territories held by the Serbs. In Bosnia, the Serbs retreated before attacks by the Croat-Moslem coalition in the north of the country, and took advantage of the situation to capture some Moslem enclaves, including Srebrenica, in the southeast. This led to the United States involvement, through NATO. Throughout the month of September, while NATO warplanes attacked Serb positions, Washington organized meetings between the Croats, the Serbs, and the Moslems. On 12 October a ceasefire was proclaimed in Bosnia, and on 21 November, in Dayton, Ohio, Presidents Izetbegovic of Bosnia, Tudjman of Croatia, and Milosevic of Serbia signed an agreement to end the war. To enforce the Dayton accord, NATO agreed to replace the Blue Helmets with a force of 60,000, which arrived at the end of December. The Dayton agreement is still holding. But the Bosnians have paid a heavy price: some two hundred thousand dead and two million refugees and displaced persons out of a total pre-war population of five million.

* * *

The UN was slow to react to the conflict in the former Yugoslavia. Careful not to intervene in the internal affairs of one of its members, it initially only passed resolutions asking the parties to settle their differences peacefully and imposed an embargo on arms shipments. Divisions among the Western countries on what position to take also delayed UN attempts at solution for several months. In the summer and fall of 1991, several countries – including Germany and Austria – favoured recognizing Slovenia and Croatia, while France and the United States were fiercely opposed, believing the survival of the Yugoslav federation was still possible. The members of the European Community finally agreed to delay recognition of the two republics until January 1992 and to propose plans for settling the conflict to the parties involved. Serbia rejected the European Community's offer and the EC turned to the United Nations Security Council.

On 8 October 1991, the UN appointed an envoy, former American secretary of state Cyrus Vance, to attempt to establish a permanent ceasefire between Croatia and the Serb forces. Vance proposed to the two parties that a peacekeeping force be deployed in the Croat territories controlled by the Serbs. This proposal was accepted, and on 21 February 1992, the Security Council authorized the creation of the United Nations Protection Force (UNPROFOR) of 15,000 Blue Helmets, to be deployed in three regions of Croatia: Krajina, Eastern Slavonia, and Western Slavonia. These regions were designated United Nations Protected Areas (UNPAs).

The mandate of UNPROFOR was multiple and complex. First, the Security Council reaffirmed its support for the territorial integrity and sovereignty of Croatia and emphasized that 'the Force should be an interim arrangement to create the conditions of peace and security required for the negotiation of an overall settlement of the Yugoslav crisis.'[8] The Security Council endorsed the secretary-general's report setting out the mandate of UNPROFOR in Croatia, which was to ensure the withdrawal of the federal army from all Croat territory and the demilitarization of the UNPAs, to supervise the local administration and the police, and to facilitate the return of displaced persons. Some months later the mandate was enlarged to authorize UNPROFOR to provide supervision by UN civilian police in the 'pink zones,' areas located outside the three UNPAs but populated largely by Serbs, and ensure the re-establishment of the authority of the Croat government in these zones; to control the entry of civilians into the UNPAs; and finally, to perform immigration and customs functions at the UNPA borders at international frontiers.[9] UNPROFOR was to do all this without the use of force and with the consent of the parties.

By spring 1995 this mandate had only been partially carried out. The federal troops did withdraw from Croatia and the three UNPAs, but in these regions, weapons were turned over to the local Serb militias. Demilitarization, which had begun with the storage of the weapons in buildings with double keys – one for UNPROFOR, the other for the Serbs – came to an end during a Croat attack in January 1993, when the Serbs came back to retrieve their weapons. Not a single displaced person, Croat or Serb, was able to return home. The Serbs who lived in the three UNPAs in Croatia systematically destroyed the homes of the Croats and continued settling there. This took place under the noses of the 15,000 Blue Helmets and civilian police, for nothing in the UNPROFOR mandate permitted them to stop the Serbs. The secretary-general of the UN acknowledged in his report of 15 May 1993 that 'the Serb side has taken the presence of UNPROFOR as a licence to freeze the status quo in place, under UNPROFOR "protection," while establishing a "state" of the "Republic of Serb Krajina" in UNPROFOR's area of responsibility.'[10]

Faced with this situation, the government of Croatia accused the UN of legitimizing 'ethnic cleansing' and asked it to modify to UNPROFOR's mandate by giving it the right to use force to compel the Serbs to respect Security Council resolutions, particularly those concerning the re-establishment of Croat authority in the UNPAs and the pink zones. The secretary-general rejected this request, declaring that 'neither the Force Commander nor I myself consider that the international community should become party to the conflict, using military force to impose a solution on one side in what remains an inter-ethnic dispute.'[11] Boutros-Ghali thus emphasized that the member states of the UN, particularly those who had sent soldiers and civilian police to Croatia (about thirty countries), did not want to use force to settle the dispute between the Serbs and Croats.

But it was force that settled the dispute. In the spring and summer of 1995, the Croat armies retook Western Slavonia and the Krajina region on the Dalmatian coast. Hundreds of thousands of Serbs were driven from their homes and forced to flee to Bosnia and Serbia. Eastern Slavonia remained in the hands of the Serbs, but the Serbs and the Croats agreed that it would be placed under UN administration until 15 July 1997, when it would begin gradually to be returned to Croat control.

* * *

As we have seen, Bosnia was also involved in the upheavals of the Yugoslav crisis. Even before Bosnia proclaimed its independence following the referendum of 29 February 1992, the three communities had begun negotiations on the constitutional future of the republic. The Croats and Moslems had agreed – although shakily – to maintain the unity of the republic. But the Serbs sought greater autonomy through the partitioning of Bosnia into three nation states; with that accomplished, fusion with Greater Serbia could more easily be achieved. These negotiations, which were carried out under the auspices of the European Community, seemed to have succeeded when the representatives of the three communities, meeting in Lisbon on 24 February, announced that they were agreed on the territorial integrity of Bosnia, although it would be divided along ethnic lines.[12]

The agreement fell apart the day after the referendum. The results, which favoured Bosnian independence, were not even known when, on the evening of 1 March, the Serbs revolted in Sarajevo, the capital, and in other Bosnian towns and cities. In the southeast, a region with a Croat majority, the Croats, who were opposed to Bosnian unity, swore they would proclaim their own republic.

As Bosnia sank into civil war, the secretary-general's personal envoy for Yugoslavia, Cyrus Vance, arrived to prepare for the establishment of UNPROFOR headquarters. For the UN had decided that the headquarters of the force deployed in Croatia would be in Sarajevo, in Bosnia, claiming that it could not be located either in Croatia or in Serbia and that its presence in the Bosnian capital would have a dissuasive effect on the Bosnian factions. Vance even stated in Belgrade on 4 March 1992, that the shooting and the danger of civil war in Bosnia would not affect the UN's decision to locate the UNPROFOR headquarters in Sarajevo.[13] The UN's disregard for reality was pointed out by the assistant commander of UNPROFOR, French general Philippe Morillon, in his memoir of Sarajevo: 'by locating the Blue Helmets in this capital we were ... attempting to maintain calm there and reassure the people of Bosnia. The road to hell is paved with good intentions.'[14] In spite of Vance's fine words, the headquarters, subjected to constant shelling, did not remain in Sarajevo for long. In May 1992, the staff was evacuated to Belgrade, and then, two months later, to Zagreb, where the headquarters remained until December 1995, when UNPROFOR was replaced by a NATO force.

But another headquarters was established in Sarajevo – that of UNPRO-FOR Sector Sarajevo, commanded by Canadian major-general Lewis MacKenzie.

At the beginning of April 1992, the Bosnian government requested the rapid deployment of a Blue Helmets mission in Bosnia. After sending Vance to the region to look into the feasibility of such a mission, the sec-retary-general of the UN rather thoughtlessly rejected Sarajevo's request, stating that it might be more appropriate for the European Community to expand its presence and activities in Bosnia-Herzegovina.[15] In his report to the Security Council, Boutros-Ghali wrote that the endemic vio-lence in Bosnia and the UN's lack of human and financial resources pre-vented him from recommending the deployment of a peacekeeping mission. He concluded his report by stating that 'the sad fact is that the present conditions in Bosnia-Herzegovina make it impossible to define a workable concept for a United Nations peacekeeping operation.'[16]

Even if Boutros-Ghali was justified from a strictly technical point of view – there was no ceasefire and no consent of the parties to the deployment of Blue Helmets – the UN was finally forced to act. After the adoption of the customary resolutions calling on the factions to end the fighting and respect the territorial integrity and independence of Bosnia and demand-ing the withdrawal of foreign forces, the Security Council decided to take action against Serbia, which was providing military assistance to the Bos-nian Serbs. On 30 May and 8 June 1992, it imposed sanctions on Serbia and Montenegro, which had formed the new Federal Republic of Yugo-slavia in January 1992, and broadened the mandate of UNPROFOR to include a new sector, that of Sarajevo. UNPROFOR was given the man-date to open the Sarajevo airport and make possible distribution of the humanitarian aid arriving there. There was no provision in this mandate for the Blue Helmets to interpose themselves between the factions to stop the fighting. General MacKenzie was put in charge of the new sector, and on 3 July the airport was reopened under the protection of Canadian and French Blue Helmets.

But in the rest of Bosnia the situation was rapidly deteriorating. The humanitarian aid sent by the United Nations High Commission for Refu-gees (UNHCR) and the non-government organizations was not getting through or was being looted by the militias, which seemed impossible to control. As the fighting spread, refugees poured into the major towns and the refugee centres. Faced with this situation, the Security Council in August and September adopted two resolutions broadening the mandate of UNPROFOR to include the protection – using force if necessary – of the humanitarian convoys throughout Bosnia and the deployment of some 6,000 Blue Helmets in four regions of the republic, over and above the 2,000 already deployed at the Sarajevo airport.

In hopes of being better able to dissuade the Serbs – and, to a lesser degree, the other factions – from continuing to fight, the Security Council on 9 October adopted a resolution banning all military flights over Bosnia. NATO was given responsibility for enforcing the ban. Then, on 16 November, to stop the infiltration of men, ammunition, and supplies into Bosnia, the council adopted a new resolution ordering the deployment of observers along Bosnia's border with the new Yugoslavia. Finally, on 16 April, 6 May, and 4 June 1993, the Security Council adopted resolutions declaring Srebrenica and five other Bosnian towns 'safe areas' and ordered UNPROFOR to protect them. (In the next chapter we will see what, precisely, 'protection' meant.)

* * *

While the UN adopted dozens of resolutions condemning 'ethnic cleansing,' it never gave the Blue Helmets the mandate to take concrete action to prevent it. The UN's Special Rapporteur on human rights violations in the former Yugoslavia, Tadeusz Mazowiecki, had recommended the adoption of such a mandate, but the only concrete measure taken by the UN to dissuade the factions from violating human rights was the creation, on 22 February 1993, of an international tribunal on war crimes. The tribunal, which is painfully short of human and financial resources, began its work in September 1994. It has laid charges against seventy-five Serbs, Croats, and Moslems, including former Bosnian Serb leaders Radovan Karadzic and Ratko Mladic. On 7 May 1997, for the first time since the Nuremberg and Tokyo trials, a person was convicted of crimes against humanity. But many observers doubt the effectiveness of a tribunal that has limited means to arrest the criminals and lacks the cooperation of governments.[17]

* * *

At the International Hotel in Zenica, Philippe Sidos was writing his report, as he did every day. He was describing one of the most horrible aspects of the war ravaging Bosnia, 'ethnic cleansing.' And he knew full well that his report would change nothing, that it would end up on a shelf in Brussels and that the Croats and Moslems who had been driven from their homes would likely never return. Sidos was one of the thousands of White Helmets and Blue Helmets who passed through Bosnia and Croatia without being able to end the war or its tragic consequences – the massacres, the rapes, the camps, and the systematic expulsion of ethnic groups by other ethnic groups. But his report remains. It will permit history to remember that, for the second time this century, the Western world lacked the courage to stand up to those who were practising physical or cultural genocide. This time, no one will be able to say, 'We didn't know.'

9

Obstruction by the Great Powers

On 4 October 1993, the fifteen members of the United Nations Security Council met to adopt a new resolution on the situation in the former Yugoslavia. The ambassadors seated around the table were visibly tired and tense. They had been meeting behind closed doors for a week, discussing the renewal of UNPROFOR's mandate in Croatia, and had just reached agreement on the wording of the resolution. As usual, there was a long list of diplomatic banalities: the resolution reaffirmed prior resolutions on the conflict, condemned the bad faith of the parties, reiterated the Security Council's concern about the gravity of the situation, warned the parties that failure to cooperate with the implementation of the peace plan 'would have serious consequences.'[1] This was the forty-fourth resolution of its kind on the situation in the Balkans. After the vote, the members dispersed to deal with their own concerns. The resolution was promptly faxed to UNPROFOR headquarters in Zagreb so that the Blue Helmets could see that it was respected.

On the third floor of those headquarters, in an old Yugoslav army barracks, the force commander, French general Jean Cot, had just read the resolution. He was fuming. Summoning the press, Cot denounced, albeit politely, the latest plan hatched by the Security Council. 'The UN has a gift for passing resolutions that become missions for the troops, but they don't provide the means to carry them out,' he declared to the journalists, who were surprised to be told officially what they had been hearing unofficially for months.[2] Cot went on to inform the diplomats – in particular, the representatives of the five great powers on the Security Council – that to apply their new resolution, he would need 4,000 men in addition to the 13,000 already deployed in Croatia. He also pointed out that the UN troops in Bosnia were still waiting for reinforcements to protect the regions the Security Council had declared emergency 'safe areas' a few months earlier.

A few hours later, Cot was gently reminded by UN officials that an officer in the service of the UN obeyed orders, and did not criticize them. The UN asked him to apply the new resolution on Croatia and to devote all UNPROFOR's resources to that task. This time, Cot complied without comment. He notified the Blue Helmets that they had to negotiate the cessation of hostilities at all levels with the military commanders of the parties to the conflict, interpose UNPROFOR troops between their forces and set up observation posts if necessary, open up crossing points, help with the evaluation of needs for humanitarian relief and with its distribution, and reinforce the protection of the local population.[3] Here was enough work for an entire army.

Cot's orders had hardly been transmitted to his men when Serb, Croat, and Moslem soldiers in the field began enthusiastically violating the ceasefire their leaders had signed, shelling civilians and harassing the Blue Helmets. With every day the situation worsened. The UN forces and the personnel of the humanitarian agencies were increasingly subjected to harassment and theft, shot at, wounded, and sometimes killed. Meanwhile, at the political level, the factions were negotiating in Geneva, and Bosnian, Croat, and Serb leaders were accusing UNPROFOR of favouring their enemies. Their propaganda machines heaped condemnation on the Blue Helmets, accusing them of smuggling, corruption, immoral behaviour, and involvement in 'ethnic cleansing.' The UN objected to the insults and harassment, but asked the Blue Helmets to put up with them and go on doing their job.

All this was too much for one of Cot's aides, General Francis Briquemont, commander of the UNPROFOR mission in Bosnia. In an interview on Bosnian radio on 16 December, he launched into a tirade. 'At the United Nations, the politicians pass resolutions almost every day, but they don't give us the means to carry out our mission. I don't even read their resolutions any more. I just try to do what I can with the troops I have.'[4] Frustrated by the fact that his men, lacking the power to intervene, were standing by helplessly witnessing 'ethnic cleansing,' looting of humanitarian convoys, shelling of civilians, and their own humiliation, he continued, 'In a few years, when the conflict in the former Yugoslavia is studied in strategic studies centres or military schools, they'll find almost every mistake you shouldn't make in crisis management. I believe that throughout this crisis ... the international community has been unable to define a clear common strategy.'

How can the Belgian general be blamed for his anger? From 25 September 1991 to the end of December 1993, the UN Security Council passed forty-five resolutions and its president made forty statements on the conflict in the former Yugoslavia. UNPROFOR's mandate was changed some fifteen times, causing a great deal of confusion for the military personnel in the field.

The UN's response to the comments of the Belgian general came quickly. The next day, a UN spokesperson stated that the top officials of the organization had noted his remarks and would reply in due time.[5] The situation seemed to calm down, particularly since the Serb, Croat, and Bosnian leaders, meeting in Geneva, announced on 22 December that a ceasefire would be declared for Christmas and New Year's, to last until 15 January 1994. But the ceasefire did not occur: the shelling continued and so did the Blue Helmets' humiliation. General Briquemont was forced to resign in January 1994, six months before the official end of his mandate, for failing to fulfil the military officer's duty to be circumspect.

Briquemont's boss, General Jean Cot, was enraged. In an interview on French radio, Cot spoke of the humiliations to which his men were subjected. 'We're not goats tied to a stake,' he said. 'We respond when we are directly attacked.' Cot acknowledged that he had little room to manoeuvre,[6] and he condemned the tactics of the Security Council: 'There are incredible gaps between the resolutions adopted by the Security Council, the will to implement them, and the means provided to commanders in the field.'

Cot had, many times, discreetly asked the secretary-general for authorization to order air strikes against the factions attacking the Blue Helmets or the humanitarian convoys, in order to win respect in the field. But Boutros-Ghali always refused to delegate to Cot this power, which he held on the basis of Security Council Resolution 836, adopted on 4 June 1993. On 8 January 1994, on the eve of the NATO summit at which France was to propose the use of air strikes against the Bosnian Serbs, Cot decided to make his dispute with the secretary-general public. Boutros-Ghali was under pressure from all sides for his hesitation to take military measures. The secretary-general justified himself by pointing out that some member states of the Security Council – Russia and China openly, United Kingdom more discreetly – were opposed to any use of force against the Serbs. But the leaders of the NATO countries, who had rejected the option of military intervention to impose a solution in Bosnia, did not want to appear to be doing nothing when public opinion condemned them for failing to alleviate the Bosnians' suffering. After two days of intense discussion, the NATO countries gave the green light to selective strikes if the Serbs opposed the opening of an airport in Bosnia (the one in Tuzla) or the replacement of the Canadian contingent in the town of Srebrenica. Cot had seemingly won.

But Boutros-Ghali had the last word. While visiting Paris on 11 January, he complained of the French general's insubordination, and asked for and received his head. Cot resigned from the command of UNPROFOR in March 1994, three months before the end of his mandate.[7]

* * *

The tug-of-war between the UNPROFOR generals and the UN secretary-general shows the difficulty of the Blue Helmets' work in the region. But while the generals' criticisms of the UN's inadequacies and Boutros-Ghali's hesitation were justified, their attacks were misplaced. The UN, after all, is what the member states are willing to make of it, and its secretary-general is only their humble messenger. The members of the Security Council – especially the five great powers – bear a heavy responsibility in this matter. The resolutions they adopted on the conflicts in the former Yugoslavia were often confused with respect both to the wording of the mandates and the means provided to carry them out. The Security Council had an infuriating propensity to produce new resolutions without taking into consideration the responsibilities involved and without allocating new resources to the forces in the field. The following examples may explain the anger of Generals Briquemont and Cot.

The Security Council had from the beginning of the conflict in Bosnia in April 1992, insisted on freedom of movement for the Blue Helmets and the employees of non-governmental organizations involved in delivering humanitarian aid. It had also requested control of the borders between Bosnia and the new Federal Republic of Yugoslavia (Serbia and Montenegro) in order to prevent the smuggling of weapons and supplies to the Bosnian Serbs. Finally, it had ordered the cessation of hostilities and the protection of civilians from attack in six designated 'safe areas.' But what actually happened on the ground?

In order to enforce the military and economic embargo against the new Federal Republic of Yugoslavia and the resolutions demanding an end to all outside intervention in Bosnia, which aimed to prevent soldiers, weapons, and supplies from the new Yugoslavia from getting into the Serb zones of Bosnia, the Security Council passed two other important resolutions.[8] Resolution 787, adopted on 16 November 1992, asked the UNPROFOR commander to act quickly. A few days later, in a report to the members of the Security Council, secretary-general Boutros-Ghali explained the scope of the task entrusted to UNPROFOR. He pointed out that in order to monitor a border 1,100 kilometres long, with 123 crossing points, UNPROFOR would need at least 10,000 more soldiers, plus civilian personnel.[9] Furthermore, this force would have to be deployed in the territories of the new Yugoslavia and Croatia, which would require the permission of these governments. He had no illusions about the reaction of the Security Council to his report.

On 10 June 1993, six months after Resolution 787 was passed, the Security Council adopted a second resolution (838), asking UNPROFOR once again to monitor the borders. In a new report to the Security Council, the secretary-general observed that it was impossible to carry out that mandate since the leaders of the new Yugoslavia refused to cooperate with the UN.[10] He also suggested that before ordering the application of the mandate, the members of the council should take into consideration the availability of additional human and financial resources, thus providing a polite reminder that it was useless to pass resolutions without ensuring that UNPROFOR would be given the means to carry them out. Disregarding Boutros-Ghali's advice, the members of the Security Council sent a letter to the secretary-general reminding him of the need to deploy the requested observers and asking him to continue to try to find personnel.[11] Seven months later, in March 1994, Boutros-Ghali wrote in his report on UNPROFOR's activities that he was still waiting for troops to carry out this new mandate from the Security Council.[12]

But the resolution that aroused the most controversy, and led eventually to General Cot being relieved of his duties, was Resolution 836, adopted on 4 June 1993. This resolution ordered UNPROFOR to provide protection for six previously established 'safe areas' and for humanitarian convoys in Bosnia.

Resolution 836 was the follow-up to resolutions passed on 16 April and 6 May, which created 'safe areas' in Sarajevo, Bihac, Srebrenica, Gorazde, Tuzla, and Zepa. Bosnian Moslems would be parked in these areas under the protection of new contingents of Blue Helmets while they waited for better times. The 'safe areas,' however, were never respected by the Bosnian Serbs, who continued their shelling. In the face of international criticism, five countries – the United States, Russia, the United Kingdom, France, and Spain – met in Washington on 22 May 1993 to attempt to reach an agreement on common action to convince the Serbs to stop their attacks. The situation had become desperate for the Moslems, who were rapidly losing ground to the Serbs. The cities and towns of Bosnia were subjected to constant shelling and the humanitarian convoys were no longer getting through to them. Their inhabitants were facing starvation and disease. Something had to be done, chorused the foreign ministers of the five powers.

The five countries agreed on a common plan of action to protect the six 'safe areas' and asked the UN Security Council to endorse their plan. But the Washington meeting was barely over when the countries began to differ on the meaning of the protection promised. For the Americans, it meant protecting the Blue Helmets from Serbian attacks. The Russians rejected the use of force against the Serbs. France, which at the outset had proposed the creation of 'reserves' for the Bosnians, recommended – somewhat ambiguously, as would later become apparent – that the Blue Helmets deter aggressors and protect the population.[13]

The plan of the five countries went to the Security Council. The members of the council were supposed to adopt a resolution describing UNPROFOR's new mandate in the six 'safe areas' and its role in the protection of the humanitarian convoys bringing in supplies to them. For ten days, the fifteen members of the Council worked on Resolution 836. The Non-aligned countries were outraged by the mere concept of 'safe areas,' which they felt would lead to the establishment of 'reserves' for the Bosnians and confer recognition on the Serbs' territorial conquests. They called for more forceful action by the Blue Helmets. The great powers yielded to the Non-aligned countries' pressure on the first point by emphasizing in the resolution that the creation of the 'safe areas' was a temporary measure. On 4 June, the Security Council met and passed the resolution.

The resolution had barely been adopted when further controversy broke out. The five Non-aligned countries interpreted the resolution to mean that the UN was sending Blue Helmets to protect the Moslem populations from attacks by their aggressors. Four of the great powers (China remained silent) disagreed with this interpretation: their understanding was that the Blue Helmets would be deployed to deter the aggressors.[14] A reading of the resolution reveals that both interpretations are possible. For example, paragraph 5 states that the Security Council has decided 'to extend ... the mandate of UNPROFOR in order to enable it ... to deter attacks against the safe areas.' A little further on, in paragraph 9, the Security Council 'authorizes UNPROFOR ... in carrying out the mandate defined in paragraph 5 above, *acting in self-defence*, to take the necessary measures, including the use of force, in reply to bombardments against the safe areas by any of the parties or to armed incursion into them or in the event of any deliberate obstruction in or around those areas to the freedom of movement of UNPROFOR or of protected humanitarian convoys [emphasis added].' Finally, paragraph 10 authorizes 'the use of air power ... to support UNPROFOR in the performance of its mandate set out in paragraphs 5 and 9 above.' Not surprisingly, even experienced diplomatic and military officials had difficulty in trying to interpret this mandate. The commander of UNPROFOR, Swedish general Lars-Eric Wahlgren, even had to return to New York to ask for clarification on the resolution.[15] What exactly did it mean?

For the Western diplomats who originally proposed the resolution, the Blue Helmets were to prevent attacks, but respond only to attacks directed against themselves. If shells hit houses or schools, for instance, they would not respond. As one military attaché put it, 'If Serb shells fly over the heads of the Blue Helmets and hit the Moslems, we won't do anything.'[16] On 13 June, nine days after the adoption of the resolution, a Serb shell hit a hospital in Gorazde, killing fifty people.[17] Not a single Blue Helmet had been deployed around this 'safe area,' which was under siege for close to a year before the UN finally intervened to genuinely protect it.

According to one Western diplomat, the resolution was passed to appease international public opinion, in particular in the Moslem countries, where it was felt that the UN was doing little to prevent the elimination of the Bosnian Moslems. Since there was increasing pressure in favour of direct military intervention against the Serbs, which neither the Europeans nor the Russians would agree to, the West chose to evade the issue by talking tough while refusing to actually strike against the Serbs. Hence the ambiguity regarding the means to be used to implement the resolution.

To protect the six 'safe areas,' the resolution provided for the deployment of Blue Helmets around them, with support from air power. According to the authors of the resolution, there was an 'emergency situation.'[18] They asked the secretary-general to submit a plan for the deployment of the Blue Helmets. Ten days after the adoption of the resolution, Boutros-Ghali submitted his report,[19] in which he specified the military forces UNPROFOR needed to carry out its mandate and indicated that he had asked NATO to prepare a plan for the use of air power. Rejecting an option that would have required the deployment of 34,000 soldiers around the 'safe areas,' Boutros-Ghali suggested adopting a 'light option' that involved the use of 7,600 soldiers with 'the consent and cooperation of the parties' in the field. Thus the Serbs, among others, would decide where, when, and how the Blue Helmets responsible for deterring them from attacking the Moslems would be deployed. The Security Council accepted the secretary-general's report and supported the 'light' option.

Resolution 836 then became the responsibility of the office of the military adviser. The officers there were faced with two problems: first, they had to find 7,600 soldiers to be dispatched to Bosnia as quickly as possible; then they had to interpret the mandate and explain it to the Blue Helmets in the field.

'It's June 9,' said one of the officers in the office of the military adviser. 'Assuming that we find all the necessary troops, it will take between four and six weeks before they arrive in Bosnia and are deployed around the areas. And that's the optimistic option. I don't believe it. I think that in two months, we still won't have found half of the 7,600 soldiers. We'll talk about this again.' In fact, it took close to eight months before a mere 5,000 soldiers were deployed around certain areas.[20]

In its search for soldiers, the office of the military adviser had to contend with recruitment problems. The Russians, who had promised to send a contingent, suddenly went back on their word, saying that the soldiers' mandate was too vague. But there were other reasons for their decision, as observers noted. Part of the Russian government was opposed to any intervention against Serbia and the Russian Blue Helmets deployed in Croatia were openly sympathetic to the Serbs. The Americans were ready to strike from the air but did not want to risk the lives of their soldiers on the ground. There was no question of sending German troops to the former Yugoslavia, which had been under Nazi control during World War II. The Turks, who had the second-largest army in NATO, were anxious to come to the aid of their Bosnian 'brothers,' but the Serbs threatened a bloodbath if the Ottomans set foot in the Balkans, a region they had ruled for four centuries. The French, the British, the Canadians, and the Spanish were already providing half of the 25,000 Blue Helmets deployed in the former Yugoslavia and balked at supplying more, although in the end France dispatched another thousand soldiers. Then there were the countries of the Third World. In his report, the secretary-general indicated that he had been able to find a few countries prepared to send troops, but they had neither military equipment to defend themselves in the field nor aircraft to transport their soldiers. Boutros-Ghali appealed to the generosity of the Western countries.

There was, however, one group of countries ready to help the UN. On

16 July 1993, the members of the Organization of the Islamic Conference (OIC), meeting in Islamabad, Pakistan, offered to supply 18,000 soldiers, including 10,000 Iranians, to carry out the mandate of Resolution 836. The Western countries immediately rejected the offer. Paris and London emphasized that they would prefer the UN to obtain soldiers from countries with peacekeeping experience, which obviously excluded the Iranian Mujahedeen. In a letter dated 2 August, Boutros-Ghali informed the OIC countries that their generosity could not be accepted in this instance.

As for the role of the Blue Helmets in the 'safe areas,' the officers in the office of the military adviser were left scratching their heads. 'What does it mean to protect the enclaves?' asked one officer. 'For me as a military man, that means ensuring that they don't have any shells dropping on them. The average range of a shell is twenty to twenty-five kilometres. If you want to defend the town, you have to deploy in a radius of about twenty kilometres around it, and therefore push back the Serb artillery, which is often only a few kilometres from the areas.'[21] The other option was to destroy the Serb artillery in place, using NATO air strikes, if the Serbs dared to shell the areas. But could they make good on that threat?

Since the beginning of the war in Bosnia, the international community and the UN had been divided on the question of military intervention to deal with the various crises that arose. On the one hand, the Americans had always argued in favour of lifting the arms embargo against the Bosnian government and taking military action against the Serbs. At various times, politicians, including President Clinton, called for unilateral air strikes against Serb targets. The Russians, French, and British, and the UN had always opposed 'adding war to war,' in the words of French president François Mitterrand. But the longer the conflict dragged on and the Bosnians suffered, while the Serbs defied the rest of the world and reneged on their commitments, the harder it became not to use the threat of force.

NATO offered to make its air force available to the UN. On 9 August 1993, responding to Boutros-Ghali's invitation, its members – led by the Americans – ratified a detailed plan on the use of air strikes to protect the 'safe areas.' The tone was confrontational and the Americans were even threatening to use force unilaterally.[22] In its press release, however, NATO emphasized that the secretary-general of the UN would have to authorize any intervention by NATO airplanes. On the strength of this threat, the UN issued a warning to the Serbs. And what happened? The attacks on Sarajevo, the 'safe areas,' and the Blue Helmets continued, without NATO air power being called on to come to the rescue.

In December 1993 and January 1994 the crisis of the generals brought the situation to a head. At a summit in Brussels on 10 and 11 January, the members of NATO decided once again to get tough with the Serbs. After laborious negotiations among the delegations and heated discussion between the Americans and the French, the final communiqué affirmed that the sixteen NATO countries were ready, under the authority of the Security Council, 'to carry out air strikes in order to prevent the strangulation of Sarajevo, the safe areas and other threatened areas in Bosnia and Herzegovina.'[23]

But this new mandate immediately created discord among the members of the United Nations Security Council. Russia and China were categorically opposed to air strikes, and Moscow demanded to be consulted prior to any NATO military action in Bosnia.[24] As for the Bosnians, they quickly became disillusioned when they read Boutros-Ghali's interpretation of 'air strikes.' After consultation with NATO and the UN's special representative in the former Yugoslavia, Yasushi Akashi (who had led the UN mission in Cambodia a few months before), Boutros-Ghali explained the distinction between 'close air support' for self-defence and 'air strikes' involving the use of air power for preventive and punitive purposes, and claimed that NATO had authorized the former but not the latter.[25] The Blue Helmets could therefore ask for the intervention of NATO aircraft *to protect themselves*, but not to protect the 'safe areas.' The UN and NATO were still trying to avoid becoming directly involved.

Why advocate and threaten to use force without genuinely resorting to it? After all, the resolutions on the protection of the humanitarian convoys and the 'safe areas' were adopted in accordance with Chapter VII of the United Nations Charter, which explicitly authorizes the use of armed force. This was also true of Resolution 678 authorizing the multinational coalition to use 'all necessary means'[26] to expel Iraqi troops from Kuwait, which was passed on 29 November 1990. And it was on the basis of Chapter VII that the UN conducted its mission in Somalia from June 1993 to March 1995, in which the Blue Helmets used force not only to protect the humanitarian convoys, but also to fight militias that did not respect the orders of the Security Council.

In Bosnia, the attitude of the UN was completely different. In spite of the resolutions passed and the public declarations of the secretary-general and high-ranking officers of UNPROFOR with respect to the possible use of force against factions which prevented the convoys from getting through or continued to shell the 'safe areas,' the members – especially the five great powers on the Security Council – never agreed to sign a blank cheque for UNPROFOR.

There are two possible explanations for this double standard on the use of force. The first is noted in the UN's experience in Somalia. After the massacre of twenty-five Pakistani Blue Helmets by General Aidid's soldiers in Mogadishu in June 1993, the Security Council had explicitly ordered the Blue Helmets to find the general and bring him to justice. This manhunt had involved a huge search operation in the neighbourhoods of Mogadishu, which continued until the end of October, and resulted in the deaths of dozens of Blue Helmets and hundreds of Somalis. In Bosnia, the Security Council never gave orders for the capture of a leader who did not respect UNPROFOR's orders or the lives of Blue Helmets, although some thirty Blue Helmets were deliberately killed by snipers. No one wanted to repeat the 'blunders' made in Somalia.

Another explanation focuses on manoeuvring by the great powers in the Balkan region. While the five great powers passed the resolutions under Chapter VII, they did not authorize the direct use of force. They felt that invoking Chapter VII and threatening NATO air strikes would be enough to induce the parties – especially the Serbs – to respect the UN's decisions. The main European mediator and representative at the Geneva negotiations on Bosnia, Lord Owen, even acknowledged that the use of air strikes could be considered a bluff.[27] Furthermore, neither the Russians nor the British, much less the French, were prepared to endorse military actions that might result in the Blue Helmets becoming directly involved in the conflict. Only the United States called for the lifting of the arms embargo against the Bosnian Moslems and the use of air strikes against the Serbs.

But a horrible massacre on Sunday, 6 February 1994 forced the UN and NATO to react vigorously. In the middle of the day, Markale, the busiest market in Sarajevo, was crowded with shoppers making their meagre purchases. Suddenly a shell exploded in the middle of the throng, killing sixty-eight people.[28] This was the deadliest attack of the war in Bosnia. Televised pictures of the mutilated corpses were seen around the world. Emotions ran high and the Serbs were widely condemned. France demanded an emergency meeting of NATO in Brussels to give the Serbs an ultimatum. At the UN, Boutros-Ghali sent a message to NATO's secretary-general asking for air raids 'against artillery or mortar positions in and around Sarajevo which are determined by UNPROFOR to be responsible for attacks against civilian targets in that city.'[29] The request was aimed at all the factions. On 9 February, after fourteen hours of acrimonious discussion, the members of NATO issued an ultimatum to all the parties, especially the Serbs, giving them ten days to withdraw their heavy weapons from a radius of twenty kilometres from the centre of Sarajevo and place them under UN control.[30] Otherwise, at midnight on 20 February, NATO airplanes would destroy those weapons and strike the direct support facilities that were essential to them.[31] This time, the Serbs complied. But while Sarajevo was saved, the other 'safe areas' continued to be shelled. The NATO ultimatum did not apply to them.

However, NATO did strike against the Serbs three times. On 28 February 1994, four Serb military aircraft were shot down for flying over Bosnia in violation of a ban decreed by the UN on 9 October 1992. But the most serious incidents occurred in April. The town of Gorazde – one of the six 'safe areas' – had been subjected to intense shelling for several weeks. The UN attempted to mediate between the Serbs and the Moslems, but without success. With public opinion running high and calls for help from the inhabitants of the town and even the UN observers on the ground, NATO launched air strikes against Serb targets on 10 and 11 April. The Serbs partially stopped their attacks, and the world thought that the UN had won a big victory. Events would prove otherwise.

The day after the air strikes, the commander of the Blue Helmets in the former Yugoslavia, French general Bertrand de Lapresle, set the record straight, with a reminder that the NATO airplanes were not there to defend the people. 'It is essential not to place too much importance on these actions of self-defence,' he said in a press conference.[32] 'The sole objective of the air support was to permit the United Nations to defend its personnel who were in danger in the town of Gorazde.' He added that the air strikes would not have taken place if no UN personnel had been in the enclave. The wily general went on to say that 'since Gorazde was designated a "safe area" by the UN, a different method would have been used to protect it.' One wonders what that would have been.

The NATO air strikes did not prevent the Serbs from continuing their campaign of humiliation of the Blue Helmets and their shelling of Gorazde. Three days later, 155 Blue Helmets, including 16 Canadians, were held hostage for several days. President Clinton made threats, but the UN negotiated discreetly and the Blue Helmets were finally freed. The shells continued to rain down on the town of Gorazde. On 22 April, NATO once again gave the Serbs an ultimatum to withdraw their heavy artillery to twenty kilometres from the town, emphasizing that its air protection would now also cover four other 'safe areas': Bihac, Srebrenica,

Tuzla, and Zepa.[33] The Serbs gave in, but they had shown they could make things difficult for the UN and NATO.

* * *

The exasperation of the UNPROFOR generals, the dispute over the use of force, and the adoption of resolutions that were impossible to apply are evidence of the great powers' lack of respect for the Blue Helmets. Of course, this attitude was not limited to the former Yugoslavia; we saw in Chapter 6 how little regard the United States showed for the UN mission in Somalia. When American military operations against General Aidid were unsuccessful, Washington blamed the decision makers at UN headquarters in New York, even though it was the Americans themselves who were commanding the operations: Washington needed a scapegoat to satisfy public opinion. In the former Yugoslavia, the UN was subjected to similar criticism. But this time the accusations came from France, and they were especially wrong-headed.

The French had not accepted the dismissal of General Cot by the secretary-general of the UN on 18 January 1994. Three days after that announcement, the Minister of Defence, François Léotard, expressed his rage on television. 'We feel that the UN is using up generals at an inordinate rate. After the Turkish one, the Italian one, and the Belgian one, now it's a French general,' he said, forgetting that on 23 June of the previous year, when the UNPROFOR commander, Swedish general Eric-Lars Wahlgren, was demoted and replaced by the Frenchman Jean Cot, he had not objected.[34] On the contrary, the nomination of Cot had been orchestrated by the French government. Léotard continued, 'The UN has to adapt instead of constantly changing the generals it has assigned to manage these crises,' and he concluded that there were 'weaknesses in the chain of command in New York, which is clearly not suited for this kind of situation.'

Léotard took the offensive again on 24 January, when General Bertrand de Lapresle was appointed Jean Cot's successor as head of UNPROFOR. He denounced 'the UN's real loss of credibility' and expressed the view that 'the term "contraption" [*machin*] that General de Gaulle once used [to describe the UN] probably falls short of reality.'[35]

The minister's criticisms were not entirely unjustified. The chain of command at the UN is particularly cumbersome, especially when military personnel, UN officials, and the diplomats of the member states all demand their say before a decision is taken. It is true that the UN is not an army headquarters, but it is working with the means at its disposal to improve the management and command of its peacekeeping missions. One might question the minister's judgment in insulting an international organization of which France is an active and respected member. When he asserted that the UN was losing its credibility, he seemed to forget that, if this is the case, it is largely the fault of countries such as his. After all, the forty-five unenforceable resolutions that the Security Council adopted on the former Yugoslavia, the ones General Francis Briquemont had stopped reading, were written in part by France and were always passed with its enthusiastic participation. If the UN is a 'contraption' incapable of properly serving the Blue Helmets in the field, one might ask why France does nothing to improve the lot of these soldiers.

'The UN is what the member states make of it,' said a spokesperson for the French minister of foreign affairs to soften the remarks of the minister of defence.[36] And what they make of it is not always equal to their declarations. On the one hand, the important member states demand greater efficiency and stricter management of UN activities. But on the other hand, the UN committees on financial matters – made up of representatives of these same great powers – are required to impose zero growth on the UN budget, and they systematically reject the requests of the Office of Peace-keeping Operations for more staff and resources to cover the expansion of its activities. This contradiction is far from being resolved.

Part Three:
An Army for the UN

10

Peacekeeping Takes a Back Seat to Politics

General Lewis MacKenzie, the Canadian officer commanding the Sarajevo Sector of UNPROFOR, was furious. It was Monday, 21 July 1992, and he was trying to reach a peacekeeping operations official at the UN headquarters in New York on the satellite telephone that allowed him to communicate throughout the world from Sarajevo. But no one was answering.

MacKenzie had barely arrived at the Sarajevo international airport at seven that morning when mortar shells began raining down on the runway and around the main building. After a brief discussion with his aides, he had ordered the airport closed to humanitarian flights until the shelling stopping. This was a difficult decision for MacKenzie. For the previous month, it had been a point of honour for him that the airport, which he had helped reopen, continued operating to ensure that the inhabitants of Sarajevo would not starve. He had been in constant negotiation with the various Bosnian factions fighting for control of the capital, trying desperately to persuade them to agree to a permanent truce. But no sooner were promises made and the ceasefire and disarmament agreements signed than they seemed to go up in smoke. MacKenzie, an old hand at peacekeeping missions, was used to this. Each time, he had had to put his blue steel helmet back on and go negotiate, passing through innumerable check points and along roads that were supposed to be neutral corridors but were often traps. That morning, a few seconds before his arrival at the airport, a mortar shell had fallen near the road he was travelling along.

Before leaving the airport, MacKenzie had learned that a detachment of Canadian Blue Helmets that was supposed to deliver food and medicine to a sector of the city controlled by the Bosnian Serbs was being held by soldiers of the Moslem-dominated Bosnian government army. The four armoured transport vehicles and three jeeps had hardly left the UN sector when government army soldiers surrounded the convoy and ordered the vehicles to halt. The Bosnian soldiers were holding the Canadians hostage, pointing anti-tank weapons at them from a distance of about twenty metres. They accused the Blue Helmets of hiding Yugoslavian weapons and ammunition in their tanks for delivery to the Serbs.

MacKenzie had rushed to the office of the president to meet the Minister of Defence, Jerko Doko, but Doko was reluctant to intervene. The Canadian officer had had an animated discussion with Doko and proposed that he himself come inspect the Canadian vehicles. Doko had suggested that they wait a bit and give things time to work themselves out, and the Canadian officer had left to contact the UN. He was thinking about the best way to get the Bosnians to give in and avoid further bloodshed. If a UN official were able to contact the Bosnian ambassador in New York, he thought, the ambassador could call President Alija Izetbegovic – whose offices were in the same building as those of the minister of defence – and ask him to put pressure on Doko. The situation was absurd, but there was nothing else he could do.

After several attempts, MacKenzie succeeded in reaching an official who was on call. In New York, at the other end of the line, it was two in the morning; the UN official pried his eyes open and tried to grasp what the excited Canadian general was saying.

'I'm from UNPROFOR!' shouted the general. 'UNPROFOR!'[1]

'What was the name of that country, sir?' asked the official, who did not seem to appreciate being disturbed at home in the middle of the night.

'I am the commander of a sector of UNPROFOR,' explained MacKenzie, becoming more and more agitated.

'What is the location of that mission?' asked the official, who worked for the UN Under-Secretary-General for Peacekeeping Operations, Marrack Goulding.

'In the former Yugoslavia,' fumed MacKenzie. 'I'm in Sarajevo now, in the Republic of Bosnia, and I need help.'

'Who are you and what are you doing there?' the official asked.

'My name is Major-General Lewis MacKenzie and I am the commander of this sector. I need you to go to the United Nations and contact the Bosnian ambassador so he can intervene with his president to get some Canadian soldiers released. They are being held hostage.'

'Yes, yes, I understand,' the official finally said. 'I'll be going to my office in a few hours, and I'll try to contact the Bosnian ambassador. Goodbye.'

MacKenzie was stunned. He might get an answer from the UN in six or eight hours, while his soldiers were surrounded and the least spark could set off a massacre. Resigned, he went back to see the Bosnian minister of defence to try to find a solution himself.

The two men talked at length, with no results. Exasperated, the Canadian general finally told Doko he was not going to wait any longer. He got up to leave.

Doko stopped him. 'All right then. I'll send one of my officers there if you do the same.'

An hour later, a Canadian major and the Bosnian officer sent by Doko returned to the president's office and informed MacKenzie and the minister that the vehicles were only transporting Canadian weapons and a shipment of food and medicine. Doko apologized, and MacKenzie went back to see his men.

* * *

A year and half later, having traded his position as general in the Canadian army for work as a military consultant, and living in a luxurious condominium in Etobicoke, northwest of Toronto, Lewis MacKenzie recounted his adventures in Bosnia with a touch of humour. He had become a star of CNN and BBC news broadcasts, and his advice was sought throughout the world.

Before we began our conversation, he pointed to the rows of apartment buildings not far away. 'There are thousands of Somalis here from both sides,' he said smiling. 'They've brought their political disputes here to the heart of Toronto. There, there's a General Aidid faction. And over there, a rival faction. And here I am, the former peacekeeper, between the two of them.'

MacKenzie was anxious to recount his conversation with the UN official – which he did not include in his memoirs published in 1993 – to illustrate how disorganized and completely isolated from their New York base the UN peacekeeping missions could be. He pointed out that the official, who was working under the senior official in charge of peacekeeping missions, seemed to be completely ignorant of what was happening in Bosnia. MacKenzie said that he had never encountered such a situation before, in the seven other UN missions in which he had taken part since 1963. But the previous missions had rarely been dangerous, and there were so few that you could count them on the fingers of one hand. Two or three officials had managed those missions from New York, and no one woke them up at night.

Difficulties communicating with his superiors were not the only problems MacKenzie had at the UN in New York. His tour of duty in the Balkans began very badly. In February 1992, after months of hesitation, the Security Council finally authorized the deployment of a force of 15,000 Blue Helmets in Serb-controlled territories in Croatia. UNPROFOR was commanded by Indian general Satish Nambiar; French general Philippe Morillon was second in command; and General Lewis MacKenzie was chief of staff. On 5 and 6 March, during their final meeting with UN officials before leaving on the mission, MacKenzie and his UNPROFOR colleagues, pressed for time, presented a two-page plan for the deployment of the Blue Helmets. They learned that the twelve battalions were to be in the field within six weeks, that the headquarters of the mission would be in Sarajevo, in Bosnia, 400 kilometres from the troops, and that their main supply base would be in Banja Luka, also in Bosnia. MacKenzie and his colleagues were surprised. They knew very well that a force of that size could not be deployed in the field that quickly. But what particularly concerned them was the isolation of the headquarters and supply base from the troops in the field. They objected vigorously, but the civilian officials of the UN replied that it was important politically that the headquarters and base be at those locations: they would be in the territory of neither the Croats nor the Serbs, the two enemies at the time, and the presence of the headquarters in Sarajevo might dissuade the Bosnians from fighting among themselves. As luck would have it, a few weeks later, Bosnia was plunged into civil war. The headquarters in Sarajevo and the supply base in Banja Luka had hurriedly to be moved to Croatia two months after they had been set up.

MacKenzie has described how discouraged he felt in the airplane en route to Sarajevo because the military expertise of the UNPROFOR commanders had been ignored in favour of political considerations and the planning of the mission had been carried out in haste. 'We were united in our common disappointment with the inadequate preparation we had received in New York. Here we were, off to a country that was in the midst of violent self-destruction, and all we had was the two-page outline of a plan that I knew in my heart would not unfold as we would like.'[2] One result was that the deployment of the Blue Helmets, the speed of which was crucial to the credibility and success of the mission, was only completed four months after the arrival of the UNPROFOR commanders in the field. The last battalion – the one from Nigeria – was not deployed until June 1992.[3]

General MacKenzie had to waste a lot of energy dealing with problems big and small. The UN airplane that the UNPROFOR commanders were supposed to use arrived five months after they did, forcing the mission commanders to use an airplane belonging to the armed forces of Yugoslavia – in other words, property of the Serbs, one of the parties involved in the conflict. Some of the Blue Helmets did not even know how to read a military map. Several contingents had no heavy equipment, and what was provided to them – from the former East Germany – came with no spare parts. Other battalions also arrived poorly equipped and some of them without food. Some did not even know which region they were supposed to deploy in and had no means of getting there. Finally, the commanders of several contingents took their orders from their national capitals and not from the UNPROFOR commander. When he commanded the Sarajevo airport sector in June and July 1992, MacKenzie discovered that his chief of staff did not speak English and that the helicopters he had requested from the UN were piloted by Russians who did not understand English and refused to obey certain orders. Every day, MacKenzie and his aides struggled and improvised in their efforts to support their soldiers and enforce the UN's authority, receiving minimal assistance from the UN bureaucrats in New York.

After his return to Canada in August 1992, MacKenzie, who had become the darling of the media since his tour in Sarajevo, used his reputation as an outspoken and personable soldier to bring the problems encountered by UN missions to public attention, setting off a small storm of controversy. In January 1993 in Ottawa, addressing the Conference of Defence Associations, a military audience sympathetic to his views, the general assailed the UN. 'Do not get into trouble as a commander in the field after 5 p.m. New York time or on weekends,' he said. 'There is no one there who will answer the phone.'[4] MacKenzie's words were reported around the world, and they did not go unnoticed at the UN. A spokesperson for the secretary-general responded that General MacKenzie had had a brilliant career in the UN peacekeeping forces, adding pointedly that during his tour in Sarajevo he was well-liked by the officials who had dealings with him 'both during the day and at night.' He extended best wishes to the general in his future career in politics.

'When I said in Ottawa that the people in the UN worked from nine to five and were unreachable in the evening or on weekends, I knew I would touch a nerve,' he said. 'I was exaggerating on purpose. But my speech was a way to shake up the organization so that it would be more serious about taking care of the Blue Helmets. Until 1992, the command and control of peacekeeping operations by the United Nations in New York were simple enough tasks. With the exception of the Congo in the sixties and Turkey's intervention in Cyprus in 1974, the United Nations commanders in the field had very little need for or, dare I say, did not want to be in constant communication with New York. We were happy to receive a mandate, a budget, and the staff to carry out a mission without having to constantly consult New York.'

Indeed, until the early nineties, the UN only maintained half a dozen peace missions throughout the world. Most were comparatively quiet, and all problems were dealt with locally. Intervention by New York was rare.

'With Bosnia, Somalia, and Cambodia, three missions established in the same year (1992) and involving some 50,000 Blue Helmets, things changed radically,' MacKenzie said. 'The UN commanders now need permanent contact with UN authorities, twenty-four hours a day, seven days a week, in order to obtain information or instructions.'

* * *

The command and control problems experienced by the UN mission in the former Yugoslavia were not new. Since 1948, all the mission commanders have complained of more or less serious problems. In recent years, UN headquarters and the governments of the troop-contributing countries suddenly discovered that there had been studies of these problems and that very precise recommendations had been made in the fifties and sixties, but no one had really done anything about them. In Canada in 1968, the Department of National Defence had commissioned Roger J. Hill, a young researcher, to do a detailed study, which had the very appropriate title *Command and Control Problems of the UN and Similar Peacekeeping Forces.* This study, which was kept secret for a long time, examined the activities and performance of certain observer missions and three large peacekeeping missions: the United Nations Emergency Force (UNEF), established after the Suez crisis in 1956; the United Nations Operation in the Congo (ONUC), established in 1960; and the United Nations Peacekeeping Force in Cyprus (UNFICYP), established in 1964. The author, rather naively, expressed the hope that his research would lead to improved planning of peacekeeping operations. Instead, it seems that no one paid much attention to it.

In order to identify the main command and control problems, Hill looked at every aspect of the peacekeeping missions: planning; the introduction of soldiers into the area of operations; the mandate, or terms of reference, and related agreements; organizational structure; unity among the troops; public relations; military training; and command and control. The inadequacies Hill identified and the solutions he proposed correspond in all points to the observations and recommendations that experts and peacekeeping operations officials in New York and elsewhere in the world have been making for several years.

Hill had no trouble pinpointing the primary shortcoming of the missions: ambiguities in their mandates. He stated that 'the Terms of Reference created for the UN forces sent to the Congo and Cyprus made both unnecessarily difficult to command and on more than one occasion led almost to disaster.' Because of the imprecise, rigid orders they received, 'some UN Commanders have found themselves at odds with the Secretary-General, because they exceeded their Terms of Reference in an effort to carry out their missions, while others failed to coordinate and support their Forces properly.'[5]

Hill observed that the chain of command was unclear and that too many leaders made decisions without consultation. 'And in Cyprus, in the early stages, there appear to have been four UN leaders to influence events: a UN mediator; a civilian Personal Representative; the Military Commander; and the Military Commander's Political Advisor,' he wrote.[6] The UN representatives in New York and in the field did not coordinate their negotiations with the various parties to a conflict, leading to tensions within the mission. 'Continuous and excessive negotiations with local power groups involve constant shifts in the UN's policy. The Secretary-General must respond to one set of pressures in New York, while the Force Commanders deal with another set of pressures in the country concerned,' he wrote. 'Faced with the manoeuvring of politicians as skillful as Tshombe [Congo] or Makarios [Cyprus], even the most advanced communications system, used in the best possible manner, will fail to maintain complete continuity of direction throughout the UN chain of command.'[7]

Analysing the political manoeuvring and the coherence of the contingents' action in the United Nations Operation in the Congo (ONUC), Hill observed that the mission was paralysed for several months because there were no longer common objectives within the UN force. After the murder of Congolese prime minister Patrice Lumumba in 1961, the contingents from four African countries and one Asian country withdrew. This politico-diplomatic problem led the author to conclude that 'it is even conceivable that an Emergency Force in certain circumstances, if deprived of adequate backing from New York, could split into rival factions pursuing different goals while paying only lip-service to the UN Commander's orders.'[8]

Finally, Hill saw the disorganized state of the missions as a result of UN officials' lack of interest in learning from their mistakes and successes. 'The UN has virtually no planning mechanism in New York to analyze past experience, monitor current operations or plan for future Peace-keeping Forces,' he wrote; it 'has proceeded by a process of trial and error, instead of taking the trouble to analyze likely situations.'[9]

It is striking how current Hill's main recommendations are today, twenty-five years after the publication of his report. He suggested that the UN give the missions clearer mandates; that the missions be under a single chain of command; that standby agreements be made to provide troops to the UN; and especially, that 'a small planning staff of perhaps 8–10 military officers should be set up at UN Headquarters in New York to analyze past experience, monitor current activities and plan for future peacekeeping operations.'[10] Only in 1992 did the UN finally decide to increase the staff of the Office of Peace-keeping Operations and the bureaucracy undertake to examine the issues of the command and control of missions and the establishment of military forces at the disposal of the organization.

Readers will have noticed that the problems identified by Hill with regard to the missions in Cyprus and the Congo are similar to those that undermined the UN mission in Cambodia in 1992–3 and to those experienced in Somalia and the former Yugoslavia. Reflecting on his tour as assistant military commander with the United Nations Transitional Authority in Cambodia (UNTAC) in 1992, French general Michel Loridon made the following revelations in the magazine of the French army.

What example and what security can people who are suffering but are filled with hope in the UN draw from Blue Helmets who are poorly educated, poorly trained, poorly commanded, and unpaid, and who in order to survive organize rackets, schemes, and illicit trade in weapons, fuel, food, or equipment?

What credibility do troops in a difficult country have when the conscripts learn upon arrival that their tour of duty will be eighteen months without leave and without pay?

Is it possible to work properly with units whose leaders have received instructions to favour such-and-such faction or even try sabotage the actions of another Blue Helmet battalion suspected of hindering its national interests?[11]

What happened during the UN mission in Somalia in 1992–3 illustrates a number of the problems identified by Hill. That mission suffered from having too many bosses. In addition, one contingent, that of the United States, commanded the military operations and it would take orders only from Washington. This attitude led to a split within the mission, with the Italians refusing to obey the commander of the UN force. Secret negotiations with certain factions also created confusion about the objectives of the mission and led, ultimately, to a bloody confrontation between General Aidid's faction and the Americans, to the dismay of some contingents.

In the former Yugoslavia, the narrowness of the mandate – protection of humanitarian aid and certain designated 'safe areas' – prevented the Blue Helmets from defending or even coming to the aid of civilians who were being shelled or subjected to 'ethnic cleansing,' with the notable exception of those in Sarajevo and Gorazde. Furthermore, even though NATO was given a mandate to make its aircraft available to the UN for air strikes, the chain of command responsible for making this decision was heavy and, more important, subject to political pressure from various quarters.

* * *

The secretary-general and his advisers thought constantly about the many political and organizational problems of the peacekeeping missions. In a report presented to the member states on 14 March 1994, Boutros Boutros-Ghali described the measures he had taken to correct problems related to the management of missions, the training of personnel, financing, and the number of staff at the Secretariat and the Office of Peacekeeping Operations. But politically, with respect to the command and control of missions, the secretary-general had to admit that his calls for more discipline on the part of the troop-contributing countries had gone unheeded. Alluding to the UN's experience in Cambodia, Somalia, and the former Yugoslavia, he wrote that 'the members of a peacekeeping operation must be under the exclusive operational command of the United Nations during the period of their assignment and must accept no orders from any outside agency in respect of their United Nations duties,' and that 'the existence of independent lines of communication between commanders and their national authorities violates the unity and integrity of the mission.'[12]

The message was clear, but by all indications it is still impossible for the

UN to solve the management problems experienced by the peace missions. The member states, especially the great powers, simply will not stop interfering in the business of running the missions, which they consider to be their business.

In organizational terms, however, the UN is working very hard to speed up the deployment of missions and to improve their management. Currently, a team of military advisors is establishing an immense structure that it hopes will revolutionize the organization and management of peace missions.

11

A Huge Lego Set

At the UN, the problems faced by peacekeeping missions are becoming more and more apparent. Obviously, the UN cannot solve them all. It is difficult to regulate the personal relations and national interests of the participants and remedy organizational and logistical deficiencies. The establishment and deployment of a peacekeeping mission will always be exceptional activities resulting from Security Council decisions which are themselves the result of political and financial compromises. Setting up a headquarters and deploying soldiers from twenty or thirty countries, organizing a communication system, repairing airports and landing strips, clearing roads, transporting material and food – all in a war zone swarming with combatants who are not always loyal to their superiors – are tasks that are not accomplished easily or according to the rules that prevail under peaceful conditions. Nevertheless, the organization and management of UN missions could be improved both bureaucratically and logistically.

As we saw in Chapter 1, Boutros Boutros-Ghali took a first step in this direction with the publication of his *Agenda for Peace* in June 1992. This document, 'analysed recent developments affecting international peace and security and introduced proposals for more effective UN operations in identifying potential conflicts, their short- and long-term resolution and post-conflict measures to build peace among former adversaries.'[1] Boutros-Ghali emphasized the prevention of conflicts, suggested new measures regarding the use of military force under the command of the UN, and appealed to the member states to place military and civilian staff and equipment at the disposal of the organization for use on short notice.

After publication of the *Agenda*, Boutros-Ghali quickly went to work. In

July 1992, he hired Canadian general Maurice Baril as military adviser and gave him full power to reorganize the military aspects of peacekeeping operations.

Once appointed, Baril immediately set to work. He asked for staff – military and civilian – for the Office of Peace-keeping Operations and responded to MacKenzie's criticisms and Boutros-Ghali's recommendations by creating a Situation Centre and forming a group of military officers in charge of establishing a system of standby forces, the embryo of a future UN army.

The Situation Centre is an essential element in the chain of command and control of peacekeeping operations. As General MacKenzie had complained, there had been no one at the UN who was responsible for answering the telephone evenings or weekends. General Baril set up a team of officers in charge of overseeing the activities of the peacekeeping missions and answering calls from their commanders twenty-four hours a day, seven days a week. Since there was no room in the Office of Peace-keeping Operations on the thirty-sixth floor of the UN building, the Situation Centre was originally located on the top floor of a small building on 47th Avenue, a short distance from UN headquarters. It is now in the main UN building. The Centre opened its doors in April 1993.

I visited the situation room, as it is called in UN jargon, in July 1993. It was a far cry from the control rooms at NORAD headquarters under the Cheyenne Mountains near Colorado Springs or those in American war movies. There were no instrument panels with flashing lights or maps on gigantic screens, and certainly no brass sitting at their command posts surrounded by advisors. With its old desks, used chairs, and old-fashioned maps of the world in two hemispheres, it looked more like a student office. Some twenty officers from various countries staffed it in round-the-clock rotations, monitoring the peacekeeping missions and, of course, answering the telephone if a commander of a mission called from El Salvador, Angola, Rwanda, or Bosnia. The most intense period of the day was from 4 a.m. to 7 a.m., when the reports came in from the different missions. The officers on duty would read and summarize them and write a complete report for General Baril's office or, if the situation was urgent, directly for the Security Council. The military staff of the Situation Centre do not plan the operations nor do they give orders to anyone: they simply collect information and transmit it to the military and political officials of the UN.

Boutros-Ghali also gave a military team the job of developing a system that would permit the UN to quickly assemble and deploy a force of Blue Helmets anywhere in the world. The secretary-general secretly dreamed of setting up an independent UN army, of which he would be in charge and which would be on call to intervene when he chose. But Boutros-Ghali knew very well that such a plan would never win the approval of an organization of independent states jealous of their sovereignty and rather particular concerning the use of armed force to settle conflicts. Indeed, the power conferred by armed force cannot be shared, and the member states of the UN are not prepared to go beyond the narrow framework they have established since 1948 by authorizing the formation of military units under UN command but the national contingents of which could be withdrawn from missions at the request of the troop-contributing nations.

In *An Agenda for Peace*, Boutros-Ghali deplored the fact that every time the Security Council decided to create a peacekeeping mission, it had to beg the member states for troops and equipment, a disorganized process results of which were far from certain. He pointed out that Chapter VII of the UN's Charter provides for a detailed approach to the use of force, and in particular, that article 43 foresees that 'Member States undertake to make armed forces, assistance and facilities available to the Security Council for the purposes stated in article 42 [use of force to maintain or restore international peace and security], not only on an ad hoc basis but on a permanent basis ... The ready availability of armed forces on call could serve, in itself, as a means of deterring breaches of the peace since a potential aggressor would know that the Council had at its disposal a means of response.'[2]

This was not the first time a secretary-general tried to establish an armed force for the UN. In 1948, Trygve Lie, the UN's first secretary-general, proposed the creation of a military corps at the disposal of the Security Council,[3] and the idea was taken up again several times in the fifties. It finally led, in 1956, to the creation of the Blue Helmets in accordance with Lester B. Pearson's recommendation.

The member states did not accept Boutros-Ghali's proposal, and he had to content himself with a solution that lay between the traditional method of establishing peacekeeping missions and having an army serving the UN: a system of standby forces. Two experienced military officers, French colonel Gérard Gambiez and his aide, Canadian lieutenant-colonel Jean-Robert Hinse, were responsible for setting up the system, assisted by a team of five officers.

The objective of this system of standby forces was to make possible the rapid deployment of a fully equipped force of Blue Helmets, which could, for example, enforce ceasefire agreements signed by belligerents. In order to act quickly, the UN had to have a database listing the human and material resources of countries willing to contribute to peacekeeping operations. But more important, it had to obtain an agreement in advance from the member states allowing it to use those resources.

In the documents Gambiez and Hinse distributed to the member states, the UN took pains to define a clear mandate for the standby forces and to explain how these forces could be used. 'The system of standby forces is based on commitments by the Member States to provide identified resources within an agreed period of time for the mounting of UN peacekeeping operations,' states one of these documents. 'It consists of arrangements negotiated in advance between the UN and each of the Member States concerning the supplying of specified resources within an agreed period of time. The resources involved remain on standby in their countries of origin; special training is provided, if necessary, for them to be able to fulfill the roles foreseen, in accordance with the directives of the UN. When they are needed, they are requested by the secretary-general, and following agreement by the Member States, rapidly deployed.'[4] The document clearly specifies that 'the resources are used exclusively for peacekeeping operations,' and not peace-enforcement operations.

Throughout 1993, Gambiez and Hinse made many presentations to the accredited diplomats of the UN and many visits to governments that wanted more information on this system. Their main task was to reassure those who believed that the standby forces constituted a roundabout way of obtaining their participation in military operations initiated under Chapter VII of the Charter.

'The member states have nothing to fear in that respect,' assured Lieutenant-Colonel Hinse, a logistics expert whose skills were greatly appreciated in the UN's mission in Namibia in 1989–90. 'We're very careful to tell everyone that the standby forces are intended for traditional peacekeeping, that is, that they would intervene with the consent of the parties or after the conclusion of a ceasefire agreement. These forces are not there to wage war.'[5]

To reassure countries participating in standby arrangements, the agreements negotiated with the UN foresee various circumstances under which those countries would not be required to send their troops, even though their soldiers are theoretically available. 'The participating states can invoke political, diplomatic, ethnic, regional, financial, meteorological, or health reasons for declining to participate in a mission,' said Hinse. 'They have to let us know the reasons in advance so that we can better plan the composition of a Blue Helmets force.'

There are many examples of refusals. Third World countries may refuse to send soldiers to regions where it is cold in winter because they do not have the equipment necessary to live in these regions. Other countries may refuse to send their soldiers to regions where tropical diseases are endemic. A state that has citizens who are ethnically related to one of the factions fighting in a country could refuse to send soldiers there. And so on. The states therefore have the last word on the use of their troops, despite being part of the standby forces.

'The system works a little like a traveller's cheque,' explained Hinse. 'The cheque comprises the contribution – an infantry battalion, a medical unit, observers, police, etc. – and the conditions. There is one signature on top by the contributing country. When the UN wants to use the cheque, the contributor must sign again.'

What is new for the UN in the system of standby forces is the existence of a catalogue of available resources and a precise commitment by the countries to furnish these resources. By 30 November 1996, sixty-two countries had agreed to place at the UN's disposal some 80,000 soldiers and military equipment. Thirty other countries were seriously studying the possibility of signing standby agreements with the UN. The UN's objective is to obtain commitments for a force of 100,000 Blue Helmets and other experts and for the equipment required for their rapid deployment. In addition, since October 1996, the UN has been working to set up an operational-level headquarters in New York that could be deployed quickly, the role of which would be to provide the supervision and direction required during the deployment and the initial phase of a peacekeeping mission.

The agreement between the UN and a member state specifies the contribution that the country is prepared to make, the equipment available, the mobilization time, the political or other conditions for the deployment of the soldiers, and any other details that could assist the UN planners in their work.

'The problem we had in the past was that such-and-such a country would offer us an infantry battalion with no equipment or means of transportation,' said Hinse. 'Today, countries that offer battalions must specify the number of soldiers, their availability, their medical condition, the equipment and spare parts they have available, etc. Nothing must be left to chance, because the day we need that battalion, it must be able to be deployed quickly and it must be prepared to operate without requiring supplies for several weeks.'

Some countries can offer soldiers but no equipment, while others can offer equipment but no soldiers. 'In our files, we'll have access to a huge Lego set with parts that can be put together to make up a Blue Helmet force for a particular mission,' explained Hinse. 'Even before the Security Council has formally voted the resolution authorizing a mission, the secretary-general will have on his desk a precise plan of the resources available. He will be able to say that mission X could consist of fifteen infantry battalions, four helicopter units, hundreds of armoured or other vehicles, medical or police units, an electoral component, as the case may be, and that these resources could come from fifteen or thirty countries and the whole force could be in the field in a few weeks.'

While the system of standby forces represents a giant step forward in the organization and management of peacekeeping missions, it still contains a significant flaw: it is applicable only to traditional operations, and the resources available remain under the authority of the contributing countries. The UN has had to deal with crisis situations that have not been between countries, but within them. In Somalia, for instance, the government had collapsed and the UN had to negotiate with armed groups that were fighting for power and that did not always keep their word. Similarly, in Bosnia, the UN had to deal with a central government that was not recognized by a substantial part of the population. In other regions, there were civil wars. The UN's action was limited by the refusal of member states to send Blue Helmets to such dangerous regions.

To counter the reservations of the member states and reinforce the UN's power to intervene, some experts have suggested the establishment of a rapid reaction force made up of volunteer soldiers, or a foreign legion. Sir Brian Urquhart, a former UN under-secretary-general for special political affairs, who was in charge of the Blue Helmets for twelve years, and the American strategic analyst Edward Luttwak are the main champions of this idea.

Urquhart proposes the creation of 'a small, elite, permanent UN force composed of volunteers that could be immediately deployed as a spearhead for a later, larger operation, if that proved to be necessary.'[6] He has pointed out, however, that such a force could even be used for traditional missions, and that its primary function would be to deter factions from continuing to fight.

'This would not be a force that would fight,' he says. 'It would enforce the resolutions of the UN. But it would have to be well enough armed to deter the hostile parties and to defend itself vigorously if necessary. I'm thinking of the French legionnaires. Usually you just tell rebels the legionnaires are coming, and they fall into line very quickly. The legionnaires don't even need to use their weapons. They appear in the streets and suddenly everything calms down.'[7]

Edward Luttwak is more categorical. A hawk among American strategic analysts, he proposes setting up a fighting force in the exclusive service of the UN. 'Instead of the present system – under which so-called UN forces are actually good, bad or indifferent national contingents supplied by member nations, usually under strict no-casualty rules that guarantee their uselessness in most cases – a UN Legion would recruit individual volunteers, whose nationality would be irrelevant, for no politician would have to answer for their fate. With that, the UN could have real military strength at its command, i.e., forces that can be exposed to combat.'[8] Luttwak feels that recruiting could be done in all the member states of the UN and that there would be no lack of personnel, since there are many warriors in the world who cannot fight for lack of their country's involvement in a war. He writes that, 'initially, a UN Legion might begin as a not-so-small force of, say, 10,000 combat-ready infantry. But if successful, that division's worth of troops could become the core of UN armed forces, complete with armored, air and naval units.'

Luttwak's scenario is ambitious but, like Urquhart's, it has failed to inspire the confidence of certain countries which, jealous of their military prerogatives, are also perturbed by the idea of an international organization setting up an armed force at their expense. The American government has stated publicly that it is firmly opposed to the creation of a permanent UN army.[9]

The cost and the administrative problems related to the establishment of such a force are daunting. For example, where would the soldiers train? Where would they live? Where would they be based? But most of all, the idea of an army that is 'uncontrollable' – from their point of view – frightens the member states of the UN. The Western countries are opposed to the existence of a UN army unless they control it; the countries of the Third World see it as a means for the great powers to intervene in their internal affairs.

Some countries have proposed the creation of a rapid reaction force that could be deployed before the arrival of a Blue Helmets mission. In 1995, the Netherlands suggested the creation of a UN rapid deployment brigade of 5,000 troops. In September of the same year, Canada submitted a report to the UN calling for the creation of a vanguard group, a

multifunctional force of no more than 5,000 military and civilian personnel that could be deployed in less than five weeks. It would be deployed
'as rapidly as possible for a brief period, either to meet an immediate crisis or to anticipate the arrival of follow-on forces or a more traditionally-
oriented peacekeeping operation.'[10] In December 1996, Canada and six
European countries concluded an agreement to establish such a group.
Called SHIRBRIG (Standby Forces High Readiness Brigade), this force
will be headquartered in Denmark and should be fully operational in
1999.

In the longer term, Canada has proposed the establishment of a Standing Emergency Group under the exclusive command and control of the
Security Council and the secretary-general. Made up of volunteer profes-
sional soldiers, this group could take on the most hazardous operations,
those in which the Blue Helmet troop-contributing countries are hesitant
to get involved. No consultation with national authorities would be
required to deploy the force.

But whatever form it takes – permanent army, foreign legion, standby
force – and whatever the future of the Blue Helmets, peacekeeping is an
instrument of international diplomacy that can no longer be ignored. It
has also been the focus of a bitter struggle for control between the UN
and certain countries. As we will see in the next chapter, France wants to
play a leading role.

12

Pressure from the French

Torrential rain was falling on Sihanoukville, the major seaport of Cambodia, on the Gulf of Thailand. It was April (1993), the beginning of the rainy season with its sudden violent storms one after another. Night had fallen. It was impossible to see where the jeep was going in this poor section of the city where there were no street lights. Chief Warrant Officer Jean-Marie Wurtz, the legionnaire at the wheel, seemed to be steering by instinct, sometimes sticking his head out the wide-open window. He came to this part of the city three times a week after work to give French classes to a handful of Cambodians. Suddenly he braked sharply. 'Here we are,' he said, water streaming down his face.[1]

The jeep had stopped in a vacant lot that the rain had transformed into one big mud puddle. We could see nothing around us, although we could hear whispering nearby.

'Follow me,' said the legionnaire. 'I'll show you my French school. There it is, right in front of you.'

A few steps from the jeep was a one-storey wooden building. The door was locked, but a dozen Cambodians had already arrived and were doing their best to find shelter from the downpour. The men were standing on one side, the women on the other. They were talking among themselves. Wurtz knew them all by name and had a greeting for each one. As soon as he opened the door, the students rushed into the single room of the building, which was pitch dark. Holding a flashlight, Wurtz looked for the cord hanging from the ceiling so he could screw in the light bulb he brought with him each time. Light flooded the room, and the students silently took their seats around the legionnaire.

These students were not the kids we saw running through the streets and markets of Sihanoukville all day long. They were all at least thirty-five years old, and they already spoke a little French. They were among those relatively few Cambodians who had learned to speak the language of the former colonial power who were not murdered by the Khmer Rouge in the late 1970s. Under the Khmer Rouge regime, which had attempted to create a 'new man,' everyone who was educated or who spoke a foreign language was persecuted. Most were executed. In 1979, following an invasion by the Vietnamese, the regime collapsed, but civil war and the international isolation of the new government did not favour a renaissance of French. Since the end of 1991, when Cambodia opened up to the world again, many Cambodians wanted to reconnect with the past.

When they arrived in Cambodia as part of the UN peacekeeping mission (UNTAC), the Blue Helmets of the Foreign Legion took it upon themselves to give French classes to a population that was becoming more and more anglicized. The legionnaires did not hide their irritation at seeing English-speaking culture gain so much ground in this formerly French-speaking country of Indochina.

Today Wurtz had his students read a one-page text on the cultural traditions of Cambodia, which had been written by UNTAC's information and education service. For two hours, the legionnaire conducted a lighthearted class, cracking jokes and getting each of the Cambodians to read, understand, and discuss the text. The women were shy and did not speak much. The men were more talkative, and as the atmosphere warmed up, willing to laugh at their mistakes. To hold his students' attention, Wurtz spoke loudly and clearly. It was not easy for these Cambodians to concentrate on a lesson for two hours after a long work day. Those who were not sitting close to the legionnaire would sometimes be caught taking a little nap, and Wurtz enjoyed waking them with his stentorian voice.

Wurtz had been giving these classes for four months. At first, he said, it was not easy to overcome the Cambodians' shyness and even fear. In this neighbourhood, the officials of the regime and people in the opposition did not want to lose control of the people, and they did not like to see Cambodians fraternizing with foreigners, especially with military personnel. Accusations of collusion with or spying for foreign powers came easily and could result in ostracism.

In spite of their good will, the struggle by Wurtz and his fellow soldiers to keep French culture intact in Cambodia seemed to be a lost cause. English was spreading like wildfire in this country. Just visiting the markets or walking through the streets of the major towns revealed the attraction of English culture for Cambodians. Merchants addressed foreign customers in English; the country's main newspaper was an English-

language weekly, and the signs of stores were in English. Even Norodom
Sihanouk, the 'god-king' newly restored to his throne in September 1993,
officially called for English to be made the first foreign language in education.[2]

Underlying the legionnaires' generous efforts to promote the French
language during their eighteen-month stay in Cambodia was a struggle
for influence between France and Australia under the cover of the UN
peacekeeping operation. Throughout the entire mission, the French and
the Australians vied for control of UNTAC's military and diplomatic activities. (As we saw in Chapter 6, the Americans had similarly competed for
control in Somalia.) In fact, the French-Australian rivalry in Cambodia is
a good illustration of the struggles that often take place for control of the
most important peacekeeping missions. While the smaller missions –
Western Sahara, India-Pakistan, and even Angola – are not much disputed, those missions in which the political, economic, and military
stakes are high – Somalia, the former Yugoslavia, and Cambodia – are the
object of bitter haggling among certain powers.

France has ambitions of being one of the big players, maybe even the
biggest, in international peacekeeping. After all, for many years, it was
the leader among countries contributing troops for peacekeeping operations. It accounted for 6,500 soldiers out of 52,000 in December 1992;
7,000 soldiers out of 70,000 in June 1994; and by the end of 1995, it contributed 7,500 soldiers out of the 58,000 Blue Helmets then deployed by
the UN in seventeen missions throughout the world.

In Cambodia, French ambitions quickly came into conflict with those
of Australia and, to a lesser degree, Japan. France had done much to find
a solution to the Cambodian problem. For years it had allowed the principal parties to the conflict to meet and talk in France. With Indonesia, it
had initiated the historic agreement of 23 October 1991, in which the
four Cambodian factions agreed on the basis for the restoration of peace
in their country. It therefore seemed natural that Paris should play a
major role in the UN mission charged with implementing the peace
agreement. But that was reckoning without the other powers waiting in
the wings.

A minor war erupted between the French and the English-speaking
countries over the military command of the UN Advance Mission in
Cambodia (UNAMIC), whose role was to prepare for the arrival of the
main mission, UNTAC. A French general, Michel Loridon, had been
approached about leading UNAMIC, which was to be deployed in
November 1991. But the United States, supported by Australia and New

Zealand, let it be known that it was opposed to the appointment of a national of one of the five permanent members of the Security Council.[3] According to tradition, in most peacekeeping missions the position of military commander is given to an officer from a neutral country or a country not directly involved in the conflict. France's colonial history in Cambodia counted against it.

The English-speaking countries favoured Australia, a long-time participant in peacekeeping missions, which had no political interest in Cambodia. The name of General John Sanderson was put forward. But Paris refused to give in. A compromise was finally found: Loridon would command UNAMIC, with its 400 soldiers, but Sanderson would take over with the arrival of UNTAC and its 15,000 soldiers in March 1992. To placate France which, after all, was contributing 1,500 Blue Helmets to the mission, compared with only 500 from Australia, Loridon would be named second in command to the Australian general.

The compromise soon proved unworkable. The deployment of UNTAC's soldiers in the field had hardly begun when a bitter dispute broke out between Sanderson and Loridon in the summer of 1992. They did not agree on the attitude to adopt toward the Khmer Rouge, which was refusing to allow its troops to be disarmed and confined to designated locations and would not let the Blue Helmets enter territories it controlled. The fiery Loridon opted for a hard line; he wanted the Blue Helmets to impose their presence in the Khmer Rouge areas and forcibly disarm the notorious Khmer Rouge soldiers. Sanderson had a completely different view of his mission. When he accepted the position, he had sworn that he would shed no blood, especially not the blood of the Australian Blue Helmets. His motto was 'zero dead, zero wounded.' This very cautious policy was also favoured by the special representative of the secretary-general and head of mission in Cambodia, Japanese diplomat Yasushi Akashi. The Japanese were participating in the first peacekeeping mission in their history; they had sent a battalion of 700 soldiers to Cambodia and under no circumstances did they want their soldiers to be attacked by the Cambodian factions. It should be noted, in Sanderson and Akashi's defence, that the UN mission in Cambodia had been set up according to the conventional rules for peacekeeping missions; that is, it provided for the use of force only in self-defence. The two UNTAC leaders could therefore say in all honesty that they were respecting the UN mandate to the letter.

After Loridon revealed to the press the extent of his disagreement with the other leaders of UNTAC, his mandate was not renewed and he had to leave the mission. But the rivalry between France and Australia continued. French diplomats and military personnel poured out their resentment in the media, accusing the Australians and the other English-speaking countries of completely dominating all the components of UNTAC. There was some basis for this view: Australia had forty-seven officers on the staff of UNTAC, while France had only fourteen.[4] Moreover, Australia completely controlled UNTAC's military and civilian radio transmissions, which allowed it to intercept and listen to all the messages sent by the various contingents to their governments. (France circumvented this problem by providing its contingent with independent transmission facilities.) Some of the civilian components of UNTAC were also controlled by allies of the Australians. For example, the information and education division was led by an American, and a New Zealander had been appointed head of the human rights component. Only the civil administration component was under the direction of a Frenchman. Upset and humiliated, the French became somewhat paranoid, constantly accusing the 'Anglo-Saxon forces' of trying to throw them out.

There were also economic and political aspects to the power struggles within UNTAC. The whole system for supplying the Blue Helmets with food, water, and various products was in the hands of Australian firms. With 15,000 Blue Helmets stationed in Cambodia for eighteen months, this was a very lucrative business. The Australians also took advantage of their presence to obtain exclusive rights on telecommunications between Cambodia and other countries. Similarly the Thai, who had always supported the Khmer Rouge, had sent a battalion of engineers to repair the roads to the Thai-Cambodian border, where Thai soldiers and businessmen were involved in the illegal traffic of precious gems and rare woods with the Khmer Rouge, who still controlled that region.

* * *

France may have had its fingers burned in Cambodia, but it took its revenge in the former Yugoslavia. In September 1994, UNPROFOR had some 38,000 soldiers deployed in three countries of the former Yugoslavia: Croatia, Bosnia, and Macedonia. Its mandate had been changed about fifteen times by the Security Council. The day-to-day management of the mission was itself a feat, given that UNPROFOR's military commander had to maintain contact with Blue Helmet contingents from thirty-six countries, all led by military commanders with the rank of colonel or general. Theoretically, they were all under the orders of the mission commander, but it is common knowledge that the leaders of national contingents in peacekeeping missions are closely supervised by their governments. When the commander of a peacekeeping force gives an order to the military leaders of the national contingents, those leaders often consult their home governments before complying. In Somalia, for example, many contingents refused to obey the orders of the mission commander when he asked for troops to capture General Mohamed Aidid, who was blamed by the UN for the massacre of twenty-five Pakistani Blue Helmets.

To ensure a minimum of respect for the position, and especially to maintain cohesiveness within a force, commanders must be experienced leaders who enjoy the confidence of all the countries participating in the peacekeeping mission. In the case of UNPROFOR, the UN believed that it had found high-quality leaders whose competence would be unanimously recognized. But they had failed to take into account French ambitions.

When the Security Council created UNPROFOR in February 1992, an Indian general, Satish Nambiar, was selected to command its military component. The choice of this career officer was hardly a matter of chance. It was made in accordance with the UN tradition of appointing an officer from a neutral or Non-aligned country with no special interests to defend in the region concerned. At the time, although France was contributing 2,700 soldiers of the 14,000 Blue Helmets that made up UNPROFOR, Paris did not apply any particular pressure to obtain this position. However, conscious of the importance of France's participation, the UN accepted the appointment of French lieutenant-general Philippe Morillon as Nambiar's second in command.

UNPROFOR's responsibilities at the time extended only to Croatia. In the summer and fall of 1992, the mission received mandates for two new areas, Bosnia and Macedonia, which required an increase in the number of Blue Helmets in the region. France immediately made it known that it was prepared to participate in these new missions. A new contingent of some 2,000 soldiers was dispatched to Bosnia, to Sarajevo and the Bihac region. Then in May and June 1993, the Security Council decreed the creation of six 'safe areas' in Bosnia and asked for more troops. On 23 June, France again answered the call, announcing it would send a contingent of about 1,000 soldiers to protect one of the areas. With this addition, French participation amounted to almost 6,000 soldiers out of the 25,000 in UNPROFOR.

In Paris, in the corridors of the Foreign Office and the Ministry of

Defence, serious questions were beginning to be raised about the role the French should play within UNPROFOR. In fact, command of the force in the former Yugoslavia had just been given, provisionally, to a Swede, General Lars-Eric Wahlgren, an old hand where international peacekeeping missions were concerned. Wahlgren succeeded General Nambiar on 3 March 1993. France then began a vigorous lobbying effort to have one of its generals put in command of UNPROFOR. Paris did not have to apply pressure for long. During a visit to the French capital on 8 and 9 June 1993, the secretary-general of the UN held discussions with President François Mitterrand, Minister of Defence François Léotard, and other French officials responsible for military questions concerning the role of the Blue Helmets in the former Yugoslavia and the French government's desire to obtain the command of the mission. Boutros-Ghali acceded to France's request, all the more readily since General Wahlgren's mandate was provisional. Moreover, the secretary-general, who had just obtained France's promise to send more troops to Bosnia, realized it was time to reward that country for its efforts in the Balkans. However, according to official UN rules, the announcement of the appointment of the Swedish general's successor could be made only after its approval by the members of the Security Council in New York. Therefore Boutros-Ghali revealed nothing for the time being.

Then events took a dramatic turn. On 23 June, Léotard said on television that French general Jean Cot would soon be leading UNPROFOR and would be in command of the entire territory of the former Yugoslavia. 'In the hours to come, in the days to come, a French general, General Cot, one of the highest-ranking officers in the army, will be exercising this extremely difficult and weighty responsibility.'[5] The next day, Boutros-Ghali, embarrassed by the French *faux pas*, issued a terse press release announcing the replacement of the Swedish general. As for the person most concerned, Wahlgren was looking for an apartment in Zagreb, the Croatian capital, and only learned the news of his replacement when a journalist asked him to comment on it. A good soldier, he replied only that it had come rather suddenly and he had had no warning.

The affair aroused indignation in Sweden, one of the most faithful participants in peacekeeping missions, particularly since one week earlier Stockholm had announced its intention to send 1,000 more soldiers to Bosnia. The Swedish representative at the UN denounced the secretary-general's behaviour, pointing out that Sweden had not been consulted. Boutros-Ghali evaded the issue; the UN had other things to worry about.

The French congratulated themselves. The Wahlgren affair had not made too many waves, and they were beginning to obtain what they had been after for close to a year: control of a major peacekeeping mission. But France had no intention of stopping there. As an officer working at the UN who was well informed on those operations pointed out, 'A few years ago, the countries that traditionally participated in peacekeeping missions (Sweden, Canada, Ireland, Finland, Nepal, etc.) offered their troops and their services without asking for anything in return. Today, the great powers look out more for their own interests and ask for more in return for their participation.'[6]

France had major ambitions in peacekeeping, and it found the management and organization of the missions deplorable. French military officers and diplomats were not shy about openly criticizing the way the UN carried out its tasks in this area. For example, in the July 1993 issue of Casoar, the magazine of the French army, members of the military condemned the UN officials' lack of professionalism and demanded an increased French presence in the UN chain of operational command. In a discussion of the frustration of the French officers, the Paris daily Le Monde said these officers harboured, but did not always dare to acknowledge, a gnawing mistrust of their fellow officers and contingents from the Third World, whom they considered lacking in competence, poorly led, or insufficiently trained, to whom the UN nevertheless entrusted responsibility for planning and organization.[7] This 'unmentionable' mistrust was revealed to me in no uncertain terms by the highest-ranking officer in France.

Jacques Lanxade, the commander of the French armed forces, received me in his luxurious office at the Ministry of Defence, on Boulevard Saint-Germain on Paris's Left Bank. The protocol was rather formal. A young officer announced the visitor, and I was led into a richly furnished room in the middle of which stood a globe of the world a metre in diameter. The admiral is a cold, reserved man, but his bureaucratic, military, and political skills are undisputed. These skills won him the command of the French fleet in the Indian Ocean and led to his joining Mitterrand's office as special chief of staff. In 1990–1, under the orders of the president, he planned and led his country's participation in the Gulf War. Immediately after that conflict, he was named to the top of the military hierarchy. A flawless career.

France, according to Admiral Lanxade, felt that UN peacekeeping missions had become more necessary than ever because of the political instability in the world. 'This instability has replaced the former bipolar pattern, which was unjust but stable,' explained the admiral. 'Under that pattern the international community had a limited role. Now that the UN has a role again, we have to give it the means to deal with situations that lead to disorder.'[8] By participating massively in peacekeeping missions, France is trying to serve as an example for other countries.

The French officer expressed the view that in order to deal effectively with conflicts, the UN needed to review the conditions under which peacekeeping operations are undertaken. He felt, for example, that countries participating directly in UN interventions should have a major role in the decision-making and command process. 'That's not how it was in the past,' he said. 'And today still, the temptation at the UN is to say, you give us troops, and after that it doesn't concern you any more.' But the day is over when a country such as Canada or Finland would offer one or two thousand soldiers for a mission under a general from the Third World.

Yet that was a way of ensuring the neutrality and impartiality of the missions, as Ghanaian lieutenant-general Emmanuel A. Erskine has pointed out, speaking of the UN mission to Lebanon, which he led from 1978 to 1981, during the worst period of the civil war in that country. 'The Middle East is an area where most countries in the world have their own economical interests and political biases,' he wrote in his memoirs. 'This can strongly influence their troops, and it is therefore important to get the minds of troops properly conditioned for UN duties on the principles of objectivity and impartiality. Troops should arrive in the mission area as UN troops under UN command and nothing else.'[9] The UN insisted that this cardinal rule be respected by all its military commanders on all its missions – at least until the events in Somalia and the former Yugoslavia.

But the French, like the Americans, hold exactly the opposite view from that of General Erskine. 'The position of the great powers is that if the UN wants us to participate heavily, we have to take part in the political management of the operations and the military command of the missions,' declared Admiral Lanxade.

When the French military look at how peacekeeping missions are managed, they do not like what they see – especially when their contingent is the largest one in a theatre of operations, as was the case in the former Yugoslavia. They feel the country that is taking the biggest risks in the field should have control of the mission. 'It doesn't make sense to entrust a mission as important as Yugoslavia to an Indian general [Nambiar] or even a Swedish general [Wahlgren] who has no troops in the field,' said the admiral. 'It's difficult for France to accept having them command and risk men's lives, since that involves decisions being taken by someone from a country that is not participating directly in the mission. Where there are large numbers of French troops, the French have to hold positions of responsibility, command positions or other positions that influence how operations are conducted. We have to make sure the French forces are used in accordance with what France is prepared to accept in the field, and without undue risk.'

At first glance the French position makes a lot of sense. After all, it seems logical that the country providing the biggest contingent should have a say in the political and military management of a peacekeeping operation. But this position conflicts with the UN tradition of avoiding giving any one country – especially one of the great powers – complete control of a mission carried out under the UN flag. When one great power dominates a mission, there are always negative consequences. In the first place, its reasons for participating are never totally altruistic. UN officials stated frankly that they take a very dim view of too much interference by one country in a mission. A country's specific interests can come into conflict with UN interests and jeopardize the neutrality and impartiality of a mission.

The idea of the countries that participate in peacekeeping missions joining together in a larger international community makes no sense to the French. 'A compromise has to be found between the notion of a UN-led international community in which the participating governments are not identified and what the Americans want, a coalition under their command,' said the admiral. 'The troop-contributing countries must have a role in the UN missions.'

France got what it wanted in the former Yugoslavia. The presence of its troops on the ground and its continuous pressure on the UN forced the secretary-general to give France command of the mission. But the negative consequences of this decision quickly became apparent. General Jean Cot, realizing that UNPROFOR was unable to carry out its mandate in Bosnia properly, openly criticized the UN and the secretary-general during the winter of 1993–4. Cot was in perfect harmony with the French government, which also assailed the UN. That was enough to provoke a reaction from the fiery Boutros-Ghali. On 11 January 1994, at a Paris meeting with the French leaders, the secretary-general expressed his anger at General Cot's insubordination and asked for his recall. Paris complied. Cot would be replaced by another French general – but one who was more malleable.

In their persistent effort to take control of peacekeeping operations, the French were not aiming merely to command certain missions in the field; they also had their eye on the office of the military adviser at UN headquarters in New York. The occupant of that office at the time was Canadian officer General Maurice Baril, who held the position from summer 1992 to summer 1995. Baril was assisted by a Malaysian second in command and a Finnish chief of staff until early 1994. This situation was not at all to the liking of either the French military or French politicians.

Paris launched its campaign in November 1992, following a report on peacekeeping operations by the French Senate which contained a harsh 'indictment of UN deficiencies and French inconsistencies.'[10] The report began by noting the unwieldiness of the decision-making structures in peacekeeping matters and the inertia of the UN, whose 'system for controlling conflicts had to work within the existing structures, which are oriented toward management, negotiation, and compromise far more than toward decision making, action, and intervention.'[11] The report also – quite rightly – questioned the abilities of the team of military advisers, who were overwhelmed by the new scale of peacekeeping operations. 'This team of military advisors currently comprises only six officers; moreover, most of them are not from countries with a strong military tradition or experience (a Canadian general assisted by five other officers: an Argentine, a Canadian, a Fijian, a Finn, and a Malaysian).'[12] The low regard of the French for military personnel from the Third World was already obvious. Noting that France had never taken much interest in peacekeeping operations, the report indicated that it was now paying for its indifference by its absence from the decision-making centres of the UN. 'This situation is serious: it deprives us of opportunities for direct influence and, in the longer term, means of reorienting and improving the functioning of the system.'[13]

France reacted to this report and to the criticisms made by its officers in specialized military magazines. On 23 June 1993, when French Minister of Defence François Léotard triumphantly announced that General Cot would be taking command of UNPROFOR, he also declared – somewhat imprudently – that General Philippe Morillon, who had led the UN mission in Bosnia with courage and flair, 'will, in coming weeks – and this will be a decision of the UN – have another command, a very distinguished one.'[14] Léotard was referring to the position of military adviser held by General Baril. If France captured this key position at UN headquarters, it would be in a position to wield considerable power in the political management of an army of Blue Helmets that numbered close to 80,000 soldiers in September 1994.

In New York, Boutros-Ghali and his advisers did not see things quite the same way. The day after Léotard's statement, the UN indicated that General Morillon would soon be returning to France.[15] The secretary-general had just renewed General Baril's contract for two years – an exceptional procedure.

But the French kept trying. On 26 November 1993, General Philippe Mercier, who was in charge of operations for the French general staff, stated after a visit to the UN that France wanted to obtain one of the three positions of responsibility in the Office of the Military Advisor, positions that were held by a Canadian, a Malaysian, and a Finn.[16] Mercier pointed out that France, with 8,000 soldiers deployed throughout the world, was the biggest contributor of Blue Helmets to the UN and insisted that for that reason it should be appropriately represented in positions of responsibility. Finally, in early 1994, France acquired one of the secondary positions.

France was tempted to assume a large role in the organization and management of peacekeeping missions quite simply because no other major power wanted to become that involved. The Americans insist on leading the important missions and will not delegate their command to the UN; this was demonstrated in the formation of multinational coalitions in the Gulf War in 1990–1 and in the first operation to aid Somalia in 1992–3. Moreover, after losing some thirty soldiers in fierce fighting with supporters of General Aidid in Somalia, the Americans carried out a complete review of their participation in peacekeeping missions. In May 1994, Washington published an unclassified version of Clinton's Presidential Directive 25, which lays down conditions for American involvement in peacekeeping missions. These conditions are so restrictive that United States participation in UN operations seems extremely improbable.[17] Russia has limited its international ambitions to its former empire and has decided to establish its own peacekeeping missions in the new republics of the former Soviet Union. Russian participation in UN missions is thus even more symbolic than that of the Americans. The United Kingdom has limited its participation to the former Yugoslavia, while China, which is opposed to all operations involving the use of force, is just beginning to take an interest in peacekeeping. France is the only one of the great powers that has realized the prestige and diplomatic influence to be gained from participating in peacekeeping operations.

* * *

The growing influence of France, and also of several other countries, in

TABLE 12.1
Largest Contributors of Blue Helmets to the UN

Rank	October 1982		October 1992		September 1994	
	Country	No. of soldiers	Country	No. of soldiers	Country	No. of soldiers
1	France	928	France	4,778	Pakistan	10,189
2	Norway	851	Canada	2,278	France	6,304
3	Austria	837	Indonesia	1,913	India	5,713
4	Netherlands	834	Poland	1,864	United Kingdom	4,315
5	United Kingdom	805	Ghana	1,858	Jordan	3,571
6	Canada	765	Pakistan	1,779	Bangladesh	3,224
7	Ireland	746	Nepal	1,672	Malaysia	2,825
8	Ghana	698	India	1,559	Canada	2,745
9	Nigeria	696	Denmark	1,338	Egypt	2,230
10	Fiji	629	Netherlands	1,305	Poland	2,134
11	Sweden	581	Finland	1,246	Nepal	2,041
12	Senegal	557	United Kingdom	1,234	Netherlands	2,008
13	Nepal	462	Bangladesh	1,152	Ghana	1,751
14	Finland	423	Nigeria	1,111	Spain	1,604
15	Denmark	356	Norway	1,102	Norway	1,576

peacekeeping operations creates problems for traditional participants such as Canada. As shown in Table 12.1, most of the countries that in 1982 made up the top fifteen participants in peacekeeping missions have been replaced by new players, the majority of whom are from the Third World and the bloc of the great powers. This reconfiguration has led to changes in the influence the participating countries can exercise in the management of peacekeeping operations.

In the late 1970s, peacekeeping was the purview of a handful of countries, mostly in the West, that could be described as neutral or Nonaligned. This select club included Canada, Australia, New Zealand, Austria, Ireland, the four Scandinavian countries, Fiji, and Nepal, all of which had no colonial past and were perceived as honest brokers without geopolitical interests – although some of them were members of military alliances. When the Security Council voted to create a mission, the UN would draw on the human and material resources of these countries to assemble a Blue Helmet force. Other countries might also contribute, according to their capabilities at the time. The needs of the UN were not that great, since there were only four or five missions in operation during the seventies and eighties, involving barely 10,000 troops and very little heavy equipment.

During that period, Canada played a primary role. Indeed, since 1948, Canadians have participated in all UN peacekeeping missions, and Canadian officers have sometimes been placed in command. Canada received constant requests from the UN, and its soldiers were always welcomed by the parties in conflict. As the American researcher Joseph T. Jockel comments in a study published in May 1994, Canadian participation in peacekeeping missions has been one of the foundations of Canadian foreign policy, and one of the ways it has distinguished itself from the United States on the international scene. Canada's dedication to peacekeeping has earned it an enduring reputation that goes beyond the resources it devotes to peacekeeping initiatives. Jockel writes: 'As a prime contributor to UN peacekeeping, Canada is entitled to a major voice in the international debates that have been under way over the future of the UN. Not only has the standing of the Canadian delegation probably been enhanced in addressing matters of international peace and security directly related to peacekeeping, but a Canadian major general has recently been named military adviser for peacekeeping to the UN secretary general.'[18]

But the end of the Cold War, the disintegration of the Communist bloc, and the increasing number of peacekeeping missions have profoundly changed Canada's role and its influence in peacekeeping operations. Jockel analyses the East-West political and military upheavals that have changed yesterday's enemies into friends and looks at the effect of budget cuts to the Department of National Defence. He points out that from 1988 to 1993, the UN established fourteen new peacekeeping missions and that sixty-nine countries contributed to those missions. He writes, 'For the first time Canada faces enormous competition from other countries that inevitably will challenge the idea of Canada's having a special international vocation as peacekeeper. Just like the Canadian Armed Forces, the national militaries have been freed from the exigencies of East-West competition. They have begun to find or be assigned new roles in the recent explosion in the number of peacekeeping operations.'[19]

Jockel's analysis identifies a challenge facing Canada with respect to its participation in peacekeeping operations. He feels that unless Canada reviews its role, it will be more and more marginalized, and that if Canada wants to preserve its international reputation as the peacekeeper par excellence, it can no longer limit itself to providing highly specialized infantry soldiers. Other countries are doing this, and some of them have a lot more resources than Canada.

However, all is not lost for Lester B. Pearson's country. The Canadian army possesses strengths and resources that, used well, can be of enormous value to peacekeeping operations. For example, its soldiers speak two of the languages most used in the missions – French and English – and thousands of them are bilingual. The peacekeeping experience that Canadian soldiers have acquired since 1948 has made Canada a leader in the organization and management of missions and the training of soldiers.

Jockel proposes a new, threefold approach for Canada. First, Canada could send specialized troops – units of engineers, communications units, medical services units, land and air transportation units – in the first months of the deployment of a mission, and withdraw them as soon as the operation could rely on other countries. Their role would be rapid intervention and preparation of the terrain.[*] Second, Canada could develop training programs for all Blue Helmets and carry out theoretical and practical research on various aspects of peacekeeping.[†] Finally, Canadian participation in peacekeeping operations could be broadened beyond the traditional military role. Since UN missions are increasingly involved in organizing elections, maintaining order, and social and economic reconstruction, civilians could be part of Canadian contingents.

Canada stands at a crossroads with respect to peacekeeping operations. It can no longer play the primary role it has played in the past. But it need not accept being relegated to the sidelines because, as Jockel has pointed out, it has access to important resources for peacekeeping.

[*]In September 1995 the Canadian government presented a document to the UN entitled *Towards a Rapid Reaction Capability for the United Nations*, in which it made several suggestions for improving the process of establishing and deploying UN forces.
[†]In 1994 the Canadian government established the Lester B. Pearson International Peacekeeping Training Centre in Nova Scotia.

Epilogue

On 25 May 1994 in front of an audience of journalists at UN headquarters, Secretary-General Boutros Boutros-Ghali discussed the civil war ravaging Rwanda. Following the assassination of the presidents of Rwanda and Burundi on 6 April, the country had plunged into anarchy, with the army and government militias massacring their Hutu opponents and members of the Tutsi minority, whom they accused of complicity in the double murder. Observers in the field estimated that at least 200,000 people had already been killed, over a period of seven weeks, at the time the secretary-general addressed the journalists. To Boutros-Ghali's dismay, the UN had been unable to convince the international community to intervene quickly to put an end to the genocide. He unleashed a tirade.

'[The situation in Rwanda] is a failure, not only for the United Nations; it is a failure for the international community,' he said. 'And all of us are responsible for this failure. Not only the great powers but the African powers, the nongovernmental organizations, all the international community. It is a genocide which has been committed.'[1] Boutros-Ghali said that he had written to some thirty African heads of state to ask them to reinforce the Blue Helmet contingent that was in Kigali when the massacre began. 'I begged them to send troops ... Unfortunately, let us say with great humility, I failed. It is a scandal. I am the first one to say it.'

Boutros-Ghali was devastated because Rwanda had been the site of a unique experiment in preventive diplomacy – which was supposed to be the first step in averting war, and was one of the key concepts of his *Agenda for Peace* – and the experiment had been on the verge of success. For several years previously, a movement of Tutsi rebels based in Uganda, the Rwandan Patriotic Front (RPF), had been involved in an open war with the Rwandan government, which was completely controlled by members of the Hutu tribe, the majority in the country. Unable to find a military solution to the dispute, the RPF and the Rwandan government had accepted mediation by the UN in 1992. A year later, on 4 August 1993, the two factions had signed a peace agreement that provided for the formation of a government of national unity, the demobilization of armed groups and the integration of their members into a national army, the organization of general elections, and the deployment of a force of Blue Helmets to control the process of political normalization. A Canadian officer, Brigadier-General Roméo Dallaire, was named commander of the United Nations Assistance Mission for Rwanda (UNAMIR) and arrived in the country in October 1993 with 2,500 soldiers.

By early April 1994, the peace process was stalled. Political leaders had been assassinated, and armed gangs of Hutus were killing Tutsis. Representatives of UNAMIR alerted world opinion that the various factions had begun a massive distribution of weapons to the Rwandan population.[2] The secretary-general of the UN made a formal appeal to the parties to reach an agreement on the establishment of the institutions provided for in the peace accord of August 1993 without further delay.'[3] Two days later, on 6 April, as the presidents of Rwanda and Burundi were returning from Tanzania, where they had attended a regional summit on the political problems in their countries, the Rwandan president's airplane was shot down over the Kigali airport, killing both politicians. It was the beginning of one of the greatest human tragedies in history. The country in turmoil, soldiers of the Rwandan army and the Hutu government militias captured and executed – usually using machetes – their Hutu opponents and any Tutsis they encountered. In addition to ordinary people, dozens of ministers – including the prime minister – and hundreds of prominent citizens were slaughtered in the streets of the capital, Kigali. At the same time, the forces of the RPF, most of which were stationed in Uganda, took advantage of the opportunity to invade the country. For weeks, General Dallaire and his Blue Helmets tried to defend the people, but to no avail. Horrified by the massacre and the refusal of the factions to respect the ceasefire, on 21 April the members of the Security Council ordered the immediate withdrawal of 2,000 Blue Helmets, while asking General Dallaire to continue his work as a mediator.

The withdrawal of the Blue Helmets did not solve anything. The slaughter continued to mount as the RPF forces took control of the territory of Rwanda. The members of the UN were completely ineffectual. On 17 May, in an attempt to avert catastrophe, the Security Council adopted a new resolution authorizing the sending of 5,500 Blue Helmets. Two countries, Ghana and Canada, offered troops. The others offered excuses. The African countries said they had no money to equip the poorly trained soldiers they were prepared to offer; but their heart was not in it. The great powers hesitated or refused outright: China showed no interest; Russia cited its massive involvement in the former Soviet republics; the United Kingdom said it was already doing a lot in the former Yugoslavia; the United States did not want to relive its Somali nightmare. The UN was once again in complete disarray. Faced with the inaction of the other member countries, France finally proposed sending a multinational force to certain regions of Rwanda and creating a secure humanitarian area where Rwandans would be protected from the various factions. On 22 June, the Security Council, which had been deeply divided over the proposal from France – some accused that country of having armed the Hutu regime and of seeking to defend its own interests in the region – narrowly passed a resolution in favour of the French proposal. Only five hundred soldiers from five African countries joined the 2,500 French soldiers who were sent. This force was deployed in south-western Rwanda, but it was too little, too late. By 1 September the blood-bath had gone on for five months; some five hundred thousand Rwandans had been killed and three million more had fled to Zaire, Tanzania, and Burundi. Cholera would kill about thirty thousand more. International relief was being organized as the Blue Helmets were just beginning to arrive in Kigali.

What can explain this abysmal response to the situation in Rwanda by the international community? Boutros-Ghali provided one possible explanation: the member states of the UN were tired of answering the constant distress calls from all over the world. But fear for the lives of their soldiers also made many governments think twice about sending troops; ten Belgian Blue Helmets who were protecting the prime minister had been murdered. However, there was more to it. With the examples of Somalia and Bosnia fresh in their minds, the member states hesitated to intervene in ethnic conflicts for which they saw no solution. This terrible reality paralysed the UN. And preventive diplomacy, which had been supposed to defuse conflicts before they flared up, had proven ineffective. Hence Boutros-Ghali's frustration.

* * *

The time has come to draw some conclusions on the establishment of peacekeeping missions, the work of the Blue Helmets, the great powers' manoeuvring around peacekeeping operations, and the role of the UN. Are the Blue Helmets still the guardians of peace or have they became the warriors of the new world order? The case of Rwanda and other missions may provide some answers to these questions.

The situation in Rwanda, as well as other, less serious, cases we have looked at in this book, demonstrates has a complex, chaotic, and hazardous the process of setting up a peacekeeping mission is. The attitude of the fifteen member states of the Security Council is the prime cause of the problems that arise during the creation of a mission and its deployment in the field. Security Council discussions can go on for days or weeks before a decision is taken. And when the members finally adopt a resolution authorizing the creation of a mission, it can take up to four months before the first military units are deployed and up to a year before the apparatus in the field is fully in place and ready to operate. These delays can be catastrophic.

In Cambodia, a peace agreement was signed by four factions on 23 October 1991, but it was only on 28 February the following year that the UN created a peacekeeping mission there. The first contingents arrived between March and June, but the entire military component of the mission did not begin to function properly until the end of 1992. In Bosnia, a similar process occurred. The UN initially rejected the idea of intervention when the government in Sarajevo requested it in April 1992. Then, in July, the Sarajevo airport was reopened, thanks to Canadian and French Blue Helmets. With the humanitarian situation deteriorating, the Security Council took action on 13 August and 10 September, deploying Blue Helmets in Bosnia to provide protection for the aid convoys. But in mid-November, seven months after the beginning of the war, only 1,500 of the planned 7,500 Blue Helmets had been deployed.

However, there are also examples of missions in which the UN was by no means slow in deploying its Blue Helmets. For example, in the Congo in 1960, Tunisian and Ghanaian soldiers arrived on the ground only forty-eight hours after the adoption of a resolution creating the United Nations Operation in the Congo (ONUC). One month later, 11,000 soldiers had been deployed.[4] In October 1973, the first contingents of the Second United Nations Emergency Force (UNEF II) arrived on the ground a few days after the end of the war between Israel and Egypt, although it is true that this was due to the availability of Blue Helmets already deployed in Cyprus a few hundred kilometres away.[5]

The extreme slowness of the UN and the participating countries in organizing the missions causes numerous problems for the Blue Helmets on the ground. Most experts consider the first six weeks to be the most important period of a mission, the time when it has to get organized in the field and establish an image of strength and credibility to the local population and the opposing factions.[6] A rapid deployment proves that the UN is serious, but even more important, it allows the situation to be stabilized. If the mission spends four to twelve months getting organized and deploying its military units, the rival groups use that time to gain as much ground as possible and stir up the people, who are frightened by the war and made desperate by hardship.

When a mission is being deployed in a territory, it frequently faces both internal and external obstacles to the implementation of its mandate and its day-to-day operations. In Western Sahara, the systematic sabotage of the Blue Helmets' activities by the Moroccan authorities jeopardized the deployment of MINURSO; in Cambodia, the Khmer Rouge refused UNTAC military personnel access to the zones it controlled. UNPROFOR contingents in Bosnia worked for three years in a violent and uncertain climate. However severe the resolutions adopted by the Security Council against factions that do not respect their commitments to the UN, a king can sabotage a mission with impunity and a little, local boss can paralyse the Blue Helmets' humanitarian activities for days or weeks without incurring the slightest sanction.

The establishment and deployment of a peacekeeping mission also encounters many administrative obstacles within the UN. First, the budget for the operation has to be approved by the UN General Assembly before the secretary-general can release the funds. Then the UN administrative machine examines the budget; it is responsible for buying the required equipment and supplies, paying the officials assigned to the mission, and reimbursing the expenses of the participating countries. The slowness and complexity of the machine are legendary. For example, in the former Yugoslavia, a contingent commander's request for supplies (such as paper, a telephone, or a truck) had to go through fifty-two different steps before it was answered.[7] In Rwanda, an urgent delivery of fifty American armoured transport vehicles to the Blue Helmets of UNAMIR was delayed for two months by a dispute between the United States and the UN on their cost and the methods of reimbursement.[8] In their frustration, the commanders of the richest contingents often obtain their supplies from local entrepreneurs, who quickly set up shop near the headquarters of the missions.

When a mission is mounted, the UN has to negotiate the recruitment of Blue Helmets with two types of participating governments: those that are well organized, with trained and equipped soldiers – and the others. The Western nations and a few other developed countries, such as South Korea, Singapore, and Argentina, easily meet the criteria the UN sets for participation in a mission. The vast majority of other countries, however, even the former Communist countries, are unable to do so. There is a long list of examples of soldiers from the Third World who reported for duty without seasonal clothing, without weapons, without equipment, without pay, and with inadequate training. Often their home countries do not even have the means to transport them to the territory where the mission is to be deployed.

Blue Helmets who arrive in a country without equipment or sufficient supplies for at least thirty to sixty days spend more time taking care of their own needs than they do carrying out their mandate and dissuading the factions. But this period is crucial, because during this time the opposing factions try to intimidate the soldiers, whose effectiveness is vital to the rest of the mission. The missions rely on the cooperation of the parties to obtain supplies, and the opposing factions never miss a chance to block the lines of land or air communication, to hold up or loot convoys, or even to put up administrative or customs barriers that slow down the distribution of supplies to the Blue Helmets. Very few missions have been able to avoid this kind of problem, and the UN does not seem to have found a solution to it.

While the organization and deployment of a mission are crucial to its operations, the actual work of the Blue Helmets on the ground is the key to its success. As noted, the first six weeks are decisive for the outcome of a mission. In Cambodia and the former Yugoslavia, the UN took from four to twelve months to fully deploy its Blue Helmets. The direct consequence was uneven implementation of the mandates of these missions. But even when the Blue Helmets manage to deploy quickly, another problem arises: the multinational make-up of the force can make a mission so dysfunctional that it cancels out the positive effects of rapid deployment.

Often the contingents come from three sources: the Western world, the former Communist countries, and the Third World. The wealth of the first group combined with the poverty of the other two prevents the harmonious functioning of the force. This situation leads to what observers have called a two-speed mission. The contingents from the rich countries work better than those from the poor countries; their soldiers are well trained and carry out their mandate effectively, while the poor contingents, despite the good will of their soldiers, work slowly, spending part of their time fighting their own poverty, and are the most vulnerable in the field. In Somalia, Cambodia, Lebanon, and the former Yugoslavia, the opposing factions tended to humiliate or harass the poorest contingents, which were the least able to defend themselves. However, the soldiers from some poor countries, particularly those of the Third World, bring to the missions a human touch that is less evident in the Western contingents. According to the former commander of the United Nations Interim Force in Lebanon (UNIFIL), Norwegian major-general Trond Furuhovde, the Blue Helmets from the Third World have a sense of team spirit and work well together, and they maintain warm relations with the local population. These qualities are undeniable assets in a mission as delicate as UNIFIL.[9]

There is an atmosphere of calm in missions made up completely of soldiers from rich countries. Of course, in many cases the opposing factions are less aggressive and more respectful of their commitments; but the fact remains that the sight of well-armed, well-trained soldiers has a certain deterrent effect; this was clearly the case in Cyprus and the Golan Heights. Of course, there are exceptions. The Somali militias did not hesitate to attack American or Belgian soldiers, but they paid with heavy losses. In Bosnia, French and Spanish soldiers and those from the Scandinavian countries were consistently targeted by Moslem and Serb snipers. But large-scale attacks were rare; since the murder of thirteen Italians in the Congo in 1961, no Western contingent has been the victim of gratuitous slaughter like that in which twenty-five Pakistani Blue Helmets died in Somalia on 5 June 1993. While the Americans lost eighteen soldiers four months later, those deaths occurred in actual combat.

Today's Blue Helmets are very different from those sent to the Suez after the crisis in 1956. At that time, the soldiers of the UN had two precise tasks: to patrol a buffer zone between the territories of the belligerents in order to prevent infiltration from either side, and to ensure that the troops of both sides withdrew from the territories they had occupied. The Egyptians and Israelis respected their obligations to the letter, and the Blue Helmets sandwiched between the two led very dull lives for ten years. Until 1978, other missions followed the same pattern, with the notable exceptions of the Congo and the second mission in Cyprus. In the former Belgian colony, the Blue Helmets were engaged in fierce fighting for four years, after which they undertook a reconstruction program. In Cyprus, the Turkish invasion and occupation in 1974 radically changed the activities of the Blue Helmets who had been deployed on the island since 1964. Since the invasion, they have had to patrol a clearly defined cease-fire line, investigate numerous incidents, assist in the reunification of families, and re-establish public services, in addition to many other tasks.

In 1978, the deployment of a peacekeeping mission in southern Lebanon took the Blue Helmets into a territory in political and social chaos. Their mandate was to monitor the withdrawal of Israeli troops and help the Lebanese government re-establish its authority in the region. But this mandate was impossible to fulfil, because the Israelis did not want to leave and Lebanon was without a true government for more than ten years. Already overwhelmed by an impossible mandate, in 1982 the Blue Helmets were given the additional responsibility of protecting the inhabitants of the region and providing humanitarian aid. Since then, they have been rebuilding what the Israeli planes and the Islamic guerrillas destroy.

This expansion of the Blue Helmets' tasks has accelerated since 1989, with the establishment of multi-role missions in Namibia, El Salvador, the former Yugoslavia, Angola, Somalia, and Cambodia, among others. Now the Blue Helmets are expected to intervene in civil wars, patrol territories, disarm militias, rebuild infrastructure, organize elections, protect minorities, evacuate threatened groups, exchange prisoners and sometimes even bodies, draw borders, etc. The list of their tasks keeps growing as new operations are mounted.

In spite of sometimes deplorable living conditions, dangerous environments, and increasingly demanding mandates, the Blue Helmets are usually up to the tasks required of them. However, the new role of these soldiers is not without hazards. Where, twenty years ago, Blue Helmets separated the armies of countries or well-identified groups that respected their commitments to the UN, today they are thrown into the midst of civil wars in which enemies are not easily distinguished from friends. As the areas of activity in which they are expected to participate expand, the Blue Helmets increasingly find themselves in direct contact with the population and with factions that often want only to see them leave.

The greater danger faced by the Blue Helmets and the desire of the UN to be able to use force to implement its decisions have forced the planners of peacekeeping missions to take stronger security measures. As the former military adviser to the secretary-general, General Maurice Baril, has observed, the soldiers' blue helmets and the white paint on their vehicles no longer protect as they once did. For decades, the Blue Helmets were only lightly armed and the UN restricted the use of force to self-defence. The soldiers were authorized to carry personal weapons and the contingents could equip themselves with armoured vehicles, but they had no heavy guns or machine-guns. Today, because of their direct intervention in civil wars and the more frequent use of force, violence against the Blue Helmets is no longer an isolated phenomenon. In 1991, fourteen Blue Helmets were killed in the eleven missions then under way. In 1993, 240 Blue Helmets lost their lives in combat or in accidents in the sixteen missions then in existence.[10] The factions do not hesitate to attack even the senior officers of peacekeeping missions. In Bosnia, Major-General Lewis MacKenzie was stopped repeatedly by representatives of all the parties to the conflict.[11]

It took the UN a long time to permit the Blue Helmets to arm themselves to deal with the increasingly violent conditions – with the exception of the UNOSOM II in Somalia, which was conducted under Chapter VII of the UN Charter. And even in Somalia, as we saw in Chapter 7, the rules of engagement were, to say the least, surprising. For example, they did not authorize the use of tear gas to control crowds; the Canadian and other Blue Helmets had to use their weapons for neutralize troublemakers. This has led to a good deal of controversy as to whether the soldiers were trigger-happy.

In 1992, at the beginning of UNPROFOR, the UN mission in the former Yugoslavia, the contingents were not authorized to deploy heavy weapons (tanks), high-explosive ammunition, anti-tank missiles, or radar. The soldiers had orders to use force solely in self-defence. But the chaotic situation in Bosnia forced the leaders of the contingents, and then the officials of the UN, to change that policy. When the Canadians opened the airport in Sarajevo in July 1992, they were under constant sniper fire. Disregarding the UN's rules on impartiality, the officers allowed their soldiers to carry out secret patrols to identify sniper positions.[12] General MacKenzie, who was in the field at the time, approved these patrols, which were intended to protect the lives of his soldiers.

MacKenzie also bent the UN rules on anti-tank missiles. In his memoirs, he tells how he took TOW missiles to Sarajevo. 'We were authorized to bring the vehicle, as I had stressed that its night- and thermal-vision enhancement systems would be a great help in detecting any developing threats around the airport,' he wrote. 'In the end, we cheated and brought the missiles anyway.'[13] He added that the same was true for mortar shells, which were also not permitted.

In 1994–5, the most exposed contingents in Bosnia had weapons with which they could return fire effectively. For example, the French Blue Helmets in Sarajevo had Sagaie tanks equipped with powerful guns, grenade launchers, armoured vehicles mounted with machine-guns, Milan anti-tank missiles, and ground-based radar. The soldiers had special guns that fired high-explosive projectiles and so were capable of detecting and neutralizing snipers.[14] At the Tuzla airport, the Danish contingent had powerful Leopard tanks and did not hesitate to use them. The British had Warrior combat vehicles, which had proven their value in the Gulf War, and trajectographic radar with a range of fifteen kilometres, which was very effective against mortar fire. When the Blue Helmets were directly threatened and could not defend themselves, NATO was authorized to use combat aircraft against the aggressors – but the usefulness of NATO air power was limited in a region as wooded and hilly as Bosnia.

Paradoxically, the question of providing the Blue Helmets with more powerful weapons has never been debated at the UN or even among the member states. The decisions were taken one at a time, with the countries of origin of the various contingents asking the UN for authorization to send heavy weapons, and the UN officials accepting without even a written agreement. Sometimes, the weapons were already in the field and the UN had to comply.[15] However, reinforcement of the Blue Helmets' military capabilities can be dangerous if it is not accepted by the factions in the region. They might think that the Blue Helmets are preparing to take sides in the conflict and to attack one of the parties.

An operation as complex as UNPROFOR in the former Yugoslavia should have been able to rely on first-hand military intelligence in order to respond effectively to threats from the warring parties and implement its mandate to force the factions to withdraw certain weapons. The Blue Helmets need an intelligence service that can provide them with information and detailed maps and photographs. But until quite recently, the very word 'intelligence' was banished from UN language, and Blue Helmets were forbidden to engage in spying, even if it could help the UN and save the lives of its soldiers. However, the need for an intelligence system has been central to the demands of many commanders of peacekeeping missions in recent decades. In 1974, several experts, including the Indian major-general Indar Jit Rikhye, who was for many years a military adviser to the UN, argued in favour of such a system, without wanting to give the UN *carte blanche* to establish an espionage service.[16] At the end of his mandate in Rwanda in August 1994, Brigadier-General Roméo Dallaire stated that the absence of security intelligence had been a huge obstacle to the evaluation of the political and military situation on the ground. 'A commander can't command if he does not have intelligence, if he is not able to prevent attacks or determine how the situation is evolving and adjust accordingly,' he said.[17]

The attitude of the UN in this regard has changed. Not that it has established its own CIA; the UN currently relies on the good will of the participating countries and the great powers to provide it with aerial photographs of the positions and objectives of the warring parties, detailed maps, and intelligence gathered on the ground by the Blue Helmets. The United States has set up radar stations and bases for pilotless reconnaissance planes in Albania and Croatia to monitor troop movements in Bosnia. American, French, and Russian satellites regularly photograph territories in which UN missions are deployed. All these data and images are given or sold to the UN. But at UN headquarters in New York, there is an awareness of the limits of the great powers' cooperation, and even that of the Blue Helmets, and a realization that Washington, Paris, and Moscow may hold back information to defend their own interests in certain regions. Some of the peacekeepers – the Russians in Croatia and Bosnia, or the Americans in Somalia – may also keep information to themselves, and there is not much the UN can do about it. And while the UN might hope one day to possess a fleet of aircraft or a satellite with which to gather its own information, there is little chance of that happening. It is unlikely that the great powers would ever allow funds to be allocated to such projects.

Perhaps the most unexpected addition to the arsenal of the peacekeeping missions is the media – written and electronic – the presence of which is revolutionizing the Blue Helmets' work on the ground. Opinions vary as to whether this is a godsend or a source of confusion, forcing diplomats and politicians to make rash and sometimes dangerous decisions. Media participation is indeed a two-edged sword.[18]

Although the media are blamed for the Americans having lost the Vietnam War, it was not until the mid-1980s that their influence really made itself felt. CNN's broadcasting of information in real time has transformed our vision of the world and our perception of events. Pressure groups and politicians quickly understood the power of this new medium and use it extensively, as we saw in 1990–1 in the former Soviet Union, when Mikhail Gorbatchev and Boris Yeltsin, engaged in a struggle for power, competed to give interviews to the American networks. During the Gulf War, television viewers throughout the world were glued to their screens to follow the live coverage of the fighting between the armies of the West and Iraq and the speeches by the leaders of both sides. But while politicians have used television to manipulate public opinion, the tactic has now been turned against them. Live news networks broadcast wars, terrorist bombings, civilians being killed by snipers, the uncovering of mass graves, and starving populations fleeing fighting. As the misery of the world invades the small screen, viewers demand immediate solutions to these problems. 'CNN diplomacy' now hangs over the heads of world leaders, pushing them to react quickly.

The presence of the media plays an important role in UN peacekeeping missions. The media make the UN's activities better known, and they can even protect populations and Blue Helmets from attacks. For example, Major-General Lewis MacKenzie has stated that the presence of the media probably prevented more atrocities in the former Yugoslavia than the troops did. 'The power of having a television camera being held by someone who you don't want to kill because another cameraman will be taking a picture of you, one of the belligerents killing the cameraman, has a tremendous impact on what goes on, a positive impact,' he said in November 1992. 'It is not just the UN force that is tempering the situation; it is that the media follows the UN.'[19] Images of the bodies strewn around the Sarajevo market after a mortar attack on 6 February 1994 pushed the Western powers, already at the end of their patience with the complicated situation in Bosnia, to issue an ultimatum to the factions to withdraw their heavy weapons to at least twenty kilometres from the city.

The power of the media also made itself felt in other regions, such as Somalia and Rwanda, where images of starving throngs of people and killing fields prompted the international community to act.

But the influence of the media can also have negative consequences. First of all, when the media are not present in a conflict, that conflict – for example, the civil war in Angola – does not seem to exist for the rest of the world. No journalists filmed the Angolan civil war, although for years it caused thousands of deaths per month. In Bosnia, where journalists were numerous, the Moslem part of the city of Mostar was reduced to ashes and its inhabitants to starvation without any protest from the world, which was completely preoccupied by the situation in Sarajevo. There were no cameras in Mostar.

Horrible images of a conflict can sensitize world opinion and it seems they can also, sometimes, impose foreign policy on governments, not always with the best results. In Somalia, for example, at the beginning of the crisis, reports of the famine and the pillaging by the factions pushed the international community to react quickly. However, on 3 October 1993, a year after the U.S.-UN humanitarian intervention, the deaths of eighteen American soldiers and the images broadcast of some of their bodies being dragged through the streets of Mogadishu caused American opinion to turn around. President Clinton immediately announced the withdrawal of American troops from Somalia, while that country still needed them. Since then, the United States and other countries have balked at sending soldiers to re-establish or maintain peace.

In spite of the problems, the power of the media remains an important tool for the Blue Helmets on the ground. The sight of a television crew or the threat of a report on their wrongdoings still has a deterrent effect on certain factions.

The control of a peacekeeping mission is a determining factor in its success or failure. Firmness of the leadership, a cohesive chain of command, the leaders' loyalty to the UN system, and the soldiers' neutrality and devotion to the UN are essential to success. Without these prerequisites a mission can degenerate into chaos even where the factions on the ground take no vigorous action against the Blue Helmets. As we have seen, command and control are a source of problems for the countries that participate in the missions and for the UN itself. In Western Sahara, the secretary-general deliberately excluded his own special representative and the commander of the force from some of the negotiations in order to deal directly with the parties. In Cambodia, some contingents sabotaged the actions of others and ignored the orders of the mission commander. In Somalia, the Americans conducted an aggressive policy against General Aidid without consulting the other contingents. In the former Yugoslavia, the French Blue Helmets dominated UNPROFOR and took their orders from Paris.

The source of these problems is, first, the refusal of governments to place their soldiers under any authority other than their own, and second, the political manoeuvring of the great powers, who defend their own national interests at the expense of those of the international community. Is there any solution to these problems? Some experts have proposed that command responsibilities in a mission be divided and shared among several countries, which would allow a certain autonomy to countries like the United States.[20] This suggestion is not feasible; there cannot be several commanders of one mission, and hybrid solutions to the problem of command and control are even less workable. In a world in which the number of peacekeeping missions is constantly increasing and their mandates are becoming more and more complex, the Blue Helmets must know who is in command, who is giving the orders, and to whom they have to answer. If the countries of the world want the UN to succeed in its peacekeeping operations, they will have to relinquish a part of their sovereignty over their soldiers.

No peacekeeping mission can be created, much less operate, against the wishes of the five great powers that have the right of veto on the Security Council. When the fifteen members of the Security Council study a resolution on the establishment of a mission, the five great powers must have their say. And for the resolution to pass, none of them must vote against it. The formulation of the resolution is the result of intense consultation and many compromises among all the members of the Security Council, and the opinions of the five great powers are decisive. Council members must take into account their political, military, ideological, and strategic interests.

Throughout the Cold War, until 1988, there was a minimum of consensus among the five great powers on the creation of peacekeeping missions. The United States, France, and the United Kingdom generally took the same position – except in the case of the Suez crisis in 1956, when Washington firmly opposed Paris and London. These three countries were supported until 1971 by Taiwan, which occupied China's seat on the Security Council; after 1971, the People's Republic of China almost always abstained in votes on the creation of peacekeeping missions. The attitude of the Soviet Union varied according to the circumstances. Moscow either abstained or voted in favour of the creation of missions, since its basic interests were never threatened by them. Since 1988, the five great powers have worked together, but the degree of their participation in peacekeeping operations has varied considerably. They have formed two blocs in the Security Council: the United Kingdom, China, and Russia play a passive role, while France and the United States play an active one.

It should be emphasized that, up until 1988, the participation of the great powers in peacekeeping missions was not extensive. The UN and its senior officials, and political leaders such as Lester B. Pearson, felt that those powers had to be excluded from participation in order to preserve the neutrality of the missions. There were, of course, some exceptions, but the attitude of the great powers toward peacekeeping was for a long time conditioned by this rule of exclusion.

The British have never shown a great deal of enthusiasm for peacekeeping. Until 1992, aside from a battalion of Blue Helmets in Cyprus, where Britain had two military bases, British Blue Helmets were rather rare. In 1992, London decided to send some 3,500 soldiers to Bosnia, and in August 1994 it sent a contingent of 600 soldiers to Rwanda. But the presence of the British in the former Yugoslavia was motivated primarily by

European political considerations. London and Paris share the same opinions on the Balkan conflict. The British are above all faithful allies of the United States and France, and they play a minor role in peacekeeping.

Since 1981, China has never opposed peacekeeping operations in their traditional form, but Chinese participation in the missions has been practically non-existent. Except for a battalion of 700 soldiers sent to Cambodia from 1992 to 1993, only a handful of Chinese have worn the blue helmet. The Chinese are cautious; before sending larger contingents, they want primarily to observe and learn. Politically, the Chinese position is that the UN must respect the principle of non-interference in the internal affairs of the member states and must not make excessive use of Chapter VII when it mounts peacekeeping missions.[21] Therefore China does not associate itself with peacekeeping missions the mandates of which are not accepted by all parties to the conflict and abstains from voting on any resolution authorizing the use of force. For example, it abstained from voting on Resolution 678 authorizing the use of force to drive Iraqi forces out of Kuwait. It also abstained when resolutions were presented on the situation in the former Yugoslavia, and when the Security Council created multinational forces for Rwanda in 1994, for Haiti in 1994–5, and for Albania in 1997. The only exceptions to this policy have been Somalia and Zaire. On 3 December 1992, when the Security Council voted to authorize the United States to put together a multinational force to intervene in Somalia, China added its voice to those of the other fourteen members, noting that the situation in that country was exceptional and it was without a government. Nevertheless, the Chinese delegate expressed his country's reservations regarding the use of force. China took the same position in November 1996 when the UN created a multinational force to assist the refuges in eastern Zaire.

Whereas China has shown little inclination to participate in peacekeeping operations, Russia has decided to limit its peacekeeping activities to the territory of the former Soviet empire. Of course, Russia has sided with the Western camp since the end of the Cold War and usually supports the creation of peacekeeping missions under Chapter VI or VII of the UN Charter. It even participates in some of them, as it did in the case of the former Yugoslavia. But since the disintegration of the Soviet Union, the Russian army has been called on to police civil wars in several former Soviet republics or conflicts between republics. In the civil wars in Georgia, Moldova, and Tajikistan, and in the war between Armenia and Azerbaijan, the Russians offered mediation and sent thousands of soldiers converted into peace-keepers.

Russia's new willingness to intervene was clearly expressed by Russian Minister of Foreign Affairs, Andrei Kozyrev, in a speech made at the UN in October 1993. Invoking the historical links among the former Soviet republics, he stated that within the borders of the former Soviet Union, 'only Russia, and no other group of nations, has the right to intervene to attempt to quell the conflicts born of a peril as dangerous as the nuclear threat of yesterday or the resurgence of aggressive nationalisms.'[22] He stressed that the 'problems [in those republics] are too serious and tragic to engage in speculation on supposed Russian neo-imperialist plans, diplomatic rivalries, or the pursuit of new spheres of influence.'

The return of the Russian army to its former domain did not fail to provoke a reaction in the new republics and throughout the world. The three small Baltic countries were not pleased, and they asked the West not to recognize Russian influence in their countries. But, after an initial negative reaction, most Western countries have given their support to the new Russian policy. Already grappling with the conflicts in the former Yugoslavia, neither the United States nor France, nor any other country, is interested in getting involved in the ethnic conflicts in some of the new republics. Moreover, on 29 March 1994, Russia made it known that it did not need the permission of the UN to conduct peacekeeping operations on its own borders. A press release issued jointly by the Russian Ministries of Defence and Foreign Affairs stated that 'all Russian peacekeeping actions to stabilize and resolve conflict situations in the Commonwealth of Independent States (CIS) are carried out so as to avoid casualties and are in keeping with the UN statutes since they occur at the request of the parties to the conflict.'[23] The international community agreed to allow Russia to play the role of policeman, but the UN refused to grant Blue Helmet status to the Russian interposition troops.[24] Busy maintaining order in its former empire, Russia is not yet ready to answer UN calls for new troops for its missions.

Like the other great powers, the United States has never participated heavily in peacekeeping operations. At most, the U.S. agreed to send a few military observers to certain missions or vigorously supported the deployment of Blue Helmets in countries where the conflicts threatened to destabilize its alliances. The latter was the case in Cyprus, where Greece and Turkey, both members of NATO, were fighting over the island. Washington has for a long time limited its role to logistical support. In most missions, from the Congo in 1960 to Rwanda in 1994, and including Somalia, the former Yugoslavia, and Angola, the United States has participated in the transportation of foreign contingents and the setting up of supply and communication systems, and provided military equipment for the Blue Helmets. When a crisis concerned them directly, the Americans have tended to organize their own multinational peacekeeping operation. For example, after the signature of the Camp David Accords by Israel and Egypt in 1978, a Multinational Force and Observers (MFO) dominated by the Americans was deployed in the Sinai Desert to monitor the withdrawal of Israeli forces. In 1982, when civil war was raging in Lebanon, the United States mounted a multinational interposition force to allow the Palestinians to leave Beirut and to separate the factions. But two years later, this force left Lebanon following a series of fatal attacks on American and French soldiers. In 1990, the United States, with the blessing of the UN, led a multinational coalition to drive the Iraqis out of Kuwait. And at the end of 1992, another UN-approved coalition intervened in Somalia to save the population from famine and protect them from fighting between opposing factions. Washington also initiated the formation of a coalition to intervene in Haiti from 1994 to 1995. Finally, in autumn 1995, the United States induced NATO to take over from the UN force in the former Yugoslavia to enforce the Dayton peace accords.

The Somali adventure led the United States to make many changes to its role in UN peacekeeping operations. When Bill Clinton took office as president in January 1993, he already had a few ideas on the role of the United States in the UN. During his campaign, he had consistently endorsed increased UN participation in conflict resolution and promised that American power would be enlisted in this cause. In April 1992, he had called for the creation of a small permanent 'rapid deployment force' by the UN to carry out such operations as 'standing guard at the borders of countries threatened by aggression, preventing mass violence against civilian populations, providing humanitarian relief and combatting terrorism.'[25] This broad program was greeted with enthusiastic support by UN Secretary-General Boutros Boutros-Ghali, who for months had been asking the United States to play a larger role in peacekeeping and send its soldiers to take part in more of the missions. The Bush administration had repeatedly rejected these requests, preferring the formula of the multinational coalition, in which the U.S. could be the leader. It refused to consider integrating American soldiers into a force under the command of a foreign officer, except of course within the framework of NATO. But Clinton claimed that he wanted to change that attitude. Throughout the spring, and even as late as August 1993, his principal advisers kept repeating the president's promises. In January, Secretary of State Warren Christopher spoke in favour of the creation of a permanent force serving the UN, while Madeleine Albright, who was then ambassador to the UN, recited the new administration's interventionist credo in all her speeches. In testimony before the House of Representatives on 3 May 1993 and in a speech to the Council on Foreign Relations in New York on 21 June 1993, Albright emphasized that maintaining collective security was of vital interest to the United States. Anarchic situations and ethnic wars had to be stopped before they degenerated, she said, invoking the moral obligation of the United States to help rebuild countries in crisis. She candidly admitted that if the UN was unable to answer the distress calls from the whole world and quickly mount peacekeeping operations, this was due in part to the fact that her country had not provided it with the necessary means.[26]

In spring 1993, responding to Boutros-Ghali's requests for greater American participation, President Clinton took his first action with respect to his ideas on a permanent force serving the UN. He announced that some 3,000 American soldiers participating in Operation Restore Hope in Somalia would be placed under the command of UNOSOM II, which was to take over from the American forces on 4 May. The American president was thus renouncing the sacrosanct principle that American troops in peacekeeping missions always be commanded by Americans. There was, however, a precedent for this: a contingent of several hundred American soldiers was serving in Macedonia as part of UNPROFOR, the Blue Helmet mission in the former Yugoslavia. But these soldiers were only guarding borders and they were not permitted to use force. The situation in Somalia, as we saw in chapter 6, was completely different.

American enthusiasm for the UN quickly gave way to disillusionment due to the turn of events in Somalia. On 14 July 1993, an American diplomat at the UN stated before the House of Representatives that the United States had never intended to promote the creation of a permanent force of Blue Helmets. A month later, when American soldiers were being killed in the huge manhunt initiated by the UN for General Mohamed Aidid, voices were raised in Washington demanding that the United States not get involved in ethnic conflicts. President Clinton backed down. Speaking at the UN on 27 September, he stated that the United States was no more able than the UN to solve all the world's problems.[27] He said the UN would have to establish precise criteria before getting involved in new peacekeeping operations. The UN, he said, had to learn to say no, and so did his own country. This change in American policy was confirmed by the events of 3 October in Mogadishu, when eighteen American soldiers were killed in an assault on one of General Aidid's strongholds. The American administration was in turmoil. It accused the UN of incompetence, saying it was incapable of mounting, managing, or commanding peacekeeping operations.

The United States then decided to carry out an in-depth review of its policy on peacekeeping. The unclassified version of the presidential directive that resulted from this review was published in May 1994. It marked a return to the broad principles of the preceding administration. For the United States to participate in a peacekeeping operation, American interests would have to be at stake; there would have to be a violation of international peace and security; the operation would have to be of predictable, limited duration; the costs and risks would have to be acceptable and they would have to be shared; the system of command and control would have to be approved by the American military; and finally, any participation would require the support of Congress and public opinion.[28] These conditions are so restrictive that one wonders under what circumstances United States would ever accept a request to take part in UN peacekeeping.

For a long time indifferent if not downright hostile to UN peacekeeping activities, France has recently rediscovered this instrument of international diplomacy. In 1991, it sent a contingent of observers to Western Sahara. The following year, France began participating in the major UN missions to such an extent that it became the biggest contributor of Blue Helmets in the world up until the fall of 1995. At a summit of the leaders of the member countries of the Security Council on 31 January 1992, in New York, French president François Mitterrand was the only leader to offer to make a thousand soldiers available to the UN within forty-eight hours following a formal request.[29] When missions in Cambodia, Somalia, and the former Yugoslavia were organized in 1992, France responded quickly to the UN's appeals. In September 1993, it accounted for 9,100 Blue Helmets in eight peacekeeping missions, or about 13 per cent of all the Blue Helmets in the world. Its greatest participation was in the former Yugoslavia.

In addition to its involvement in peacekeeping operations, France followed the American policy of unilateral intervention in Rwanda. In part to defend its interests, but also in response to appeals by humanitarian organizations, and with the blessing of the UN, it established a secure humanitarian area in southwest Rwanda between June and August 1994.

Finally, in terms of theory and organization, France has proposed ideas and concrete measures to improve efficiency and cohesiveness in the organization and operation of peacekeeping missions. For example, it suggested that the areas of action for peace presented in *An Agenda for Peace*, which range from traditional peacekeeping to peace-enforcement, be supplemented 'in order to reflect more accurately the nature of operations that are deployed before a conflict has ended and are intended to restore peace or moderate the conflict by methods that involve both securing the parties' consent (principally through negotiation) and constraint.'[30] France also suggested mechanisms to improve the quick reaction capability of the UN and proposed strengthening the capabilities of the headquarters and the command structures.

We saw in Chapter 12 the interest France has taken in peacekeeping missions. It should be remembered that the French government sees these missions as one more instrument in the broader diplomatic manoeuvring to maintain France's status as a great power in Europe and in part of the world.

Many questions can be raised with respect to the influence of the great powers in the process of mounting peacekeeping missions and the appropriateness of their participation in them. In his memoirs, Brian Urquhart, who was for many years head of peacekeeping operations for the UN, cited the example of the creation of a peacekeeping operation in southern Lebanon in 1978 to show how the great powers rid themselves of a problem they could not solve by passing it on to the UN. When Israel invaded southern Lebanon in March 1978 in response to Palestinian incursions into Israeli territory, the United States was embarrassed. For several months, it had been promoting peace talks between Israel and Egypt. President Jimmy Carter was concerned about the possible impact of this invasion on Arab and international public opinion. He arranged for a UN mission to be created in southern Lebanon to separate the parties and re-establish peace – without, however, tackling the underlying problems. Urquhart, who was working for the UN at that time, was worried. 'I explained my concern that once the Security Council, under American pressure, had decided to send forces to southern Lebanon, the United States and others would rapidly lose interest, ignore the problems which our soldiers would inevitably face, and leave us and the troop-contributing countries without the necessary political support to do the job. Subsequent events amply justified this pessimistic evaluation,' he wrote.[31]

Without question, the same evaluation could be made of the recent missions in Western Sahara, Angola, Somalia, and the former Yugoslavia. In all these places, the deployment of the Blue Helmets locked the status quo into place, and political negotiations between the factions proceeded at a snail's pace. The Blue Helmets have been constant targets of the frustration of the warring parties and even the local people. This has not prevented the great powers from denouncing the UN's lack of effectiveness. But the great powers are themselves largely responsible for this state of affairs; it is they who write the ambiguous mandates, pare away at the budgets, and try to influence the activities of the Blue Helmets in the field. In fact, it can reasonably be said that the massive participation of the great powers, especially the United States and France, has not in any way helped the UN to solve the tragic problems in Somalia, Bosnia, and Rwanda. The same is true of Russia's action in the former Soviet republics. The intervention of the great powers in the peacekeeping missions has two negative effects. First, their massive participation is never without a price; ulterior political and military motives can be seen behind their every effort in Somalia, Bosnia, Rwanda, and in some of the former Soviet republics. Second, on the ground, the opposing factions always try to get the great powers on their side. In Somalia, the heads of two major clans did everything they could to gain favour with the Americans. In the end, the Americans chose to fight General Aidid, and we have seen the consequences. In Bosnia, the Moslems did not hesitate to stir up major incidents and even kill Western Blue Helmets to provoke international military intervention, because they felt it would be favourable to them. The Serbs did the same, but their aim was to frustrate the Western nations and force them to withdraw. In the former Soviet republics, the intervention of Russian peacekeeping forces suits those who want to see Russia return to its former empire or at least provide protection to it.

The great powers should review their participation in peacekeeping operations to see how improvements could be made. For example, instead of contributing many contingents of soldiers – whose mere presence in the field creates tension among the factions and power imbalances within the missions – the great powers should reduce the scale of their participation. It does not make sense that 75 per cent of the peacekeepers sent to Somalia for UNITAF were from the United States, or that one third of the UN force in Bosnia was made up of French soldiers. A better balance of contingents from the various countries would allow the UN to avoid power struggles within missions, as well as command and control problems. The UN could also choose the mission commanders according to competence alone, and not according to nationality. Finally, the great powers could play a leading role in providing troops specialized in intelligence or logistics work and in training and equipping soldiers from other countries.

Imposing a limit on the number of soldiers from the great powers in any one mission does not run counter to meeting the increasing needs of the UN. Contributions of personnel by the great powers could be better divided among the peacekeeping operations, with their consent of course. Many missions in Third World countries are sorely lacking in the specialized, well-trained troops that only the Western countries can supply. The Western countries' participation in training and equipping soldiers from poor countries could both strengthen the capacity of those countries to participate in the missions and increase the number of troop-contributing countries, which currently seems to have peaked at about 70 out of the 185 member states.

* * *

When the UN secretary-general proposes an action to promote peace – an activity that the members of the Security Council strongly recommended he reinforce at a special summit held on 31 January 1992 – he is told more and more often by the member states, rich or poor, that they do not have the money or the soldiers, and that the UN manages its missions poorly. These three myths have no basis in fact, but they allow the member states to avoid facing up to their responsibilities.

The member states claim they cannot afford to finance the budget of the UN which, in the 1994–5 fiscal year reached U.S.$2.5 billion for the regular budget and U.S.$4 billion for peacekeeping operations. Some countries, among them some of the richest, accuse the UN of spending too much. In July 1994, Boutros-Ghali pointed out a paradox. 'During the cold war, [the U.S. was] ready to have its bombers flying 24 hours a day, which cost you $1 billion a day. But [now] U.N. members will not agree to spend $50 million to send troops on a mission to avoid conflict.'[32] Boutros-Ghali was exaggerating the daily expenditures for the bombers. But he could have added that the member states of the UN had still managed to find U.S.$60 billion to finance the seven-month U.S.-UN operation against Iraq in the Gulf War in 1990–1.

The member states claim they do not have enough well-trained, well-equipped soldiers ready to be deployed quickly when the secretary-general of the UN asks for them. Whenever the Security Council establishes a mission, the secretary-general has to go begging to the member states to recruit Blue Helmets, a process that can take months. Contrast this with the mobilization that followed the invasion of Kuwait by Iraq in August 1990: in a few months, the multinational coalition assembled 700,000 over-equipped soldiers, 2,000 combat aircraft, and hundreds of tanks and ships. In June 1994, there were about twenty-five million soldiers – including ten million in the West and the former Soviet Union – in the barracks of the member states, and the UN had huge problems recruiting 5,500 Blue Helmets for Rwanda.

Finally, it is said that the UN is incapable of managing its peacekeeping operations financially and militarily. This was the accusation made by the United States after the debacle in Somalia in October 1993, and by France when Boutros-Ghali fired a French general in the former Yugoslavia in January 1994. The facts do not bear it out. When the UN obtains the resources it needs and receives active political support – without interference or sabotage – its actions are successful, as was shown in the missions in Namibia in 1989–90 and Cambodia in 1992–3, and in the mission that led to free elections in El Salvador in 1994.

Even if we acknowledge that there is some justice in the criticism of excessive bureaucratization, waste, the proliferation of commissions and committees, the incompetence of some staff, and the lack of the human and technical resources required to manage the peacekeeping operations, we have to ask who bears the responsibility for these problems. According to Maurice Bertrand, a member of the United Nations Joint Inspection Unit for eighteen years, the fault lies first and foremost with the member states, especially the great powers. He points out that the UN is not a free agent on the world scene, and that the organization and its components – the Secretariat, the General Assembly, and the Security Council – 'are bodies in which the governments of the member states, especially those of the most powerful countries, use their influence to obtain the official cover of the UN for certain actions.' It is these countries that authorize the recruitment of officials, debate budgets, create commissions and committees, and decide on peacekeeping missions.[33] Bertrand's criticism is harsh, but it shows that the accusations against the UN are aimed at the wrong target. If there is blame to be laid, it should be laid at the feet of the member states and the great powers, because they are the ones who refuse to grant the UN the human and financial resources it needs to fulfil the mandates that they so generously bestow in votes in the General Assembly and Security Council.

Are the Blue Helmets still the guardians of peace so esteemed by Lester B. Pearson, or have they become the warriors of the new world order that Boutros-Ghali dreamed of in 1993 and 1994? This book has provided ample evidence of the fact that their original mission has changed a great deal over the past forty years. Indeed, in June 1997, there remain only seven missions in which the Blue Helmets are acting as true peacekeepers: Western Sahara, Cyprus, the Golan Heights, India-Pakistan, Kuwait-Iraq, Macedonia, and the UN Truce Supervision Organization in Jerusalem. The mandates of ten other current missions place the Blue Helmets at the centre of civil conflicts where the line between peacekeeping and peace-enforcement is, to say the least, a thin one. And the UN continues to answer calls for help, as conflicts, especially those within states, are becoming more numerous every year.

There has been a spectacular rise in the number of peacekeeping operations since 1991. At that time, there were some 11,000 Blue Helmets from forty-six countries in eleven missions. On 1 June 1997, the UN was managing seventeen missions with about 25,000 Blue Helmets from seventy countries. This expansion has created technical and political problems for the managers at the UN. The former could be solved with some effort by the international community. The allocation of additional resources to peacekeeping operations would facilitate UN officials' tasks of mounting and managing peacekeeping missions, recruiting Blue Helmets, and seeing that the troops are deployed quickly. It would also permit the development of programs for military, language, and cultural training, and for supplying equipment to troop-contributing countries that are less affluent but have human resources they can devote to peacekeeping. There is no doubt that solutions can be found to all the technical problems related to peacekeeping operations.

The political problems are more delicate. First of all, the great powers must realize that peacekeeping missions are above all multinational operations reflecting the will of the international community to intervene in a conflict with complete neutrality and impartiality. Neutrality and impartiality are essential to the political success of the missions, which constitute a diplomatic instrument of the international community that must not be perverted by the manoeuvring of the great powers. These powers could facilitate peacekeeping operations by redirecting their participation to supplying transportation, equipment, and certain specialized troops, and refraining from dominating missions by sending too many Blue Helmets.

The member states of the UN should also reconsider whether it is appropriate to intervene in every conflict by sending the Blue Helmets to resolve it. In his *Agenda for Peace*, first published in June 1992, Secretary-General Boutros-Ghali stressed that the international community had to face new responsibilities in a world freed of the Cold War but entering a transitional phase marked by contradictory trends. 'Fierce new assertions of nationalism and sovereignty spring up, and the cohesion of States is threatened by brutal ethnic, religious, social, cultural or linguistic strife,'[34] he wrote, and he proposed a series of measures ranging from traditional peacekeeping to the complete reconstruction of countries. The UN should certainly not learn to say no, as President Clinton suggested it do in September 1993. That would be both an admission of weakness and an evasion of responsibility. But is it reasonable that the UN set as the objective for its Blue Helmets the complete reconstruction of countries devastated by civil war – such as Somalia – when the local elites refuse to cooperate? Is it reasonable to expect the UN to intervene and separate the belligerents in ethnic conflicts and set up courts to judge war crimes, when even the great powers balk at cooperating in capturing the accused? Can the Blue Helmets be expected to separate groups that are enraged and determined to exterminate other groups, and impose peace on them – using force if necessary? In other words, can the Blue Helmets be warriors in the cause of peace, as former secretary-general Boutros-Ghali had so fervently hoped at the beginning of his mandate? In January 1995, Boutros-Ghali answered that question, and many others, in the negative. In his Supplement to *An Agenda for Peace*, he stated categorically that peace cannot be imposed.

Bitter about the way the great powers used peacekeeping operations for their own ends in Somalia and Bosnia, Boutros-Ghali reasserted that the success of peacekeeping depends on three important principles: consent of the parties, impartiality, and non-use of force except in self-defence. 'Analysis of recent successes and failures shows that in all the successes those principles were respected and in most of the less successful operations one or other of them was not,' he wrote.[35] On the delicate question of the use of force to impose peace, he stated that 'peacekeeping and the use of force (other than in self-defence) should be seen as alternative techniques and not as adjacent points on a continuum, permitting easy transition from one to the other' (paragraph 36, pp. 15–16). 'However,' he said, 'neither the Security Council nor the secretary-general at present has the capacity to deploy, direct, command and control [enforcement action]' (paragraph 77, p. 28). He called for respect for the special nature of peacekeeping. 'The logic of peace-keeping flows from political and military premises that are quite distinct from those of enforcement; and the dynamics of the latter are incompatible with the political process that peace-keeping is intended to facilitate. To blur the distinction between the two can undermine the viability of the peace-keeping operation and endanger its personnel' (paragraph 35, p. 15).

Elsewhere in his Supplement, Boutros-Ghali expressed the view that the UN cannot 'impose a new political structure or new State institutions,' as it had attempted to do it in Somalia. 'It can only can help the hostile factions to help themselves and begin to live together again' (paragraph 14, p. 9). Noting that the current system for establishing a peacekeeping mission did not work during the Rwanda crisis, he suggested the creation of a rapid reaction force under the control of the Security Council, which could be deployed in emergencies (paragraph 44, p. 18).

If the Blue Helmets are to return to their traditional role, what should be done in situations that may require the use of force? Some observers feel that when the use of force is necessary, a multinational coalition should be created, sanctioned by the UN. This option has been gaining favour in the international community since the Gulf War, the most recent case being the creation in March 1997 of a multinational force to re-establish order and monitor elections in Albania. Boutros-Ghali admitted that entrusting enforcement functions to a multinational force had positive aspects, but also negative ones. In his Supplement, he wrote that 'this arrangement provides the Organization with an enforcement capacity it would not otherwise have and is greatly preferable to the unilateral use of force by Member States without reference to the United Nations. On the other hand, the arrangement can have a negative impact on the Organization's stature and credibility. There is also the danger that the States concerned may claim international legitimacy and approval for forceful actions that were not in fact envisaged by the Security Council when it gave its authorization to them' (paragraph 80, p. 29).

* * *

Boutros-Ghali's observations and recommendations are instructive and full of common sense. The Blue Helmets cannot permit themselves to wage war. When they do, they fail, and lose all credibility. In several conflicts to which the Blue Helmets have been sent, the UN was employing a good tool for the wrong job. In Somalia, Bosnia, Rwanda, and even southern Lebanon, the Blue Helmets' inability to stop the fighting and the slaughter made them targets of the anger of the local population, targets of the warring parties, and the object of contempt in world opinion. Elsewhere, particularly in Namibia, Cambodia, El Salvador, Cyprus, the Golan

Heights, Mozambique, and Angola, where true peacekeeping missions were deployed, the Blue Helmets were well received.

While waiting for the member states of the UN, and in particular the great powers, to agree on a clear and coherent philosophy on military intervention and how it should be implemented, the UN must return to the great principle that governed the creation of the Blue Helmets: to keep the peace when this is what the parties concerned really want. This is no doubt a less spectacular, less heroic mission, but returning to it is the only way that the Blue Helmets will be able to continue to be an effective instrument of international diplomacy in the settlement of conflicts and a credible hope for thousands of people caught up in the turmoil of war.

APPENDIX A

United Nations Peacekeeping Missions to 1 September 1994

Agency created by the UN	Establishing resolutions	Date of end of operation or current operation (Sept. 1994)	Cumulative or projected cost in $U.S. (1994)	Fatalities	Personnel	Canadian personnel
United Nations Truce Supervision Organization (UNTSO)	Res. 46 and 50 (S.C.) 17 April and 29 May 1948	current operation	30 million	28	218	14
United Nations Military Observer Group in India and Pakistan (UNMOGIP)	Res. 47 and 210 (S.C.) 21 Apr 1948 and 6 Sept. 1965	current operation	8 million	6	38	0
United Nations Emergency Force I (UNEFI)	Res. 998 (G.A.) 4 Nov. 1956	17 June 1967	214 million	90	6,073	1,007
United Nations Observation Group in Lebanon (UNOGIL)	Res. 128 (S.C.) 11 June 1958	9 Dec. 1958	3.6 million	0	591	77
United Nations Operation in the Congo (ONUC)	Res. 143 (S.C.) 14 July 1960	30 June 1964	400 million	234	19,828	421

Agency created by the UN	Establishing resolutions	Date of end of operation or current operation (Sept. 1994)	Cumulative or projected cost in $U.S. (1994)	Fatalities	Personnel	Canadian personnel
United Nations Temporary Executive Authority (UNTEA) and UN Security Force in West New Guinea (West Irian) (UNSF)	Res. 1752 (G.A.) 21 Sept. 1962	30 Apr. 1963	32.3 million paid by the Netherlands and Indonesia	0	1,576	16
United Nations Yemen Observation Mission (UNYOM)	Res. 179 (S.C.) 11 June 1963	4 Sept. 1964	1.8 million	0	189	36
United Nations Peacekeeping Force in Cyprus (UNFICYP)	Res. 186 (S.C.) 4 Mar. 1964	current operation	47 million	164	1,221	19
Mission of the Representative of the Secretary-General in the Dominican Republic (DOMREP)	Res. 203 and 205 (S.C.) 14 and 22 May 1966	22 Oct. 1966	0.2 million	0	2	1
United Nations India-Pakistan Observation Mission (UNIPOM)	Res. 211 and 215 (S.C.) 20 Sept. and 5 Nov. 1965	22 Mar. 1966	1.7 million	0	200	112

Agency created by the UN	Establishing resolutions	Date of end of operation or current operation (Sept. 1994)	Cumulative or projected cost in $U.S. (1994)	Fatalities	Personnel	Canadian personnel
United Nations Emergency Force II (UNEF II)	Res. 340 (S.C.) 25 Oct. 1973	24 July 1979	446 million	52	6,973	1,145
United Nations Disengagement Observer Force (UNDOF)	Res. 350 (S.C.) 31 May 1974	current operation	35 million	36	1,043	220
United Nations Interim Force in Lebanon (UNIFIL)	Res. 425 (S.C.) 19 Mar. 1978	current operation	138 million	199	5,240	0
United Nations Good Offices Mission in Afghanistan and Pakistan (UNGOMAP)	Res. 622 (S.C.) 31 Oct. 1988	15 Mar. 1990	14 million	0	50	5
United Nations Angola Verification Mission I (UNAVEM I)	S.20338 17 Dec. 1988	25 May 1991	17 million	0	70	0
United Nations Angola Verification Mission II (UNAVEM II)	Res. 696 (S.C.) 30 May 1991	current operation	25 million	1	78	0

Agency created by the UN	Establishing resolutions	Date of end of operation or current operation (Sept. 1994)	Cumulative or projected cost in $U.S. (1994)	Fatalities	Personnel	Canadian personnel
United Nations Transition Assistance Group in Namibia (UNTAG)	Res. 435 (S.C.) 29 Sept. 1978 and Res. 629 16 Jan. 1989	31 May 1990	383 million	15	5,593	301
United Nations Iran-Iraq Military Observer Group (UNIMOG)	Res. 598 (S.C.) 27 July 1987	28 Feb. 1991	167 million	1	828	525
United Nations Observer Group in Central America (ONUCA)	Various Resolutions (S.C.) 7 Nov. 1989, 27 Mar. 1990, 20 Apr. 1990, 5 Nov. 1990, and 16 Nov. 1991	17 Jan. 1992	89 million	0	1,098	175
United Nations Observer Group for the Verification of Elections in Haiti (ONUVEH)	Res. 45/2 (G.A.) 10 Oct. 1990	7 Feb. 1991	13 million (of which 0.4 million was provided by the UN)	0	257	11
United Nations Iraq-Kuwait Observation Mission (UNIKOM)	Res. 687 and 689 (S.C.) 9 Apr. 1990	current operation	70 million	3	1,139	5

Agency created by the UN	Establishing resolutions	Date of end of operation or current operation (Sept. 1994)	Cumulative or projected cost in $U.S. (1994)	Fatalities	Personnel	Canadian personnel
United Nations Mission for the Referendum in Western Sahara (MINURSO)	Res. 690 (S.C.) 29 Apr. 1991	current operation	40 million	5	299	0
United Nations Observer Mission in El Salvador (ONUSAL)	Res. 693 and 729 S.C. 20 May 1991, and 14 Jan. 1992	current operation	24 million	2	198	0
United Nations Advance Mission in Cambodia (UNAMIC)	Res. 717 and 728 S.C. 16 Oct. 1991, and 8 Jan. 1992	28 Feb. 1992, replaced by UNTAC	33 million	0	222	2
United Nations Transitional Authority in Cambodia (UNTAC)	Res. 747 (S.C.) 28 Feb. 1992	24 Sept. 1993	1.4 million	56	19,628	214
United Nations Protection Force in Yugoslavia (UNPROFOR)	Res. 743 (S.C.) 21 Feb. 1992	current operation	1.9 million	105	38,715	2,060

Agency created by the UN	Establishing resolutions	Date of end of operation or current operation (Sept. 1994)	Cumulative or projected cost in $U.S. (1994)	Fatalities	Personnel	Canadian personnel
United Nations Operation in Somalia (UNOSOM)	Res. 751 and 775 (S.C.) 24 Apr. and 25 Aug. 1992	Apr. 1993	110 million	0	893	3
United Nations Operation in Mozambique (UNUMOZ)	Res. 797 (S.C.) 16 Dec. 1992	current operation	327 million	13	5,427	4
United Nations Operation in Somalia II (UNOSOM II)	Res. 814 (S.C.) 26 Mar. 1993	current operation	1 billion	123	18,776	0
United Nations Observer Mission in Liberia (UNOMIL)	Res. 866 (S.C.) 22 Sept. 1993	current operation	65 million	n.a.	335	0
United Nations Observer Mission Uganda-Rwanda (UNOMUR)	Res. 846 (S.C.) 22 June 1993	current operation	Costs included in UNAMIR	0	66	0
United Nations Assistance Mission for Rwanda (UNAMIR)	Res. 872 (S.C.) 5 Oct. 1993 and Res. 911 (S.C.) 17 May 1994	current operation	225 million	13	3,764 expected to increase to 5,000	450

Agency created by the UN	Establishing resolutions	Date of end of operation or current operation (Sept. 1994)	Cumulative or projected cost in $U.S. (1994)	Fatalities	Personnel	Canadian personnel
United Nations Observer Mission in Georgia (UNOMIG)	Res. 858 (S.C.) 24 Aug. 1993	current operation	5 million	0	55	0
United Nations Aouzou Strip Observer Group (UNASOG)	Res. 915 (S.C.) 4 May 1994	13 June 1994	0.4 million	0	9	0
United Nations Mission in Haiti (UNMIH)	Res. 867 (S.C.) 23 Sept. 1993	current operation	n.a.	n.a.	n.a.	n.a.

Source: This table was produced by the Centre québécois de relations internationales (Laval University) using information provided by the United Nations.

Excerpts from the Charter of the United Nations

Chapter VI

Pacific Settlement of Disputes

Article 33

1. The parties to any dispute, the continuance of which is likely to endanger the maintenance of international peace and security, shall, first of all, seek a solution by negotiation, enquiry, mediation, conciliation, arbitration, judicial settlement, resort to regional agencies or arrangements, or other peaceful means of their own choice.

2. The Security Council shall, when it deems necessary, call upon the parties to settle their dispute by such means.

Article 34

The Security Council may investigate any dispute, or any situation which might lead to international friction or give rise to a dispute, in order to determine whether the continuance of the dispute or situation is likely to endanger the maintenance of international peace and security.

Article 35

1. Any Member of the United Nations may bring any dispute, or any situation of the nature referred to in Article 34, to the attention of the Security Council or of the General Assembly.

2. A state which is not a Member of the United Nations may bring to the attention of the Security Council or of the General Assembly any dispute to which it is a party if it accepts in advance, for the purposes of the dispute, the obligations of pacific settlement provided in the present Charter.

3. The proceedings of the General Assembly in respect of matters brought to its attention under this Article will be subject to the provisions of Articles 11 and 12.

Article 36

1. The Security Council may, at any stage of a dispute of the nature referred to in Article 33 or of a situation of like nature, recommend appropriate procedures or methods of adjustment.

2. The Security Council should take into consideration any procedures for the settlement of the dispute which have already been adopted by the parties.

3. In making recommendations under this Article the Security Council should also take into consideration that legal disputes should as a general rule be referred by the parties to the International Court of Justice in accordance with the provisions of the Statute of the Court.

Article 37

1. Should the parties to a dispute of the nature referred to in Article 33 fail to settle it by the means indicated in that Article, they shall refer it to the Security Council.

2. If the Security Council deems that the continuance of the dispute is in fact likely to endanger the maintenance of international peace and security, it shall decide whether to take action under Article 36 or to recommend such terms of settlement as it may consider appropriate.

Article 38

Without prejudice to the provisions of Articles 33 to 37, the Security Council may, if all the parties to any dispute so request, make recommendations to the parties with a view to a pacific settlement of the dispute.

Chapter VII

Action With Respect to Threats to the Peace, Breaches of the Peace, and Acts of Aggression

Article 39

The Security Council shall determine the existence of any threat to the peace, breach of the peace, or act of aggression and shall make recommendations, or decide what measures shall be taken in accordance with Articles 41 and 42, to maintain or restore international peace and security.

Article 40

In order to prevent an aggravation of the situation, the Security Council may, before making the recommendations or deciding upon the measures provided for in Article 39, call upon the parties concerned to comply with such provisional measures as it deems necessary or desirable. Such provisional measures shall be without prejudice to the rights, claims, or position of the parties concerned. The Security Council shall duly take account of failure to comply with such provisional measures.

Article 41

The Security Council may decide what measures not involving the use of armed force are to be employed to give effect to its decisions, and it may call upon the Members of the United Nations to apply such measures. These may include complete or partial interruption of economic relations and of rail, sea, air, postal, telegraphic, radio, and other means of communication, and the severance of diplomatic relations.

Article 42

Should the Security Council consider that measures provided for in Article 41 would be inadequate or have proved to be inadequate, it may take such action by air, sea, or land forces as may be necessary to maintain or restore international peace and security. Such action may include demonstrations, blockade, and other operations by air, sea, or land forces of Members of the United Nations.

Article 43

1. All Members of the United Nations, in order to contribute to the maintenance of international peace and security, undertake to make available to the Security Council, on its call and in accordance with a special agreement or agreements, armed forces, assistance, and facilities, including rights of passage, necessary for the purpose of maintaining international peace and security.

2. Such agreement or agreements shall govern the numbers and types of forces, their degree of readiness and general location, and the nature of the facilities and assistance to be provided.

3. The agreement or agreements shall be negotiated as soon as possible on the initiative of the Security Council. They shall be concluded between the Security Council and Members or between the Security Council and groups of Members and shall be subject to ratification by the signatory states in accordance with their respective constitutional processes.

Article 44

When the Security Council has decided to use force it shall, before calling upon a Member not represented on it to provide armed forces in fulfillment of the obligations assumed under Article 43, invite that Member, if the Member so desires, to participate in the decisions of the Security Council concerning the employment of contingents of that Member's armed forces.

Article 45

In order to enable the United Nations to take urgent military measures Members shall hold immediately available national air-force contingents for combined international enforcement action. The strength and degree of readiness of these contingents and plans for their combined action shall be determined, within the limits laid down in the special agreement or agreements referred to in Article 43, by the Security Council with the assistance of the Military Staff Committee.

Article 46

Plans for the application of armed force shall be made by the Security Council with the assistance of the Military Staff Committee.

Article 47

1. There shall be established a Military Staff Committee to advise and assist the Security Council on all questions relating to the Security Council's military requirements for the maintenance of international peace and security, the employment and command of forces placed at its disposal, the regulation of armaments, and possible disarmament.

2. The Military Staff Committee shall consist of the Chiefs of Staff of the permanent members of the Security Council or their representatives. Any Member of the United Nations not permanently represented on the Committee shall be invited by the Committee to be associated with it when the efficient discharge of the Committee's responsibilities requires the participation of that Member in its work.

3. The Military Staff Committee shall be responsible under the Security Council for the strategic direction of any armed forces placed at the disposal of the Security Council. Questions relating to the command of such forces shall be worked out subsequently.

4. The Military Staff Committee, with the authorization of the Security Council and after consultation with appropriate regional agencies, may establish regional subcommittees.

Article 48

1. The action required to carry out the decisions of the Security Council for the maintenance of international peace and security shall be taken by all the Members of the United Nations or by some of them, as the Security Council may determine.

2. Such decisions shall be carried out by the Members of the United Nations directly and through their action in the appropriate international agencies of which they are members.

Article 49

The Members of the United Nations shall join in affording mutual assistance in carrying out the measures decided upon by the Security Council.

Article 50

If preventive or enforcement measures against any state are taken by the Security Council, any other state, whether a Member of the United Nations or not, which finds itself confronted with special economic problems arising from the carrying out of those measures shall have the right to consult the Security Council with regard to a solution of those problems.

Article 51

Nothing in the present Charter shall impair the inherent right of individual or collective self-defense if an armed attack occurs against a Member of the United Nations, until the Security Council has taken measures necessary to maintain international peace and security. Measures taken by Members in the exercise of this right of self-defense shall be immediately reported to the Security Council and shall not in any way affect the authority and responsibility of the Security Council under the present Charter to take at any time such action as it deems necessary in order to maintain or restore international peace and security.

Notes

Chapter 1: In the Glass Tower

1 United Nations press release SC/5769, 6 January 1994.
2 United Nations document S/24333, 21 July 1992, 4; *Le Monde*, 26 July 1992; *New York Times*, 24 July and 3 August 1992.
3 Interview by the author, 20 January 1993. (*Translators' note: our translation.*)
4 Boutros Boutros-Ghali, *An Agenda for Peace 1995*, 2nd ed. (New York: United Nations, 1995), 43.
5 Ibid., 6.
6 Interview by the author, 10 June 1993. (*Translators' note: our translation.*)
7 Shashi Tharoor, *The Great Indian Novel* (New York: Penguin, 1989), 373.
8 Indar Jit Rikhye, *The Theory and Practice of Peacekeeping* (New York: St Martin's Press, 1984), 208.
9 Interviews with the author, 19 January 1993, and 18 January 1994.
10 Figures obtained from the office of the military adviser to the UN, 20 July 1994.

Chapter 2: A Nobel Prize for Canada

1 John English, *The Worldly Years: The Life of Lester Pearson 1949–1972* (Toronto: Vintage, 1993), 137.
2 Geoffrey A.H. Pearson, *Seize the Day: Lester B. Pearson and Crisis Diplomacy* (Ottawa: Carelton University Press, 1993), 141.
3 Article 34, *Charter of the United Nations*.
4 Pearson, *Seize the Day*, 143.
5 English, *The Worldly Years*, 135.
6 Pearson, *Seize the Day*, 147.

7 Quoted in Pearson, *Seize the Day*, 147.

8 Pearson, *Seize the Day*, 70.

9 Brian Urquhart, *Ralph Bunche: An American Life* (New York: W.W. Norton, 1993), 266–7.

10 Ibid., 266.

11 Ibid., 269.

12 English, *The Worldly Years*, 141.

13 Pearson, *Seize the Day*, 153.

14 United Nations, *United Nations Peace-keeping* (New York: 1993), 8.

15 Ibid., 8.

16 Ibid., 10.

Chapter 3: The Soldier-Diplomat

1 Interview by the author, 17 September 1993. (*Translators's note: our translation.*)

2 *Le Figaro*, 28 July 1993.

3 United Nations, *United Nations Peace-keeping*, 19.

4 United Nations document A/34/1, 5.

5 Speech given at Carleton University in 1964, quoted in *The Citizen*, 13 August 1988, B-4.

6 United Nations document S/1994/856, 20 July 1994, 3.

7 United Nations document S/26111, 20 July 1993, 4.

8 Agence France-Presse, 27 December 1993.

9 Reuters, 6 June 1994.

10 Interview by the author, 19 January 1994.

11 Peter Gizewski and Geoffrey Pearson, *The Burgeoning Cost of UN Peace-keeping: Who Pays and Who Benefits?* Aurora Papers 21 (Ottawa: Canadian Centre for Global Security), 31.

12 United Nations document ST/ADM/SER.B/420, 8 November 1993.

13 United Nations document A/47/776, 11 December 1992.

14 Interview by the author, 31 August 1994. (*Translators' note: our translation.*)

15 Figures provided by the Department of National Defence, 17 February 1994.

16 William J. Durch, 'Paying the Tab: Financial Crises,' in *The Evolution of UN Peacekeeping: Case Studies and Comparative Analysis*, ed. William J. Durch (New York: St. Martin's Press, 1993), 50.

17 Figures obtained from the office of the military adviser to the secretary-general on 12 September 1994. It should be noted that some countries that the UN considers developing countries for purposes of determining their financial contribution – such as South Korea, Singapore, Venezuela, Chile, Argentina, Kuwait, and Saudi Arabia – pay their military higher salaries than poorer countries.

18 Karl Th. Birgisson, 'United Nations Peace-keeping Forces in Cyprus,' in
    Durch, ed., *The Evolution of UN Peacekeeping*, 227.

Chapter 4: Cambodia: The Fairies around the Cradle

1 For a description of the situation in Cambodia between 1970 and 1991, see
   Nicolas Regaud, *Le Cambodge dans la tourmente* (Paris: L'Harmattan-FEDN,
   1992).
2 Resolution 745, 28 February 1992. UNTAC press release, 26 February
   1993.
3 Boutros-Ghali, *An Agenda for Peace 1995*, 50
4 Interview by the author, 12–15 April 1993. (*Translators' note: our translation.*)
5 Interview by the author, 12 April 1993. (*Translators' note: our translation.*)
6 United Nations document S/26777, 22 November 1993, 5.
7 *Guideline Standard Operating Procedures for Peace-keeping Operations*, UN restricted
   document 91-15137. No publication date.
8 Interview by the author, 21 April 1993. (*Translators' note: our translation.*)
9 United Nations document S/25913, 10 June 1993, 1.

Chapter 5: Sabotage and Betrayal in Western Sahara

1 Jarat Chopra, testimony before the U.S. Senate Committee on Foreign Relations, October 1992, and before the Fourth Committee of the United Nations
   General Assembly, 19 October 1992.
2 The geographic, historical, and political information presented here is based
   on an unofficial MINURSO document entitled *History of the United Nations Mission for the Referendum in Western Sahara* (1993), and from William J. Durch,
   'Building on Sand,' *International Security* 17, no. 4 (1993): 151–71.
3 Armand Roy, interviews with the author on 14 January, 3 February, and 7 July
   1993. (*Translators' note: our translation.*)
4 *United Nations Peace-Keeping Operations, Information Notes*, Update no. 1, 1993,
   29.
5 Alain Forand, interview by the author, 3 June 1993. (*Translators' note: our translation.*)
6 U.S. Senate Committee on Foreign Relations, *The Western Sahara: The Referendum Process Is in Danger*, S. Prt. 102–75, January 1992.
7 William J. Durch, 'The United Nations Mission for the Referendum in Western Sahara,' in Durch, ed. *The Evolution of UN Peacekeeping*, 412.
8 Ibid., 429.
9 United Nations document S/1997/742, 24 September 1997.

10 Interview by the author, 1 March 1993. (*Translators' note: the interview was recon-structed from the author's notes.*)
11 Interview by the author, 1 March 1993. (*Translators' note: our translation.*)

Chapter 6: The New Warriors

1 United Nations document S/23829, 21 April 1992, 9, and Resolution 751, 24 April 1992.
2 *Le Monde,* 9 April 1992. (*Translators' note: our translation.*)
3 United Nations document S/24480, 24 August 1992.
4 Resolution 775, 28 August 1992.
5 *Le Monde,* 31 October 1992.
6 United Nations document S/24859, 27 March 1992, 5.
7 United Nations document S/24868, 30 November 1992, 5.
8 United Nations document S/23829, 21 April 1992, 12.
9 United Nations document S/24343, 22 July 1992, 13.
10 United Nations document S/24992, 19 December 1992, 7–8.
11 United Nations documents S/23693, 11 March 1992, 3; S/24343, 22 July, 1992, 3; S/24859, 27 November 1992; and S/24868, 30 November 1992, 2.
12 *New York Times,* 4 January 1993.
13 *New York Times,* 6 January 1993.
14 United Nations document S/25354, 3 March 1993, 14.
15 Quoted in *New York Times,* 7 June 1993.
16 United Nations document S/Res/837, 7 June 1993, 2.
17 *New York Times,* 10 August 1993.
18 United Nations document S/26022/, 1 July 1993, 7.
19 *Le Monde,* 4 July 1993.
20 *New York Times,* 12 July 1993.
21 *Le Monde,* 15 July 1993.
22 Agence France-Presse, 13 July 1993. (*Translators' note: our translation.*)
23 *Financial Times,* 15 July 1993.
24 United Nations document S/26317, 17 August 1993, 20–1.
25 *New York Times,* 29 September 1993.
26 *New York Times,* 1 October 1993.
27 Quoted in the *New York Times,* 18 October 1993.
28 *New York Times,* 13 May 1994.
29 United Nations document S/26738, 12 November 1993, 18.
30 Resolution 885, 16 November 1993.
31 Report of the Commission of Inquiry Established Pursuant to Security Council Resolution 885, n.d.; *Le Monde,* 17 May 1994.

32 *New York Times,* 6 December 1992.
33 United Nations document S/1994/12, 6 January 1994, 15.

Chapter 7: Murder in Somalia

1 Interviews by the author, 18–22 February 1993.
2 *Canadian Airborne Regiment Fact Sheet,* summer 1993.
3 *Translators' note: our translation.*
4 Department of National Defence, *Board of Inquiry on the Canadian Airborne Regiment Battle Group,* Phase 1, vol. 11, 19 July 1993 (hereafter Board of Inquiry on the Canadian Airborne Regiment Battle Group), A-9/33.
5 *Translators' note: the interview was reconstructed from the author's notes.*
6 Kim Campbell, Minister of National Defence, speech, 26 April 1993.
7 *Backgrounder: Summary of Incidents* (Department of National Defence, April 1993), 3–4.
8 *Globe and Mail,* 21 May 1993.
9 *Board of Inquiry on the Canadian Airborne Regiment Battle Group,* C-2/8.
10 Ibid., C-4/8.
11 Ibid., A-20/33.
12 Ibid., G-1/5.
13 Ibid., G-4/5.
14 *Le Devoir* and *The Gazette,* 14 April 1993.
15 *Board of Inquiry on the Canadian Airborne Regiment Battle Group,* 3329.
16 *Toronto Star,* 10 July 1994, F-5.
17 *Dishonoured Legacy: The Lessons of the Somalia Affair,* Report of the Commission of Inquiry into the Deployment of Canadian Forces in Somalia (Ottawa, 1997).
18 Ministère de la Défense de Belgique, *Commission d'enquête Somalie,* 24 November 1993.
19 Transcript of the radio program 'Actuel,' 24 August 1993.
20 *Commission d'enquête Somalie,* 28. (*Translators' note: our translation.*)
21 Agence France-Presse, 24 August 1997.
22 Agence France-Presse, 24 January 1994.
23 Ibid., 25 February 1994.
24 Confidential interview, 21 October 1993.

Chapter 8: The Unhappy Warriors

1 Interview by the author, 31 July 1993. (*Translators' note: our translation.*)
2 Interview by the author, 31 July 1993. (*Translators' note: the interview was reconstructed from the author's notes.*)

3 Interview by the author, 2 August 1993. (*Translators' note: the interview was reconstructed from the author's notes.*)

4 Bob Stewart, *Broken Lives: A Personal View of the Bosnian Conflict* (London: HarperCollins, 1993), 265.

5 United Nations document S/25792, 10 May 1993, 20.

6 Paul Garde, *Vie et mort de la Yougoslavie* (Paris: Fayard, 1992), 367. (*Translators' note: our translation.*)

7 United Nations document S/24766, 4.

8 Resolution 743, 21 February 1992, paragraph 5.

9 Resolution 762, 30 June 1992, and Resolution 769, 7 August 1992.

10 United Nations document S/25777, 15 May 1993, 5–6.

11 Ibid., 7.

12 *Le Monde*, 26 February 1992.

13 *Le Monde*, 6 March 1992.

14 Philippe Morillon, *Croire et oser. Chronique de Sarajevo* (Paris: Éditions Grasset, 1993), 25. (*Translators' note: our translation.*)

15 United Nations document S/23836, 24 April 1992, 1.

16 Ibid, 6.

17 Christian Lambert, 'Ex-Yougoslavie : une erreur et une faute,' *Le Monde des Débats*, November 1993, 13; and Agence France-Presse, 29 July 1994.

Chapter 9: Obstruction by the Great Powers

1 Resolution 871, paragraph 5, 4 October 1993.

2 *Le Monde*, 12 October 1993. (*Translators' note: our translation.*)

3 Agence France-Presse, 22 October 1993.

4 Quoted by Agence France-Presse, 17 December 1993. (*Translators' note: our translation.*)

5 Agence France-Presse, 18 December 1993.

6 Quoted by Agence France-Presse, 3 January 1994. (*Translators' note: our translation.*)

7 *Le Monde*, 19 January 1994.

8 *United Nations Peace-keeping Operations, Information Notes, Update No. 2*, 1993, 43 and 50.

9 United Nations document S/25000, 21 December 1992, 5.

10 United Nations document S/26018, 1 July 1993.

11 *United Nations Peace-keeping Operations, Information Notes, Update No. 2*, 1993, 50.

12 United Nations document S/1994/300, 16 March 1994, 9.

13 *New York Times*, 25 May 1993. *Le Monde*, 25 and 26 May 1993.

14 *Le Monde*, 3 August 1993.

15 Xavier Gauthier, *Morillon et les Casques bleus. Une mission impossible?* (Paris: Édition no. 1, 1993), 162.

16 Confidential interview at UN headquarters, 9 June 1993. (*Translators' note: our translation.*)

17 *New York Times*, 14 June 1993.

18 Resolution 836, 4 June 1993.

19 United Nations document S/25939, 14 June 1993.

20 United Nations document S/1994/300, 16 March 1994, 12.

21 Confidential interview at UN headquarters, 9 June 1993. (*Translators' note: our translation.*)

22 *New York Times*, 10 August 1993.

23 Quoted in United Nations, *The Blue Helmets: A Review of United Nations Peacekeeping*, 3rd ed. (New York: United Nations Department of Public Information, 1996), 528

24 Agence France-Presse, 7 February 1994.

25 Agence France-Presse, 28 January 1994.

26 29 November 1990, paragraph 2.

27 Agence France-Presse, 11 January 1994.

28 *New York Times*, 8 February 1994.

29 Quoted in United Nations, *Blue Helmets*, 529.

30 *New York Times*, 10 February 1994.

31 Agence France-Presse, 13 February 1994.

32 Agence France-Presse, 12 April 1994. (*Translators note: our translation.*)

33 *New York Times*, 23 April 1994; *Le Monde*, 24 April 1994.

34 *Le Monde*, 23 January 1994. (*Translators' note: our translation.*)

35 Agence France-Presse, 26 January 1994. (*Translators' note: our translation.*)

36 Ibid.

Chapter 10: Peacekeeping Takes a Back Seat to Politics

1 Quoted in an interview by the author, 16 October 1993. (*Translators' note: the interview was reconstructed from the author's notes.*)

2 Lewis MacKenzie, *Peacekeeper: The Road to Sarajevo* (Vancouver: Douglas and McIntyre, 1993), 108–9.

3 *UNPROFOR Magazine,* January 1993, 24.

4 Quoted in *The Gazette*, 30 January 1993.

5 Roger J. Hill, *Command and Control Problems of the UN and Similar Peacekeeping Forces* (Ottawa: Department of National Defence, 1968), 2.

6 Ibid., 26.

7 Ibid., 25.

8 Ibid., 27.
9 Ibid., 24.
10 Ibid., 29.
11 *Le Casoar,* July 1993, 30. (*Translators' note: our translation.*)
12 United Nations document S/26450, 14 March 1994, 8.

Chapter 11: A Huge Lego Set

1 United Nations, *United Nations Peace-keeping,* 10.
2 Boutros-Ghali, *An Agenda for Peace 1995,* 56.
3 Brian Urquhart, 'For a UN Volunteer Military Force,' *The New York Review of Books,* 10 June 1993, 3.
4 *Forces en attente* [Standby forces] (N.p.: United Nations n.d.). (*Translators' note: our translation.*)
5 Interview by the author, 19 January 1994. (*Translators' note: our translation.*)
6 *New York Times,* 22 May 1994.
7 Interview by the author, 13 July 1993. (*Translators' note: our translation.*)
8 'Unconventional Force,' *The New Republic,* 25 January 1993, 23.
9 United States, State Department, *The Clinton Administration's Policy on Reforming Multilateral Peace Operations,* Presidential Directive 25, May 1994, 3.
10 Canada, *Towards a Rapid Reaction Capability for the United Nations* (Ottawa: 1995), 52.

Chapter 12: Pressure from the French

1 *Translators' note: our translation.*
2 Agence France-Presse, 5 November 1993.
3 *Le Monde,* 8 November 1993.
4 *Le Figaro,* 30 May 1993.
5 Quoted in Agence France-Presse, 23 June 1993. (*Translators' note: our translation.*)
6 Confidential interview, 8 June 1993. (*Translators' note: our translation.*)
7 *Le Monde,* 28 July 1993. (*Translators' note: our translation.*)
8 Interview by the author, 9 November 1993.
9 Emmanuel A. Erskine, *Mission with UNIFIL* (New York: St Martin's Press, 1989), 46.
10 Quoted in *Le Monde,* 3 December 1992. (*Translators' note: our translation.*)
11 *Sénat français,* no. 56, 24 November 1992, 64. (*Translators' note: our translation.*)
12 Ibid., 66. (*Translators' note: our translation.*)
13 Ibid., 69. (*Translators' note: our translation.*)

14 Quoted by Agence France-Presse, 23 June 1993. (*Translators' note: our translation.*)
15 Agence France-Presse, 24 June 1993.
16 Agence France-Presse, 26 November 1993.
17 United States, *Policy on Reforming Multilateral Peace Operations*
18 *Canada and International Peacekeeping* (Washington: CSIS-CISS, 1994), 15.
19 Ibid., 24.

Epilogue

1 Quoted in *New York Times*, 26 May 1994.
2 Agence France-Presse, 17 February 1994.
3 Agence France-Presse, 4 April 1994.
4 Indar Jit Rikhye, Michael Harbottle, and Bjorn Egge, *The Thin Blue Line: International Peacekeeping and Its Future* (New Haven: Yale University Press, 1974), 76.
5 Ibid., 52.
6 William J. Durch and Barry M. Blechman, *Keeping the Peace: The United Nations in the Emerging World Order* (Washington: Henry L. Stimson Center, 1992), 34.
7 Mats R. Berdal, *Whither UN Peacekeeping?* Adelphi Paper no. 281 (London: IISS, 1993), 36.
8 *New York Times*, 16 April 1994.
9 Interview by the author, 17 September 1993.
10 Figures provided by the Office of the Military Adviser to the Secretary-General, 28 August 1994.
11 Proceedings of the Standing Committee on National Defence and Veterans Affairs, 18 February 1993, Issue no. 33, 23.
12 *Winnipeg Free Press*, 21 December 1993, 1.
13 MacKenzie, *Peacekeeper*, 205.
14 Agence France-Presse, 4 August 1994.
15 Confidential telephone interview with a UN military adviser in New York, 20 July 1994.
16 Rikhye et al., 95–6 and 117.
17 Quoted in *La Presse*, 14 August 1994. (*Translators' note: our translation.*)
18 See *Courrier International* 195, 28 July to 17 August 1994, 35–8, and Warren Strobel, *Late-Breaking Foreign Policy: The News Media's Influence on Peace Operations* (Washington: United States Institute of Peace Press, 1997).
19 Proceedings of the Standing Senate Committee on Foreign Affairs, Subcommittee on Security and National Defence, 24 November 1992, Issue No. 8, 18.

20 *Peacekeeping and the US National Interest*, Report no. 11, Henry L. Stimson Center, February 1994, 15.

21 John Ruggie, 'The United Nations and the Collective Use of Force: Whither or Whether?' *International Peacekeeping* 3, no. 4 (Winter 1996): 14.

22 Quoted in *Le Monde*, 1 October 1993, and by Reuters, 14 October 1993. (*Translators' note: our translation.*)

23 Quoted in Agence France-Presse, 29 March 1994. (*Translators' note: our translation.*)

24 Agence France-Presse, 4 April 1994.

25 Quoted in *New York Times*, 23 September 1993.

26 Documents obtained from the American consulate in Montreal in July 1993.

27 *Le Monde*, 29 September 1993.

28 United States, *Policy on Reforming Multilateral Peace Operations*.

29 *New York Times*, 1 February 1992.

30 United Nations document A/50/869, 2.

31 Urquhart, *A Life in Peace and War* (New York: W.W. Norton, 1991) 288.

32 Quoted in *Time*, 1 August 1994.

33 Maurice Bertrand, *L'ONU* (Paris: La Découverte, 1994), 48. (*Translators' note: our translation.*)

34 Boutros-Ghali, *An Agenda for Peace 1995*, 41.

35 Supplement to Boutros-Ghali, in *An Agenda for Peace 1995*, paragraph 33, 14. Subsequent references to this document are indicated in parentheses in the text.

Selected Bibliography

Ballaloud, Jacques. *L'ONU et les opérations de maintien de la paix*. Paris: Éditions A. Pedone, 1971.

Berdal, Mats R. *Whither UN Peacekeeping?* Adelphi Paper no. 281. London: IISS, 1993.

Bertrand, Maurice. *L'ONU*. Paris: Éditions La Découverte, 1994.

Blechman, Barry M., and Matthew J. Vaccaro. *Training for Peacekeeping: The United Nations' Role*. Washington: Henry L. Stimson Center, 1994.

Boulden, Jane. *Prometheus Unborn: The History of the Military Staff Committee*. Aurora Papers 19. Ottawa: Canadian Centre for Global Security, 1993.

Boutros-Ghali, Boutros. *An Agenda for Peace 1995*. 2nd ed., with new supplement and related UN documents. New York: United Nations, 1995.

Burns, E.L.M. *Between Arab and Israeli*. Toronto: Clarke, Irwin, 1962.

Cahill, Kevin M., ed. *Preventive Diplomacy: Stopping Wars Before They Start*. New York: Basic Books, 1996.

Canada. House of Commons. *The Dilemmas of a Committed Peacekeeper: Canada and the Renewal of Peacekeeping*. Report of the Standing House of Commons Committee on National Defence and Veterans Affairs. Ottawa, June 1993.

Canada. Senate. *Meeting New Challenges: Canada's Response to a New Generation of Peacekeeping*. Report of the Standing Senate Committee on Foreign Affairs. Ottawa, February 1993.

Chaumont, Charles. *L'O.N.U.* 13th ed. Que sais-je? Series no. 748. Paris: Presses universitaires de France, 1992.

Choprat, Jarat. *United Nations Authority in Cambodia*. Occasional Paper 15. Providence: Thomas J. Watson Jr Institute for International Studies, Brown University, 1994.

Cot, Jean. *Dernière Guerre Balkanique?* Paris: Éditions L'Harmattan, 1996.

Coulon, Jocelyn. 'Le maintien de la paix au Cambodge: la victoire de la diplomatie tranquille.' *A Part of The Peace*. Edited by Maureen Appel Molot and Harald von Riekhoff. Canada among Nations Series. Ottawa: Carleton University Press, 1994.

Cox, David. *Exploring An Agenda for Peace*. Aurora Papers 20. Ottawa: Canadian Centre for Global Security, 1993.

Cox, David, and Albert Legault, eds. *UN Rapid Reaction Capabilities: Requirements and Prospects*. Clementsport, N.S.: Canadian Peacekeeping Press, 1995.

Daniel, Donald C. F., and Bradd C. Hayes, eds. *Beyond Traditional Peacekeeping*. New York: St. Martin's Press, 1995.

Diehl, Paul F. *International Peacekeeping*. Baltimore: Johns Hopkins University Press, 1993.

Durch, William J., ed. *The Evolution of UN Peacekeeping: Case Studies and Comparative Analysis*. New York: St Martin's Press, 1993.

– ed. *U.N. Peacekeeping, American Policy, and the Uncivil Wars of the 1990s*. New York: St Martin's Press, 1997.

Durch, William J., and Barry M. Blechman. *Keeping the Peace: The United Nations and the Emerging World Order*. Washington: Henry L. Stimson Centre, 1992.

Erskine, Emmanuel A. *Mission with UNIFIL*. New York: St Martin's Press, 1989.

Gaffen, Fred. *In the Eye of the Storm: A History of Canadian Peacekeeping*. Toronto: Deneau and Wayne, 1987.

Gauthier, Xavier. *Morillon et les Casques bleus. Une mission impossible?* Paris: Éditions No 1, 1993.

Gizewski, Peter, and Geoffrey Pearson. *The Burgeoning Cost of UN Peace-keeping: Who Pays and Who Benefits?* Aurora Papers no. 21. Ottawa: Canadian Centre for Global Security, 1993.

Goulding, Marrack. 'The Evolution of United Nations Peacekeeping.' *International Affairs* 69(3) (1993): 451–64.

Granatstein, J.L., and Douglas Lavender. *Shadows of War, Faces of Peace: Canada's Peacekeepers*. Toronto: Key Porter, 1992.

Harbottle, Michael. *The Blue Berets*. Harrisburg: Stackpole, 1971.

Hill, Roger J. *Command and Control Problems of the UN and Similar Peacekeeping Forces*. Ottawa: Department of National Defence, 1968.

Jockel, Joseph T. *Canada and International Peacekeeping*. Washington: Center for Strategic and International Studies, 1994.

Johnstone, Ian. *Aftermath of the Gulf War: An Assessment of UN Action*. International Peace Academy Occasional Paper Series. Boulder, Colo.: Lynne Rienner Publishers, 1994.

King, Charles. *Ending Civil Wars*. Adelphi Paper 308. London: IISS, 1997.

Léonard, Yves. *L'ONU à l'épreuve*. Paris: Éditions Hatier, 1993.

MacKenzie, Lewis. *Peacekeeper: The Road to Sarajevo*. Vancouver: Douglas and McIntyre, 1993.

Makinda, Samuel M. *Seeking Peace from Chaos: Humanitarian Intervention in Somalia.* International Peace Academy Occasional Paper Series. Boulder, Colo.: Lynne Rienner Publishers, 1993.

Morillon, Philippe. *Croire et oser. Chronique de Sarajevo.* Paris: Éditions Grasset, 1993.

O'Brien, Conor Cruise. *To Katanga and Back.* London: Hutchinson, 1962.

Parsons, Anthony. *From Cold War to Hot Peace: UN Interventions 1947–1995.* Harmondsworth: Penguin, 1995.

Pearson, Geoffrey A.H. *Seize the Day: Lester B. Pearson and Crisis Diplomacy.* Ottawa: Carleton University Press, 1993.

Rikhye, Indar Jit. *The Theory and Practice of Peacekeeping.* New York: St Martin's Press, 1984.

— *The Sinai Blunder: Withdrawal of the United Nations Emergency Force Leading to the Six-day War of June 1967.* London: F. Cass, 1980.

Rikhye, Indar Jit, Michael Harbottle, and Bjorn Egge. *The Thin Blue Line: International Peacekeeping and Its Future.* New Haven: Yale University Press, 1974.

Rohde, David. *Endgame: The Betrayal and Fall of Srebrenica.* New York: Farrar, Straus and Giroux, 1997.

Siilasvuo, Ensio. *In the Service of Peace in the Middle East, 1967–1979.* New York: St Martin's Press, 1992.

Simons, Geoff. *The United Nations: A Chronology of Conflict.* London: Macmillan, 1994.

Stewart, Bob. *Broken Lives: A Personal View of the Bosnian Conflict.* London: Harper-Collins, 1993.

Stjernfelt, Bertil. *The Sinai Peace Front.* New York: St Martin's Press, 1992.

Sutterlin, James S. *Military Force in the Service of Peace.* Aurora Papers 18. Ottawa: Canadian Centre for Global Security, 1993.

Tavernier, Paul. *Les Casques bleus.* Que sais-je? Series no. 3169. Paris: Presses universitaires de France, 1996.

United Nations. *The Blue Helmets: A Review of United Nations Peace-keeping.* 3rd ed. New York: United Nations Department of Public Information, 1996.

United Nations. *United Nations Peace-keeping.* New York: United Nations Department of Public Information, 1993.

United Nations Institute for Disarmament Research. *The Guardian Soldier: On the Nature and Use of Future Armed Forces.* Research Paper 36. New York: United Nations, 1995.

Urquhart, Brian. *A Life in Peace and War.* New York: W.W. Norton, 1991.

— *Ralph Bunche: An American Life.* New York: W.W. Norton, 1993.

Vilalta, Georges. *Les Casques bleus : une nouvelle fonction pour les armées nationales?* Paris: Fondation pour les études de défense nationale, 1977.

Willame, Jean-Claude. *L'ONU au Rwanda.* Bruxelles: Éditions Maisonneuve-Larose, 1996.

Index